AF594319

George Graham Vest

George Graham Vest

The Life and Times of Dog's Best Friend

By

Stephen M. Vest

MORLEY, MISSOURI

P.O. Box 238
Morley, MO 63767
(573) 472-9800
www.acclaimpress.com

Book & Cover Design: Frene Melton

ISBN: 978-1-956027-79-2 | 1-956027-79-3
Library of Congress Control Number: 2024930938

First Printing: 2024
Printed in the United States of America
10 9 8 7 6 5 4 3 2 1

This publication was produced using available information.
The publisher regrets it cannot assume responsibility for errors or omissions.

Contents

This book is dedicated to Toby, Alfie,
Friskies I, II and III, Annie, Patches and Lucy,
the best friends this man has ever known.

"It is not meaningless, then, that one was born, as Vest was, on that beautiful tableland of Kentucky fondly called the Blue Grass; for it is stoutly asserted on one side and generally allowed on the other that the sky there is a little bluer, the grass a little greener, the air a little more vitalizing, the water a little purer than elsewhere and that not only the women and the men but the very horses of this favored spot bear distinguishing marks."

— Henry Lamm, ESQ., 1904

Introduction

George Graham Vest is best known for coining the phrase "Man's best friend is his dog" or "Dog is man's best friend," but he was much more.

Henry M. Rose (1858-1932), chief clerk of the U.S. Senate, called Vest "one of the most remarkable and picturesque men this country has produced. His remarkable and original genius, his conspicuously independent intellect, and his absolute fearlessness have placed him peculiarly in a class by himself."

During his 73 years, he was one of a select group of men to serve as both a United States and Confederate senator. He was a friend and a fishing buddy of presidents, Supreme Court justices, and the world's most famous bank and train robbers. He attended the first Sunday school west of the Alleghenies and is the only legislator in American history to be assaulted by a woman during an open legislative session.

As a politician, he was a friend to Native Americans, especially the Choctaw, Chickasaw and Plains tribes, and is credited with saving and establishing Yellowstone National Park.

He was slow to support the rights of Blacks and women and opposed Chinese and Italian immigration.

As a speaker, he is also said to have coined the phrase "history is written by the victors," a truism he butted his head against most of his life.

"He had his faults as he was a human; he had his virtues as he was mortal," said T.T. Crittenden, his friend and rival for more than 50 years. "There were some strange peculiarities about the man which could not be understood or interpreted by even his closest friends. Such is always the case with men of genius. There has never been an exception."

As a young man, Vest established a community newspaper and, in his retirement, he penned a series of articles for the *Saturday Evening Post*, the first of which appeared on August 8, 1903, following the publication's serialization of *Call of the Wild* by 27-year-old Jack London (1876-1916). Vest wrote 17 essays, the last two published after his death. "Imagine a man who has read much of the best and remembered it well. Imagine a man who has seen many men and things, has run the gamut of experience, and appropriated to himself something of all that he had seen and experienced, and could tell it—and you have Vest," said future Missouri Chief Justice Henry Lamm (1846-1926) in a 1904 speech to the Missouri Bar Association, of which Vest was a member for nearly 50 years.

George Graham Vest

George Graham Vest

The Life and Times of Dog's Best Friend

CHAPTER ONE

A Young Gentleman of Promise

Planted in a limestone-lined Kentucky River valley, Frankfort, Kentucky's state capital, remains one of the nation's most charming seats of government—the fifth smallest, to be exact. Still, Frankfort is a metropolis compared with the frontier village of fewer than 2,000 into which Vest was born on December 6, 1830.

"The old hills and the shining river, with the bridge hanging across it, and the road running up and around the cliffs like a serpent and undulating through the trees and the rocks" was how Vest described his memories of the place in *The Saturday Evening Post*. "The schoolhouse and the old [Presbyterian] church with the high pulpit and the hard, hard seats, where we sat on each recurring Sabbath, with eyes fixed on the preacher until our cervical vertebrae seemed to be parting."

Vest was the only son of John Jay and Harriet Graham Vest and the second of their three children. George was born in the home of his grandfather and namesake, George Washington Graham (1780-1863), on the south side of the Kentucky River, adjacent to the Singing Bridge. Vest's father, a carpenter and contractor, built what is now known as the Old State Capitol (erected in 1830), the Franklin County Courthouse (finished in 1835), the city's public school (completed in 1839), and much of the main campus of the Kentucky Military Institute (now the Stewart Home and School). He was a city trustee and commander of the State Arsenal (now the Kentucky Military History Museum) and an elder of the First Presbyterian Church. In 1845, J.J. Vest and his father-in-law, George Washington Graham, were members of the committee that disinterred the pioneer Daniel Boone (1734-1820) in Warren County, Missouri and reinterred him and his wife, Rebecca (1739-1813), in the Frankfort Cemetery.

Boone had been dead 25 years and Rebecca nearly 30. "When the coffins were opened, it was found that the large bones were perfect in size and shape … but so far decomposed … could not be raised in form," the committee reported. "Their coffins were entirely rotten except for the bottom planks."

The committee, with the remains, reached Frankfort in August. On September 13, 1845, businesses were closed for the ceremonies, which drew representatives from each Kentucky county and all surrounding states.

The gravesite has an unobstructed view on a high outcropping above the Kentucky River. Of the site, Vest wrote, "The river wends its way between majestic hills and the

Kentucky Military Institute as it appeared in the 1800s. Much of the main campus was built by Vest's father, John Jay Vest. Library of Congress photo.

spires of the classic old town are seen in the distance. The evergreens which stand above their last resting place constantly remind the wayfarer of the soul's immortality and these lofty pines above their grave, keep green the memory of the brave."

The hearse carrying the Boones' remains was drawn by four white horses, decorated with evergreens and flowers. J.J. Vest was captain of the Frankfort Lancers, one of eight military groups in the massive parade. The Vests' pastor, Rev. Joseph James Bullock (1812-1892), delivered the closing prayer.

Reverend Joseph James Bullock (1812-1892)

George was 14 when Daniel and Rebecca's remains were moved to Frankfort, but the scene was captured in an 1886 letter Vest wrote to Frankfort Mayor Col. Edmund Haynes "E.H." Taylor Jr. (1830-1923), the namesake of the small-batch bourbon produced by Buffalo Trace Distillery, and Col. John Lafayette Scott (1829-1903) of the Frankfort Centennial Association, tentatively accepting an invitation to return to Frankfort that October 6. "On that summit, I sat, thinking of the great world beyond the little valley beneath me," Vest wrote. "If it is possible, I will accept your invitation."

By July, Vest's schedule would not permit him to leave Washington, D.C.

"I regret very much that it will be out of my power to attend your celebration. It would afford me great pleasure to visit my birthplace and meet again the friends of my youth and early manhood. There are reasons, however, which inevitably prevent my accepting your invitation, and all I can do is to send my kindest regard to all my old friends, and to express my regret that I cannot be with them."

Vest's childhood memories stayed with him. "The cold, hard features of that austere Presbyterianism, under whose teaching we were reared, became softened by the dim twilight of years ago," Vest wrote. "Father, mother, teacher, minister, where are they? Ask the marble gleaming in the moonlight on those Kentucky hills. And how they taught us our duty both to God and to man! We thought it was hard, severe, tyrannical then, but now, mellowed by time, we see the surpassing love in it all."

As with most of Vest's relationships, he crossed paths with his friends again and again. One example: Rev. Bullock, who Vest described having a "massive and towering physical frame [that] formed a fit abode for his noble and lofty spirit, and gentleness and strength were exquisitely blended in his countenance and bearing." Bullock pastored Vest's church from October 1837 until the summer of 1847, when impaired health forced him to resign. Bullock recovered and returned to ministry, eventually landing at the Second Presbyterian Church in Alexandria, Virginia. From 1879, the year Vest joined the U.S. Senate, until 1883, Bullock served as the senate's chaplain.

From all descriptions, Vest's father expected the most from his children, not just in religious upbringing but also in education. He sent his children to the best schools, including the academy of Professor Burwell Bassett Sayre (1810-1879), whose rigorous teaching methods were apparent in his students' achievements. At one time, seven of Sayre's former students, including Vest, were in the United States Senate simultaneously.

"So inflexible was the father's determination to educate George that he once pulled his gold watch from his pocket and gave it in pledge for his son's tuition—an incident making an indelible impression on the boy and often tenderly mentioned by him," Lamm said.

By the age of 10, Vest had read the many works of Sir Walter Scott (1771-1832) and was well-versed in the tales of *Ivanhoe* and *Rob Roy*. Clearly, he knew "Epitaph to a Dog" by Lord George Gordon Byron (1788-1824), the author of *Don Juan*. Byron wrote of his dog, Boatswain, that he "possessed beauty without vanity, strength without insolence, courage without ferocity and all the virtues of man without his vices."

Vest was also a political student of Senator Henry Clay (1777-1852), Representative Benjamin Hardin (1784-1852) and Kentucky Governor John Jordan Crittenden (1787-1863), two of whom attended his childhood church.

His introduction to politics came when his father took the precocious boy to a political picnic near Frankfort to hear Crittenden speak. "I remember attending a burgoo at a locality on Benson Creek known as the Punch Bowl, near what is now the track of the Lexington and Louisville Railroad," Vest said of the strictly Kentucky institution surrounding a come-what-may stew. "Mr. Crittenden was advertised to speak, and my father, an ardent Whig, took me to the burgoo to allow me to learn the great principles of the Whig party.

"An immense kettle of many gallons capacity was placed over a fire at the foot of a large sycamore tree, and Uncle Larkin, a celebrated burgoo maker with a white apron and a large wooden spoon with a long handle, was superintending the preparation of the burgoo soup, assisted by some dozen able citizens, who were busy preparing the necessary ingredients," wrote Vest, who found the cooking spectacle entertaining. "No one can tell you what burgoo is for the simple reason that no two kettles were ever made alike.

"I soon made my escape from the speaking and joined the hungry crowd of boys who stood at a respectful distance and watched with great interest the movement of Uncle Larkin, whom we considered a much more important personage than Mr. Crittenden," who, when not in Washington, lived a block from the house where Vest was raised, and attended the same church, as did Hardin. "The wind was blowing a sharp breeze, and about the time the soup was ready for consumption, a jaybird's nest was overturned in the upper branches of the sycamore, and three recently hatched young jays, whose personal appearance was eminently disgusting, dropped into the kettle. An exclamation of horror was heard from the spectators, who considered the burgoo at an end, but Uncle Larkin was equal to the emergency.

"With a dexterous twist of his wooden spoon, he submerged the unfortunate birds and calmly said, 'Just in time, gentlemen, just in time.'

"I swallowed a large quantity of the soup," Vest wrote, "which was furnished in a tin cup with a pewter spoon and a chunk of bread to everyone in attendance, and thanks to youth and perfect health, I experienced no bad effects; but this is the last and only time I tasted jaybird soup."

An avid reader, Vest had an eye for a good story—even when he was a participant. His account of a Sunday pigeon hunt, accompanied by his father's horse, Old Put, and his childhood friend and cousin, Charley, has the sound and feel of Mark Twain (1835-1910), a Vest contemporary on the Missouri frontier. Vest's youth could have easily served as inspiration for Twain's Tom Sawyer.

"Put was an old horse belonging to my father and named, from patriotic motives, after the New England hero, General Israel Putnam [1718-1790], whose famous gallop down a precipice in his apocryphal escape has served to illustrate every school history for 50 years and has sent that illustrious warrior down to posterity indissolubly connected with a horse," Vest's tale begins. "In color, Old Put was white; in disposition amiability itself. Never in all the outrages and freaks committed upon him by whole troops of children was he ever known to exhibit the slightest impatience, whilst he was the palladium of safety to the old and infirmed.

"Dignified, affable, and venerated both on account of his age and character, Old Put was an institution," said Vest, describing Old Put as the embodiment of Presbyterian ideals in the shape of a horse. "One thing only, in his personal appearance, did not sustain his general character as it was known to all. In early life, probably while owned by some irreligious horse fancier, Put's tail had been docked, and, from my earliest recollection, it presented the appearance of a ghastly weeping willow, being always carried at an angle of 45 degrees, the white hair floating down from it like the locks of some venerable patriarch.

"Now, like all boys, Charley and I were mighty hunters, and in the fall, when wild pigeons passed over the woods of Kentucky in vast droves, we reveled in the sport of hunting."

The Kentucky of the 1840s is beyond the imagination of those living today or even at the turn of the last century when he committed the tale to print. "It is hardly possible to believe how vast the flights of wild pigeons were, which appeared every autumn in the middle and western states. The larger portion of them was migrating to some locality farther south and in such numbers as to obscure the sun, their habitat in the summer months being in British or Russian America," he wrote. "There were immense roosts in Kentucky, Tennessee, and Missouri, some covering thousands of acres."

One such roost was in Owen County, Kentucky, 20-plus miles north of Frankfort.

"The pigeon season lasted only for a few weeks, and every Saturday, therefore, was eagerly and gloriously spent," Vest wrote. "On one Friday afternoon, when we could look from the schoolhouse window and see drove after drove of birds darkening the sky, Charley came to me with the information that he had, by a masterly stroke of enterprise, a large amount of powder, with shot in proportions for the next day, and we proceeded to map out the details of the hunt. The envy of every other boy in school was excited by our boasts of what we proposed to do on the morrow, and in our anticipated success, we went back to past exploits, many of them imaginary."

As is often the case in the Bluegrass, when Saturday morning arrived, rain came with it, ruining young George and Charley's plans.

"We were just in that condition of mind when the devil always makes his appearance and, in a bland, respectable, gentlemanly way, as [Johann Wolfgang von] Goethe

[1749-1832] tells us, proposes some infernal scheme of ruin. On that eventful day, his satanic majesty, true to his antecedents, intruded himself and prompted Charley to suggest we slip off and go hunting the next day—Sunday."

Vest received Charley's suggestion in mock horror. "Then we discussed it with 'bated breath,' and finally we illustrated the truth of that much-hackneyed quotation: 'Vice is a monster of such frightful men … by arranging all the preliminaries.' Charley was to take charge of the ordnance department and have the guns and ammunition at a secluded spot early the next morning. I was responsible for the transportation and to meet him with an ancient family chase [horse carriage] and Old Put."

That night, young George struggled to sleep, partly due to guilt and the excitement of the hunt.

"A dozen times, I determined to abandon the unholy enterprise, and even after I fell into a troubled sleep, all sorts of spectral visions floated around me.

"A Negro boy, whom I suborned for the purpose, waked me at an early hour, and, my courage having partially returned, I managed to secure the chase with Old Put and met Charley.

"In safety, without being seen by a single person, we reached the open country, and then, elated by the prospect of a successful hunt, we proceeded to light two enormous common cigars, known in Kentucky as 'Long Nines,' and, having elevated our feet on the dashboard of the chase, felt entirely secure, when at a sudden turn in the road we were startled by the appearance of Elder Joe Thompson on his way to church with his two maiden daughters at an unprecedented early hour.

"Uncle Pomp, a white-haired Negro, was driving two dignified family horses that never ventured into any faster gait than a stately walk. We knew a crisis was upon us, for Elder Thompson belonged to the session as did our fathers and, like all orthodox Presbyterians, felt it his duty to apprehend any children of the church house on the Sabbath day, just as he would secure to their owners so many cattle or sheep.

"Instinctively feeling that the cigar I was smoking gave me a lawless appearance, I endeavored to thrust it into the side pocket of my coat, but unfortunately, I placed it in Charley's pocket—who sat by my side—where he had deposited the powder, tied up in two wrappings of strong, thick paper.

"At the exact moment, Elder Thompson discovered the extraordinary turnout, comprising Old Put and two children of the church, out for a hunt on Sunday morning! The Thompson vehicle stopped, and as Pomp proceeded to dismount from his perch to open the carriage door, there was an explosion such as my nervous system has never experienced. Charley and I separated immediately. He went over the fence into a meadow, and I passed clear over or through the Thompson carriage—I have never been certain of which. Amidst the shrieks of the Misses Thompson and yells of the Elder and Pomp, I staggered to my feet, burning and half dead, to behold a scene of utter ruin.

"Both vehicles were wrecked: Pomp was amid the debris, and Elder Thompson looked like the captain of an exploded steamboat, but the central figure was that of Old Put. True to his military title, that venerable animal stood his ground but was terribly demoralized. He had been blown forward on his forequarters, his rump presenting the appearance of an elephant, whilst his tail stuck straight up, bald and blackened like a charred stump after a forest fire.

"Carried back in disgrace on that bright Sabbath morning, we were swathed and bandaged with cruel kindness for days afterward. Special prayers were made for us at church and prayer meetings. All the Sunday school scholars were brought to see us as a 'horrible example,' whilst the doctor and minister alternated in physicking us bodily and spiritually."

Both boys recovered. Charley migrated to Mississippi and fought for the Confederacy in the Civil War, and George went west seeking fame and fortune. Old Put was never the same. "From having been the kindest and best and safest animal in Kentucky, he became the 'devil's own,' and at Christmas, when firecrackers began their annual fusillade, he was perfectly frantic," said Vest.

Vest no doubt developed his literary skills and use of vocabulary at B.B. Sayre's academy. A forerunner of Lexington's esteemed Sayre School from 1842 to 1848, it was located at Main and Saint Clair streets in Frankfort, two blocks from Vest's boyhood home, a rambling boarding house at the northwest corner of Wapping and Washington streets, called the Corner in Celebrities. Historical accounts report that Sayre was loved and feared and demanded thorough mastery of English, Latin, Greek and mathematics. Vest excelled under Sayre's tutelage. A classmate to future Supreme Court Justice John Marshall Harlan (1833-1911), U.S. Senator Joseph Clay Stiles Blackburn (1838-1918), and Missouri Governor Benjamin Gratz Brown (1826-1885), Vest held Sayre in high

Far left: *Judge John Marshall Harlan, ca. 1870-80. Brady-Handy Photograph Collection, Library of Congress, Prints and Photographs Division.*

Left: *Hon. Joseph Clay Stiles Blackburn of Kentucky, who served as a lieutenant colonel in the Confederate Army, ca. 1860-75. Brady-Handy Photograph Collection, Library of Congress, Prints and Photographs Division.*

Vest's childhood home in Frankfort, Kentucky, known today as the Vest-Lindsey House. Top photo courtesy of Capital City Museum, Frankfort, Kentucky.

regard. "He (Vest) always bore witness that to Sayre, he attributed any success he attained in life," Lamm said.

Sayre was one of Kentucky's most celebrated teachers. Among Sayre's students was Thomas Theodore "T.T." Crittenden (1832-1909), who would serve as Missouri governor from 1881-1885 and act as Vest's opposing counsel in the "Dog Trial." Vest and Crittenden's lives were intertwined, beginning with Sayre but extending to Centre College and their lives in Missouri.

Another of Sayre's students was Union General Daniel Weisiger Lindsey (1835-1917), a future adjutant general and the eventual owner of Vest's childhood home, now known as the Vest-Lindsey House.

Vest left Sayre's school so advanced that he entered Centre College in Danville, Kentucky, as a member of the junior class under Dr. John Clarke Young (1803-1857), a Columbia graduate, Presbyterian minister, teacher and administrator, who came from Princeton and is credited with establishing Centre as Kentucky's premier institution of higher education. Centre alumnus John Todd Stuart (1807-1885) encouraged Abraham Lincoln (1809-1865) to become an attorney, and Adlai Stevenson I (1835-1914), another Centre student, was vice president under Grover Cleveland (1837-1908).

According to *The Senatorial Career of George Graham Vest,* Elaine Dawes' successful 1932 dissertation for a Master of Arts degree at the University of Missouri, Vest's circle of friends consisted of Stevenson; his future law partner, John Finis Philips (1834-1919); Crittenden, and future real estate magnate and philanthropist Thomas Hunton Swope (1827-1909).

"One of Vest's traits was being unusually fortunate in being associated with people of character and ability," Dawes claimed. Another was maintaining friendships over the course of decades. In an 1896 speech at the dedication of Swope Park in Kansas City. Vest said of Swope, "He was a slender, delicate boy, devoted to study, and exceedingly popular," recalling their days at classmates. "I remember his fainting in the recitation room when reading an essay and loving the solicitude of professors and students as we gathered around him. He had a great respect for the Christian religion. It has gone with him throughout his life, although he has never connected with any church.

"I am aware of many generous acts by him to good people and one of his first donations was a thousand dollars to repair the old Presbyterian church in Danville, where we listened to orthodox sermons as students." Swope later gave Centre $25,000 to help build a new library.

Vest was ill much of his senior year, but the 17-year-old graduated with the highest honors.

After leaving Centre, Vest taught briefly in a country school near Frankfort and worked as the capitol correspondent for the Louisville-based *Journal* under editor George Dennison Prentice (1802-1870), a well-known Whig Party newspaper. Prentice was known for his fiery editorials, which some blamed for a bloody election day riot in 1855, and he obviously rubbed off on his young reporter.

Vest also read law in the office of Kentucky Attorney General James Harlan (1800-1863), the father of his grade school, Sunday school, and law-school classmate, John Marshall Harlan. The elder Harlan was an early Whig supporter of Henry Clay who became a strong Unionist and a Lincoln district court appointee.

In 1849, Vest heard a speech by the senior Harlan that he remembered for the rest of his life. The point of the address was that a public man with no enemies was either a mere figurehead or a routine drudge. "Even [George] Washington had enemies," Harlan said. "When you look for the best fruit in an orchard, always hunt for the tree around which can be found the largest number of sticks and stones."

As Vest's instructor, Harlan, instead of having Vest read William Blackstone's commentaries of English law, had Vest read the political papers of Alexander Hamilton (1755-1804), John Jay (1745-1829), and James Madison (1751-1836), saying Vest would learn more about statesmanship.

As a young man, Vest was described as 5-foot-6, a boyish 110 pounds with fiery red hair and freckles. He had a short neck, an uncommonly large head, and blue-gray eyes. "He had a form of the singular makeup of being almost as tall when sitting as standing and the breadth of shoulder and reach of the arm of a larger man," Lamm said.

In 1850, 19-year-old George was "reading law" and living at home with his parents and 17-year-old sister, Louisa (1833-1900). His older sister, 25-year-old Mary Ellen (1834-1882); her husband, James Warsham Batchelor (1819-1896), and their daughter, Emma C. (1847-?), shared the home with nine boarders, which included a clerk, a newspaper editor, a merchant, and a bookbinder.

On February 13, 1851, 53-year-old J.J. Vest died. In his will, written October 23, 1850, he provided for Mana, an older Black woman. He requested his children provide her with "everything necessary"—clothing, food, shelter, and medical attention, and $20 per year (roughly $800 in today's value) for the rest of her life "in consideration for her long and faithful service to me and my family." He also provided for his wife, Harriet, Mary Ellen, George, and Louisa.

J.J. and Harriet's graves are east of the Kentucky War Memorial on a high point in the Frankfort Cemetery, near the graves of Nicholas Smith (1802-1839) and his wife, Mary Johnson Smith (1808-1854), the parents of Colonel Nicholas Smith (1836-1919), editor of the *New York Tribune*. The younger Smith, once called "the handsomest man in America," married Ida Lilian (1848-1882), daughter of Horace Greeley (1811-1872), whose presidential bid Vest supported in 1872.

In his book *Senator Vest: Champion of the Dog*, Edwin Malcolm Chase French (1870-1949) apologetically writes, "Vest was born with negroes, as he once expressed it, nursed by them, owned them, and never sold one for profit, he declared. He treated them as he did members of his own family, and his former slaves, after the war, came to him in every adversity and for financial assistance. Two of them, one an old nurse [Mana] who fondled him in her arms, were recipients of his daily bounty and lived upon the means he provided them. Senator Vest was a sincere friend of the negroes and showed it in a humane manner."

When Mana [Maria] Fenwick died, she was buried in the Glenn's Creek section of the Frankfort Cemetery. Her tombstone reads: "My devoted nurse and friend.—G.G. Vest."

On December 18, 1851, Louisa married Captain Robert Samuels Triplett (1830-1905). Four months later, in April, George, Louisa, Robert, and printer Joseph H. Mayhall (1812-1854) moved west from Frankfort to "the thriving town" of Owensboro to start *The Owensboro Gazette*, a weekly broadsheet newspaper.

When it debuted, *The Gazette* was praised, described as "beautiful in appearance" by *The Louisville Times* and "well-edited" by *The Bardstown Herald*. *The Eddyville Telegraph* wrote, "*The Gazette* is a good-looking paper, well printed, and the only fault we find with it is its politics, which we cannot swallow."

The Gazette did not attempt to hide its Whig leanings. In an early editorial, Vest made this clear. "[I] prefer an open and honest foe to a lukewarm friend."

Within days of the first issue, April 30, 1852, Vest's mother, Harriet, died in Frankfort. He returned to Frankfort for the funeral and again for several weeks in June. Vest's ability to express emotion is no more compelling than in his mother's obituary.

"When we lose friends who have endeared themselves to us by kind words and actions, the heart suffers severely, but when a mother's love is added to the other ties that unite us with the lost one, no earthly affliction can be greater. She, to whose memory we now pay the last sad tribute of respect, possessed in a preeminent degree those traits of character that win admiration and love. Her disposition was loving and gentle, with the finest sensibility to the sufferings and frailties of others. Believing and practicing the Christian religion, she lived a useful and exemplary life, giving with a liberal hand to those who needed charity and sympathizing deeply with those who suffered affliction. What more can we say than that she lived and died an earnest believer and professor of that faith which was taught to us by one who took upon himself, for a time, the garb of humanity and suffered for the sins of our fallen race? And he, to whom she had given the service of her Life, upheld and supported her when passing into that unknown world from which no spirit returns.

"When her eye had been glassed, and her cheek paled by approaching dissolution, she murmured not at the will of Providence but devoted her death, as she had her life, to the good of those around her. Calling her children and friends to her side, she spent the last hours of her life advising them on how to live, that their departure from earth might not be in agony with no future hope but rather the commencement of a more glorious existence. Cold skeptic! You who would take from the suffering that religion, which alone supports them in the darkest hours of human existence, learn from such a deathbed the fallacy of your belief, learn that death is not the portal to a dark and gloomy world, where disembodied spirits wander through the vastness of eternity, but that it is the birth of another and brighter spirit to the society of heaven."

Vest's writing in *The Gazette* was direct. Readers were left with little doubt of his views as he aptly used sarcasm and wit, as exemplified in a July 10, 1852, exchange with the editor of a paper in neighboring Indiana.

"The editor of a sort of hermaphrodite sheet at Cannelton, neither Whig, Democratic, Christian, Jew, or Pagan, was excessively irritated at a statement in our paper, some weeks since, that the coal at Hawesville [Kentucky] was superior to that at Cannelton. All Hoosierdom, no doubt, is perfectly astounded at the tremendous abilities this gentleman has exhibited in defense of their mineral wealth. If he continues in the same ratio, he may someday be elevated by his grateful countrymen to the dignity of constable."

Vest's ability to convey humor showed in a correction in an early issue. "The report of the death of Wm. C. Marshall, Esq., proves utterly false. Mr. M. is, at present, in good health and is very grateful, we understand, for the flattering notices he received in all portions of the State. Our Democratic friends were peculiarly kind on the occasion and seemed anxious to make up for the political burial they inflicted upon Mr. M. last summer."

While Vest wrote for *The Gazette*, the final product also reflected his interests, whether a selection from his and Triplett's favorite authors or items gleaned from the numerous papers with which *The Gazette* exchanged.

During Vest's return to Frankfort in June of 1852, the paper ran the following notice: "The Editor of the 'Gazette' is absent at present and has left the 'Local' with the bag to hold. We hope our subscribers will make due allowance for want of editorial matter until his return."

Within six weeks, struggles to build circulation and advertising got to Vest. As Vest described it, he was more than ready to return to law school, the law being "a scarcely less laborious, but to us, a much preferable profession. While our editorial experience has been an exceedingly pleasant one, it is, we must confess, amply sufficient to convince us that there are other more profitable employments," Vest wrote in his final column on August 12, 1852.

While reports, including the *1883 History of Daviess County*, said Vest and Triplett ran *The Gazette* for several years, it was, in fact, less than four months. The brothers-in-law sold their interests to Mayhall, who continued publishing the paper until he was thrown from a buggy and killed in the fall of 1854.

With the assistance of U.S. District Judge Thomas Bell Monroe (1791-1865), chair of the Transylvania University law department, Vest returned to Lexington to complete law school. Under the guidance of Monroe, Vest learned the importance of Blackstone and graduated as valedictorian in 1853 in a class that included future Supreme Court Justice John Marshall Harlan. *The Kentucky Statesman* (Lexington's newspaper) of February 25, 1853, reported: "The Law Class of Transylvania University held their commencement exercises at the Chapel of Morrison College this evening. The occasion is an interesting one, and we trust there will be a large audience of ladies and gentlemen present. Mr. G.G. Vest of Owensboro is to deliver the valedictory address, which, we have no doubt, will be a production well worth hearing, as he is a young gentleman of fine promise."

The graduation committee members included Harlan, J.C. Wickliffe and V.H. Lynn.

The connections Vest made at Transylvania came into play throughout his life. From his years as a Missouri attorney to his terms in the Confederate and United States Senates, his story is sprinkled with the names of native Kentuckians and fellow Transylvania graduates.

Transylvania, which traces its beginnings to the 1780s, was the school of choice for many gifted young Southern men. Among Transylvania's alumni list are esteemed

Kentucky politicians Henry Clay, Jefferson Davis, and Albert Sidney Johnston (1803-1862). Other Transylvania graduates include numerous senators, including Blackburn and Vest; two associate justices of the U.S. Supreme Court, and two vice presidents of the United States.

Nearly 175 years since his graduation, Vest is ranked the 14th most significant Transylvania graduate, just ahead of his friend Joseph O. "Jo" Shelby, general of the Confederates' Iron Brigade (No. 15). Other Vest associates included President Davis (No. 1), John Crittenden Breckinridge (No. 5) and Harlan (No. 8). Other Transylvania graduates on the list include The Father of Texas, Stephen Fuller Austin (1793-1836); U.S. Ambassador to Russia Cassius Marcellus Clay (1810-1903), and Francis Preston Blair (1791-1876), the father of Vest's future colleague in the United States Senate.

Two-time Republican presidential candidate James Gillespie Blaine (1830-1893), "The Plumed Knight" of Maine, who nearly defeated Grover Cleveland in 1884, said of Vest in later years that, during his career in the Senate, he had "certain peculiarities of style and phrase characteristic of graduates of Transylvania University."

During a 1908 visit to Transylvania, Justice Harlan described the school he and Vest attended:

"I remember sitting at the feet of some of the greatest judges and lawyers that ever appeared in this or, I believe, in any other country. [Congressman] George Robertson [1790-1874], [Kentucky Chief Justice] Thomas Alexander Marshall [1794-1871], [Judge] A.K. Woolley [1799- 1849], and [Major] Madison C. Johnson [a graduate, professor, and president of the law school] were in the law school when I had the honor to be a member. I undertake to say that no law school that has ever existed in this country, or, in my judgment, in any other country, has had at the same time as professors and teachers of the science of law four greater lawyers than those four I have named."

In Harlan's estimation, if Robertson and Marshall had been placed on the Supreme Court in their early years, they would have left a reputation as remarkable as his namesake, Chief Justice John Marshall (1755-1835): "No greater lawyer, in the largest sense of the word, ever lived in this country, in my judgment, than Major Madison C. Johnson," Harlan said. "He deserves to be ranked by the side of Daniel Webster [1782-1852], Rufus Choate [1799-1859], and lawyers of that kind."

It could be argued that if it had not been for his stint in the Confederate government—at war, in a fundamental sense, against the Constitution—Vest, too, could have found his way to the high court.

At Centre and Transylvania, Vest learned the importance of hard work. "All other education amounts to nothing without the great lesson of self-control and continuous effort," he wrote to the editor of *The Savitar*, the University of Missouri yearbook, in March 1903. "These magic words—self-control and continuous effort—should be placed above the doorway of every university, college, and school and over the hearthstone of every home."

The Tripletts remained in Owensboro, and in 1881, their son, George Vest Triplett (1856-1931), founded *The Saturday Post*, which in 1883 was described as a "sprightly gazette."

Judge George Vest Triplett III (1922-2007) said in a July 1, 2002, interview that Judge Triplett's great-grandfather and Vest's brother-in-law, Robert, founded a railroad between Owensboro and the rustic retreat at Falls of Rough. In the late 1890s, the uninsured railroad burned, bankrupting the family. In January 1897, Vest returned to Owensboro and bought the family's home, a Steamboat Gothic-style house on Frederica Street, at the Commissioner's sale on the courthouse steps for $2,702.54 ($96,481 in 2022), securing the family's home for Judge Triplett's grandmother, Nannie (1861-1948), Vest's niece.

Vest deeded the house to Nannie the day before Christmas 1903.

CHAPTER TWO

Frontier Lawyer to Secessionist

Within months of graduation from Transylvania, the 22-year-old Vest headed west to seek his fortune, making it as far as Missouri. From all reports, his departure from Kentucky was abrupt. One theory is that he was despondent because the parents of his college sweetheart, Sallie Elizabeth Sneed, refused them permission to marry.

Another says he fled after angering an old man named Whitaker by setting adrift the houseboat on which the aged sot was playing poker. Whitaker and his friends floated more than 130 miles downriver when the game broke up around dawn.

According to Blackburn, Vest and a few other young men had been out relatively late, and, while wandering along the riverbank—presumably Owensboro's—they came upon a tattered flatboat tied to the plank landing with two ropes.

"Vest thought it would be a good joke to cut the ropes and let the old scow drift downstream," Blackburn said. "It was, but the scow drifted faster than expected. The fellows inside never felt the scow move and kept playing and hitting the jug quite often." As the game broke up around dawn, it was intensely foggy, and no one noticed they were in mid-stream. "Old Whitaker stepped off the boat, and instead of onto the wharf, he found himself 20 feet deep in the rapid Ohio River."

Old Whitaker's friends fished him out, and all were surprised to see they were approaching Cairo, Illinois. They quickly attracted the attention of a northbound riverboat, which agreed to tow them back upstream, which is when they realized their ropes had been cut.

"As soon as they landed," Blackburn said, "Whitaker went home and took down his squirrel rifle" and announced he would kill the fellow who cut the ropes.

"That night, Vest, with his earthly belongings tied in a handkerchief, stole a small skiff and paddled down the Ohio and across the Mississippi and into the Missouri wilderness," said Blackburn, who said Vest's departure was significant for both states because Missouri gained a brilliant senator and Kentucky had an equal leader in Blackburn. "There was no room [in Kentucky] for two of us."

Whatever the reason, we do know what Vest chose to share. "In the spring of 1853, I left my native state for the west. My worldly possessions consisted of a trunk containing some wearing apparel and a few elementary law books, a small amount of money, and a double-barreled shotgun."

He traveled to Saint Louis on the Louisville packet, passing Owensboro, and secured passage on the *F.X. Aubrey* (named after Francois Xavier Aubrey (1824-1854), the fastest distance rider in the West) on her second trip up the Missouri River. "The Saint Louis levee scenes were exciting, with a dozen steamers leaving port," Vest said in retelling the adventure. "Their bills of fare would put an appetite into the jaws of death."

From Saint Louis, Vest traveled up the Missouri River to Independence.

Lamm said, "Tradition has it that he and two traveling companions, friends from Kentucky, quickly ran out of money by some misadventure [most likely an unfortunate card hand], and Vest was constrained to return home by coach, the water falling below navigation on the river."

Stopping in Boonville, Vest and his fellow passengers divided patronage between the two leading inns—the City Hotel (later the base of operations for the Missouri Home Guards) operated by Edward McPherson (1805-1869), "a cultivated, intellectual Marylander," and Pierce's, owned by Colonel Peter Pierce (1794-1871), "a large, genial, hospitable Virginian."

Vest described the Boonville hotels as "worthy of the best days of the republic ... I have traveled many a mile, but never looked on their like again."

Vest stayed at the Capital Hotel for several days. "There was a crowd on the veranda, and the central figure was a fine-looking man of massive form with an antique, classic face," Vest wrote. "He talked loudly and aggressively while his audience listened respectfully, often demanding approval.

"While waiting for dinner, I asked an old gentleman the speaker's name. With a look of contemptuous pity, he replied: 'You are evidently a stranger, sir. That is Thomas Hart Benton, the greatest man in the United States.'"

Senator Thomas Hart Benton of Missouri from c. 1821-51. Brady-Handy Photograph Collection, Library of Congress, Prints and Photographs Division.

U.S. Senator Benton (1782-1858) was the first senator to serve five terms, elected first as a Republican (until 1825), then a Jacksonian (1825-1837) and then a Democrat (1837-1858). Nicknamed "Old Bullion," he was the architect of westward expansion and the champion of what became known as Manifest Destiny. He is one of the eight senators profiled in *Profiles in Courage* by President John Fitzgerald Kennedy (1917-1963).

"Colonel Benton was not on a regular canvas but had come to visit his daughter, Sarah McDowell Benton [1821-1863], wife of Kentucky Lieutenant Governor

Richard Taylor Jacob [1825-1903], who owned a farm 12 miles west of Boonville," Vest wrote. "That Benton was a great man; there can be no question. He was haughty, violent [in 1813, he wounded his employer, future President Andrew Jackson (1767-1854), in what some called a duel and others a brawl], and uncompromising. Still, his mind was strong, analytical, and untiring. He was inclined to verbose speeches and was the vainest man living, but his vanity was not repulsive. His courage was of the highest order. He was destroyed politically by his opposition to the expansion of slavery, which he honestly believed was a curse."

According to Vest, "From Boonville, I went by boat to Lexington, and after remaining there for two days, traveled by stage to Georgetown, then the seat of Pettis County."

Missouri's interior counties were sparsely settled, and transportation was limited to coaches, wagons and one line of the Missouri Pacific Railroad.

"The journey from Lexington to Georgetown was a revelation," Vest wrote. "I had never seen a prairie, and its undulating billows covered with wildflowers and virgin grass with bunches of deer timidly gazing at us as we passed along, furnished a landscape of rare interest and beauty. The country abounded in game. Deer, turkeys, prairie chickens, pheasants, quail, and rabbits could be found everywhere, and to a young, eager sportsman, there was on all sides a veritable paradise."

As the story goes, the coach, traveling at high speed, overturned near Georgetown. Vest suffered a broken shoulder. During his brief recovery, he grew fond of Georgetown. "I found myself in the midst of Kentuckians. The county was filled with Thompsons, Majors, Gentrys, Scotts, Joneses, Ferriss, all coming from the Bluegrass part of Kentucky, and they received me with open arms."

A tragic event occurred on July 3, 1853, in Heath's Creek Township in the northern part of the county that haunted Vest for the rest of his life.

"A man named [Henry] France (1799-1886) had removed from [Todd County] Kentucky some years before and purchased a fine farm, together with a few slaves," Vest wrote. "He was not popular with his neighbors and had little to do with them."

France lived on socially equal terms with those he enslaved and talked with them about his neighbors in such a way as to inflame and poison their minds against the white population. One of France's sons and a farmer named Rains married sisters. A family quarrel split the family, and the Frances took sides against the Rainses, whose house was situated at the end of a prairie canyon a mile away from the nearest neighbor.

On Sunday, July 3, 1853, Henry Rains left his family, consisting of his expectant wife, a 5-year-old boy, and a 3-year-old daughter, to attend church 2 1/2 miles away.

"On his return, he found his wife [Elizabeth] and little girl dead in the yard, their brains beaten out, and evidence of a desperate struggle in the house and the grass outside," Vest wrote. "The little boy was alive and, although badly beaten on the head, could tell who had been there, 'France's Sam.' To add to the horror, Mrs. Rains had been brutally violated."

Rains alerted the neighborhood, and 19-year-old Sam was quickly arrested and brought to Georgetown Monday morning. The two resident attorneys were away at the newly opened land office in Warsaw, Missouri, and France hired Vest to defend Sam.

"The next day, the prisoner was arraigned before an examining court, consisting of three justices, in the courthouse at Georgetown, the building being packed with an excited crowd, many of them carrying rifles," Vest wrote. "The prosecution placed their only witness on the stand, the little boy, who was mangled and only half alive. I promptly questioned his competency because, from his tender years, he could not know the nature and obligation of an oath."

After questioning the child, the judge, General George Rappeen Smith (1804-1879), agreed with Vest. "The attorneys for the prosecution seemed bewildered and demoralized. As they had no other evidence, and no attempt was made to have the little boy instructed regarding the nature of an oath, I arose to move my client's discharge and, at that instant, heard the rattling of a chain."

General George Rappeen Smith (1804-1879) served as a judge in Georgetown, Missouri, and later founded the town of Sedalia in 1857.

A shout came from behind, "Make way for the Heath's Creek Statute!"

The mob rushed the prisoner, threw a log chain around his body, and dragged him from the courtroom. "Believing he was about to be hanged, Sam confessed to the crime with all the horrible details." Sam also said his violence had been encouraged by his enslaver.

The mob appointed one of its members a jailer and relieved the sheriff of his keys. They set the execution for two weeks off and sent notice to all slaveholders in Pettis and the adjoining counties to bring their slaves to Georgetown, where in a natural amphitheater north of town, more than 2,500 witnessed "the miserable wretch" burned alive. "Everything was done in so systematically and deliberately a fashion that it seemed to be a lawful proceeding," Vest wrote. "The two saloons in Georgetown were closed by order of the mob, and no concealment as the identity of the actors in this tragedy was attempted."

Vest said the vigilantes lacked the irrational thinking generally associated with mob mentality.

General Smith pleaded with the gang not to proceed. His attempt to intervene lowered the community's opinion of the local stalwart, partially prompting Smith's move west, where he founded the railroad town of Sedalia in 1857.

The gang's original plan was to hang Sam, but after Smith's urging, hanging was not enough.

Despite being only 65 miles from the state capital, Georgetown was isolated enough that state officials knew nothing of the incident until long after Sam's death.

"The leaders were neither barbarians nor ruffians," Vest claimed. "They were the best citizens of the county—members of orthodox churches. They came from that Scot Irish stock that has furnished many illustrious men. Living upon the border, with the institution of slavery in their midst, their homes isolated, and their women unprotected, the husbands and fathers determined that punishment would be such as to prevent a recurrence."

Following Sam's execution, community leaders met and resolved that Henry France, his family, and William Daniel France (1832-1865) be ordered to leave Missouri within 10 days. "We do not feel that our families and interests are safe whilst they remain in the neighborhood," reported *The Missouri Statesman*. "We believe France was guilty of aiding and abetting … in the murder of Elizabeth Rains." Among the 17 committeemen was Elizabeth's husband, Henry. Furthermore, they accused France of committing "various and diverse depredations" to his neighbor's livestock, threatening to harm his neighbors, and influencing his slaves to "commit deeds of crime and rapine."

France did not leave Missouri but moved 90 miles west to Bates County, near the Kansas state line.

Before the trial, Vest contemplated accepting an offer to practice law in Santa Fe. When death threats began circulating for "the lawyer who defended the negro," Vest chose to settle in Georgetown, established in 1835 by General David Thomson (1775-1861), an Indian fighter and Judge Smith's father-in-law, who immigrated to the Missouri Territory from Georgetown, Kentucky.

"It had to be so," *The Saint Louis Post-Dispatch* said of Vest's choice to stay in Georgetown. "A man raised under the Kentucky code of that day was tied to Georgetown the firmer by every threatening word."

When Vest opened his office the day after the execution, one of his first clients was the leader of the gang who called for his lynching. "Such was my entrée into the practice of law, and although nearly 45 years have passed, I look back upon this awful experience with no pleasurable emotions," said Vest.

Coming to Missouri as a young stranger, braving such harsh public opinion at the outset of his career, Vest immediately attracted attention, and his political party soon began to shower him with offers.

Vest was firmly educated in the Bible, winning numerous prizes for memorizing verses and, at times, entire chapters. "By the aid of a prodigious memory and a mother's gentle ministrations, he laid the foundation of that Biblical knowledge which, ever-present and at command, thrilled and charmed both Bar and Senate," said Lamm, a member of the Missouri Supreme Court.

The Bible was just one of the books Vest committed to memory, and when he used it, he used it well. "Once there was a bitter, pugnacious man, no friend of Mr. Vest, who had the habit of muttering to himself and shaking his head as he walked along the streets of Sedalia," Lamm said. "Vest needed to allude to this man in a speech to a jury in a case in which the head-shakings and muttering man had been a hostile witness, and he boldly offered a daring explanation of the mannerisms. To the surprise of the court, jury, and bar, he quoted verbatim *Matthew* 12, verses 31-32. He then said that his theory behind these headshaking and mutterings was that the witness had committed the 'unpardonable sin' and was subject to the dreadful maledictions outlined in the quoted verses."

In 1854, Vest returned to Kentucky and, on June 6 in Boyle County, he married Sara Elizabeth "Sallie" Sneed (1833-1906), whom he had first met at Centre College. Sallie was described as one of the belles of Danville, and Vest, a master of self-deprecation, often told a tale of the reaction the couple received upon his return to Georgetown.

"She is better appearin' than you be, for she is right-down good-looking," said Captain Oswald Goldsmith Kidd (1800-1878), who owned the hotel where Vest lived before the wedding. "All I can say is that you must have caught her in a pinch for a husband." As for Vest, he was described as having a fair face with boyish freckles.

"Mr. Vest had a noble countenance, a wise and kindly eye, and a voice in perfect command. It had a resonant tremor, far-reaching and effective, with the powers of imitation and personifications such as you hear in great actors," Lamm said. Coupled with an astonishing wit, Vest was a grand raconteur and conversationalist. He was equally at home in the side room of a country courthouse, by a roaring campfire on a fishing trip, or in the cloakroom of the United States Senate.

In 1856, the couple moved 35 miles to Boonville, which had a stronger bar association, as Mrs. Vest wanted her husband to spend less time hunting and fishing and more time working. "She knew him and knew him well," Lamm said, well enough to know he could rise and fall to any environment.

"Why move?" said Vest. "I can shoot enough meat for my family and win any case that comes my way."

Her case was aided by a cholera epidemic that sharply decreased Georgetown's scant population, and her neighbor's Sunday morning hunting horns had grated on her Presbyterian ears long enough.

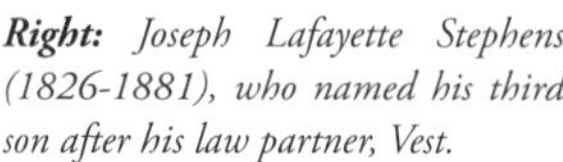

Right: *Joseph Lafayette Stephens (1826-1881), who named his third son after his law partner, Vest.*

Far right: *Lon Vest Stephens, named in honor of George Graham Vest.*

Vest first partnered with J.W. Draffen (1824-1896), who led a pro-slavery company of the Missouri State Guard to Kansas in 1856, and later with Joseph Lafayette Stephens (1826-1881), who in 1858 named his third son Lawrence "Lon" Vest Stephens (1858-1923) in honor of his father, a judge (Lawrence), and his law partner (Vest). The younger Stephens would become a newspaper editor and banker before becoming state treasurer from 1890 to 1897 and Missouri's 29th governor from 1897 to 1901.

Vest became prominent in his opposition to the Know Nothing Party, which sought to organize native-born Protestants against foreign influence—especially Catholics politically. The Know-Nothings were also anti-Irish and anti-German. Vest's withering sarcasm, witty rejoinders, and masterful illustrations of the shortcomings of its policy did more to drive the party out of Missouri than anyone.

> *"He who defers to another time to do what he ought to do at the present time must take to himself all the consequences of his negligence."*
>
> – G.G. Vest, 1857

In 1858, Missouri elected Robert Marcellus Stewart (1815-1861) governor. According to Vest, Stewart was a gentleman of great ability but with many remarkable eccentricities, including riding a horse into the governor's mansion. "It had been for many years the unwritten law of our state that the governor should on each Christmas Day pardon a convict who was thought by the penitentiary's warden to be worthy of executive clemency," Vest said. "On the first Christmas Day after his inauguration Gov. Stewart, with his private secretary, went to the penitentiary and, after causing the convicts to be brought out and placed in line, proceeded to ask each of them for what crime he was convicted and whether he was innocent or guilty.

"All of them vehemently asserted their innocence until a stalwart young fellow near the end of the line said he had been convicted of horse-stealing and was guilty. 'What?' said the governor. 'You didn't mean to say that you stole the horse?'

"'Yes, your excellency,' replied the man. 'I stole the horse and pleaded guilty afterward in open court.'

"'Mr. Secretary,' said the governor, 'issue a pardon to this wretch at once. His presence here is an insult to all these innocent gentlemen, and unless turned out, he will poison the moral atmosphere of the prison.'"

It was sometime before 1859 when Vest first met Ulysses S. Grant (1822-1885), whose fortunes, according to Vest, were at their lowest ebb. "He had just resigned his commission in the regular army and was living with his young and rapidly increasing family on the White Haven estate of his father-in-law"—Colonel Frederick Fayette Dent (1787-1873)—about six miles from Saint Louis. Grant and the self-proclaimed Colonel's son, future General Frederick Tracy Dent (1820-1892), were roommates at West Point, and he met and eventually married Fred's sister, Julia (1826-1902), when stationed at Jefferson Barracks, five miles from White Haven.

"He [Grant] impressed me as a modest, reticent, intelligent man who had the unmistakable appearance of having been unsuccessful in the battle of life," Vest said. "I was told that he was endeavoring to build up a business as a real estate agent in Saint Louis, but his efforts in that direction had been unsuccessful."

When Vest and Grant first met, Grant had unsuccessfully applied for appointment as county surveyor despite the efforts of Colonel Samuel Bullitt Churchill (1812-1890), a prominent Southern Democrat with whom Vest would become well acquainted in the Missouri legislature.

"After the Civil War, I met Colonel Churchill, and he related to me an episode in the life of General Grant that was entirely characteristic," Vest said. "Colonel Churchill said that after General Grant had failed to be appointed county surveyor, he met him one day on the street, and Captain Grant, as he was then termed, told him that his father-in-law, Major Dent, had given him permission to cut and haul firewood to the city for sale, and asked as a great favor that Colonel Churchill would loan him $30, which he would repay by hauling firewood to Churchill's residence."

Samuel B. Churchill (1812-1890) served as Secretary of State of Kentucky from 1867-71 and 1879-80.

After more failed efforts to find employment, Grant relocated to Galena, Illinois, where he worked as a clerk in his brother's tannery business. When the war began, he was appointed colonel over Illinois volunteers and began his phenomenal rise through the military ranks. In the meantime, Colonel Churchill, a well-known Southern sympathizer, was arrested for disloyalty and placed on house arrest in the old Planters House Hotel, of which he was part owner, and his rents, the most significant part of his income, were confiscated.

Following the fall of Fort Donelson, Tennessee, General Grant, with his staff, visited Saint Louis, taking rooms at the Planters House. The following day, Colonel Churchill sent a card requesting an interview. "Moments later, the general walked into Churchill's room and, after greeting him warmly, asked Churchill what he could do for him, expressing his earnest desire to render any service in his power," Vest recalled. "Colonel Churchill told him he was very anxious to leave Missouri for Kentucky, his native state, and would be glad to have his rents returned, which the local Federal authorities had confiscated."

Grant had a permit allowing Churchill to return to Kentucky made out immediately and had the Colonel's confiscated rents repaid. He and his family left Missouri at once. After the war, Colonel Churchill served as Kentucky's secretary of state from 1867-71 and 1879-80.

"He [Churchill] told me that official business called him to Washington during General Grant's first administration, and on learning of his arrival in the city, the President ordered the state carriage to be sent to his hotel and had him brought to the White House, where he remained a guest until the conclusion of his business," Vest wrote.

In 1860, Vest's interests in public matters and growing popularity led him to run for a seat in the Missouri General Assembly, and he won. He was made chairman of the Federal Relations Committee, appointed an elector on the Stephen Douglas ticket, and was not considered an extremist on the issue of slavery. "He became a lawyer and Kentuckian with a liberal education, with the gloomiest outlook on the looming war. He did not, at least then, belong to the extreme Breckinridge school," Lamm said.

In 1860, Judge John Finis Philips, a college friend and Vest's future law partner, heard Vest speak at Warrensburg that summer and delivered what he called "the most impassioned appeal for the preservation of the Union that ever fell from human lips."

Within a year, Vest drafted the "Vest Resolutions," denouncing the federal government's coercion of the Southern states; authored Missouri's "Ordinance of Secession," and joined the Missouri State Guard. Once the die was cast, he went "with all his fiery zeal with his people and stood with them for the integrity of a state's power to secede," Lamm wrote. Vest quickly found himself separated from his wife and three children, and they would remain apart for most of the next seven years.

Vest served in the Missouri House of Representatives until advancing Federal troops forced the divided legislature at Jefferson City to take up arms. Each member was furnished a musket and cartridge box and continued legislating with muskets across their laps.

Alexander Jones of Independence, Missouri, told *The Washington Post* in a 1903 interview that, as Federal troops advanced, Missouri Gov. Claiborne Fox Jackson (1806-1862), a pro-slavery Democrat, was outside the capitol building with his pistols strapped to his waist and rifle on his shoulder, prepared to flee south.

Missouri Governor Claiborne Fox Jackson, ca. 1861. Bryan Obear Collection, The State Historical Society of Missouri.

Vest rose from his seat inside the capitol, stacked his musket, and held up a newspaper. "Mr. Speaker, I notice a dispatch which reads as follows: 'The bodies of the soldiers that were killed in Baltimore, belonging to a Massachusetts Regiment [the 6th], have been placed on ice and shipped to New England for burial.' I say, Mr. Speaker, if this Yankee government expects to put the body of every soldier killed to coerce the South on ice, Lincoln had better make a contract for Greenland's icy mountain, and damn quick! The undertakers will need it all before they finish burying the dead."

Four soldiers and 13 civilians were killed during the Baltimore Massacre on April 19-20, 1861, as the 6th Massachusetts attempted to reach Washington following Lincoln's call for troops.

According to Jones, "About the time Vest closed his remarks, a messenger rushed into the house, handed a telegram to the presiding officer, who passed it to the clerk. The dispatch was as follows: 'Nathaniel Lyon [1818-1861] and Frank [Preston] Blair [1821-1875] are en route to Jefferson City with three regiments to capture the legislature and hang all the secessionists of that body.'

"'Thank God for that,' exclaimed a Union member from the backcountry. 'A few pairs of plow lines well used on some House members will cause the Union some good.'

"The wildest excitement prevailed. Members reached for their muskets; some were for defending the state house, while the majority thought prudence the better part of valor and favored going further south," Jones relayed.

After the panic subsided, the message proved to be a hoax to test the legislature's courage. In later years, Vest, according to Kentucky congressman John Wesley Langley (1868-1932), confirmed the authenticity of his "Greenland" quote and relayed to him a story that it was General John Charles Frémont (1813-1890), then head of the Missouri State Militia, who entered the House chamber and compelled the legislature to adjourn.

In addition to the "Vest Resolutions," he essentially formulated the legislative report stinging the May 10 seizure of Camp Jackson, just north of Saint Louis, by Federal forces under Captain Lyon.

When news reached Jefferson City that Lyon's command had taken 639 prisoners at Camp Jackson, Vest called the move "illegal, unchristian, and an inhuman violation of our rights."

Over the next month, several attempts to reach a compromise failed. On June 14, Lyon's troops entered Jefferson City and seized the capital, replacing the elected state government with a provisional one appointed by the Federal Government in Washington.

When negotiations broke off, Lyon said before he would "concede to Missouri for one instant the right to dictate to my government in any matter … I would see you and every man, woman, and child in the state dead and buried. In an hour, one of my officers will call for you and conduct you [referring to Gov. Jackson and governor's aide Thomas Lowndes Snead] out of my lines."

Snead (1828-1890) later wrote in his book *Fight for Missouri* that Lyon's actions were a rebellion against the state and the Constitution of the United States.

On June 16, Lyon, now a general, and his forces attacked the state militia headquarters in Boonville—effectively taking control of the state.

In a panic, the legislature adjourned and, with Gov. Jackson, fled south to Neosho, 200 miles southwest of Jefferson City, where they used a Presbyterian church as a legislative hall. Vest wrote the "Ordinance of Secession" adopted by the Southern wing of the legislature while still at Neosho.

According to Jones, the moving legislature became tired and demoralized. The camp followers grew so large that "Old Pap" Price (1809-1867) ordered able-bodied men to enlist or leave the camp. Some legislators joined Price's army, Vest as a judge advocate—a colonel on Price's staff.

By August, Lyon controlled Springfield, but on August 10, his force of 5,500 men was overtaken by 8,000 Missourians under Price and 5,000 Confederates led by General Benjamin McCulloch (1811-1862). At Wilson's Creek, near Springfield, Lyon, recently promoted to brigadier general, was killed trying to lead the last charge in a battle generally considered a Confederate victory, making him the first Union general killed in the war. The Rebels inflicted 1,235 casualties while suffering 1,095, making it the most significant battle fought on Missouri soil.

Vest's most direct combat experience came in the Battle of Lexington, the "Battle of the Hemp Bales", on September 13-20. Price's army lost 100 men in defeating Colonel James Adelbert Mulligan's Union "Irish Brigade" (1830-1864) and capturing the Missouri River port.

Governor Claiborne responded after the victories, "With such soldiers and a just cause we cannot fail to achieve our liberties."

After the week-long battle, in which 1,774 Union soldiers fell, Vest said he would never be in another fight.

"I am not a soldier but a statesman," Vest said. "I am not built for a soldier."

Vest's "Ordinance of Secession" was introduced to 23 state senators and 77 representatives on October 28 in Neosho and unanimously approved on November 2 in Cassville, 45 miles southeast.

Missouri's Ordinance of Secession

AN ACT declaring the political ties heretofore existing between the State of Missouri and the United States of America dissolved.

WHEREAS, the Government of the United States, in the possession and under the control of a sectional party, has wantonly violated the compact originally made between said government and the State of Missouri by invading with hostile armies the soil of the state, attacking and making prisoners the militia whilst legally assembled under the State laws, forcibly occupying the State capital, and attempting, through the instrumentality of domestic traitors, to usurp the State government, seizing and destroying private property, and murdering with fiendish malignity peaceable citizens, men, women, and children, together with other acts of atrocity, indicating a deep settled hostility toward the people of Missouri and their institutions; and,

WHEREAS, the present administration of the government of the United States has utterly ignored the Constitution, subverted the government as constructed and intended by its makers, and established a despotic and arbitrary power instead thereof; Now, therefore,

Be it enacted by the general assembly of the State of Missouri as follows:

That all political ties of every character now existing between the government of the United States of America and the people and government of the State of Missouri are hereby dissolved, and the State of Missouri, resuming the sovereignty granted by compact to the said United States upon admission of the said state into the Federal Union, does again take its place as a free and independent republic amongst the nations of the earth.

This act to take effect and be in force from and after its passage.

On November 2, "In the northeast room of the courthouse, we elected delegates to the Provisional Congress of the Confederacy," Vest said later.

Kentucky-born John Bullock Clark (1802-1885) and Colonel Robert Ludwell Yates Peyton (1822-1863) were elected senators, and Vest, Thomas Alexander Harris (1826-1895), Caspar Wistar Bell (1819-1898), Aaron Hackett Conrow (1824-1865), Thomas W. Freeman (1824-1865), and William Mordecai Cooke (1823-1863) representatives. Dr. John Hyer (1810-1890), a retired physician and surgeon, was also elected but never took his seat.

On November 4, the legislature passed a bill thanking the militia for the "brilliant victory at Lexington" and the "brilliant victory over the Federals and the Battle of Blue Mills."

Vest won his election to the Confederate legislature over Colonel George Solon Rathbun (1829-1907), a member of Price's staff. The two were distinctly different in physical appearance and temperament, and Vest used it to his advantage. As described in *The Lexington Intelligencer* at the time of Rathbun's death in 1907, Vest left little to chance.

"At the opportune moment, Vest had one of his supporters start the cry for a speech. It was the Little Giant's opportunity, and he made the most of it. His portrayal of the soldierly qualities of his friend Rathbun made him loom on the military horizon like a Napoleon. The cap-sheaf of his eloquent speech was when he pointed to the magnificent and nearly perfect figure of Colonel Rathbun and said, 'Boys, are you going to allow the Confederate service to lose such a soldier when a damned runt like me, who is of no earthly use to the military, can serve you in the Confederate congress just as well?"

Vest spent his last night in camp with Jones, who did not see Vest again until the conclusion of the war. Years later, Jones told *The Washington Post* a story relayed to him by Vest of how he nearly did not make it to Montgomery to take his seat.

At Fort Smith, Arkansas, Jones said Vest was mistaken as "a damned Yankee" spy and about to be hanged by the 16th Missouri under the command of Colonel Sidney Drake Jackman (1826-1886), who later served under Vest's Transylvania College friend, General Joseph Orville "J.O." Shelby (1830-1897), who was considered the most capable Confederate general in the Western Theater.

McCulloch's second in command was Shelby, who joined the Missouri State Guard after Lyons killed 28 civilians at Camp Jackson, near Saint Louis. Like Vest, Shelby fought at the Battle of Wilson's Creek.

Most of Shelby's troops were from Lafayette County and would make up much of his famed "Iron Brigade," which refused to surrender at the end of the Civil War.

As the rope was placed around his neck, Vest pleaded, "Boys, I am from Missouri and have been elected to the Confederate Congress, and here is the certificate of Gov. Jackson."

Luckily for Vest, one of the soldiers recognized him. "I know this little rascal," he said. "He is the chap who raised so much hell in the legislature. He's the one who told the Yanks if they expected to put all their dead soldiers on ice, Abe Lincoln would need to make a contract for Greenland's icy mountains."

Vest was reportedly raised from his saddle, greeted with a Rebel Yell, and taken to Jackman's tent. Another Kentuckian, Jackman happened to be a friend of the congressman-elect.

CHAPTER THREE

Confederate Congressman and Senator

Vest was at home in the Confederate legislature. He made friends quickly and had few, if any, enemies. He was in a familiar crowd in Montgomery, Alabama, and Richmond, Virginia, many of whom were from his college days in Kentucky. Also in the Confederate Congress were George Washington Triplett (1809-1894), his sister's father-in-law, and Waldo Porter Johnson (1817-1885), a fellow Boonville attorney expelled from the U.S. Senate on January 10, 1862. Johnson returned home to Missouri and was commissioned as a Confederate Army colonel before joining the Confederate Senate, serving alongside Vest from 1863-65.

One of Vest's early colleagues was Lucius Quintus Cincinnatus Lamar (1825-1893), future associate justice of the U.S. Supreme Court and U.S. Secretary of the Interior, who wrote Mississippi's *Ordinance of Secession.* "He was an intense pro-slavery man and made no apology for the institution," said Vest, discounting a claim by James Gillespie Blaine that Lamar reluctantly voted for secession. "They [pro- slavery men] thought American slavery was instrumental in civilizing and Christianizing [those they enslaved]."

After the Provisional Congress, Lamar was named lieutenant colonel of the Nineteenth Mississippi Infantry, serving until July 1862, when he developed vertigo while reviewing his troops. He resigned his command and was sent on a diplomatic mission to France, where he failed to secure recognition of the Confederacy.

The Provisional Congress, held in Montgomery from February 4, 1861, to February 17, 1862, elected Jefferson Davis president of the Confederacy. Davis (1808-1889) was elected by a 6-5 vote over General Robert Augusta Toombs (1810-1885) of Georgia, who, along with William Lowndes Yancey (1814-1863) and Louis Trezevant Wigfall (1816-1874), opposed Davis at every turn throughout the war. A native Kentuckian and Transylvania University graduate who rose through the political ranks in Mississippi and Washington, D.C., Davis played a significant role in Vest's life.

Louis Trezevant Wigfall (1816-74) was a Confederate State Senator from Texas.

Vest took his seat in the Confederate Congress in February 1862 and found the hostilities within the government and legislature in full force. "[Toombs] and Mr. Davis were colleagues in the United States Senate when the Southern States seceded but were political antagonists upon every question except slavery," Vest said. "Toombs was a Whig and Davis a disciple of John Caldwell Calhoun [1782-1850], but both were extremists on the slavery question."

The rivalry between Toombs and Davis continued even years after the war, when Vest served in the United States Senate. In Davis' *Rise and Fall of the Confederacy*, the former president wrote that his election was unanimous.

In an 1884 address on the life and public service of C.S.A. and U.S. Senator Benjamin Harvey Hill (1823-1882), who had recently died, Vest, who had not read Davis' multi-volume set, said the Provincial Congress in Montgomery elected Davis by a single vote. "A few days after my speech appeared in the *Congressional Record*, Senator James Zachariah George [1826-1897], Mississippi's 'Great Commoner,' who was Davis' close friend and political ally and served in his regiment during the Mexican War, came to me with a letter written him by Davis in which he complained of my statement in the Senate, as it contradicted the assertion in his book," Vest said.

James Zachariah George (1826-1897) was a United States Senator from Mississippi from 1881-1897.

In response, Vest wrote of his admiration for his former leader. "I expressed my sincere regret that I had said anything on the subject which even annoyed him and that I not only sympathized with him in his misfortunes but had taken every opportunity to defend his conduct as President of the Confederate States, in which position I knew he had done nothing unworthy of a brave and honorable man."

He explained that his information on Davis' election came from second-hand sources and that he (accurately, it appears) heard that, in executive session, the eleven Confederate states, each casting one vote, voted 6-5 in favor of Davis over Toombs.

Hon. Benjamin Harvey Hill of Georgia, Brady-Handy Photograph Collection, Library of Congress, Prints and Photographs Division.

Toombs was called the "Mira Beau of the South," drawing comparisons to the Frenchman Honoré-Gabriel Riqueti, compte de Mirabeau (1749-1791).

"To present a unified front on such an important issue, when the doors of the executive session opened, it was announced that Davis was unanimously chosen," Vest wrote. "About these facts, about which there could be no doubt, it was evident, as I wrote Mr. Davis, that the statements made by both him and me were true, and I intended to do him no injustice."

Within days, Vest received the following hand-written response from Davis, then living at Beauvoir, his oceanfront retreat near Gulfport, Mississippi, where he spent his later years and wrote most of his memoirs.

Hon. G.G. Vest:

My Dear Sir: The misconstruction placed upon a sentence of your address has been the happy cause of a letter which I sincerely prize. Since the War, so many persons have made complaint against me to whom I felt sure of never having intentionally given offense or done injustice that I have no doubt been rendered prone to believe myself the subject of unfriendly criticism. Your letter is more than satisfactory, and I cordially thank you for the vindication you have had occasion to make of one who had no other claim upon you than that of fidelity to the cause to which you gave your heart and your conviction.

I cannot regret my mistake since it has made me the recipient of very gratifying information which I might not otherwise have had.

Faithfully yours, Jefferson Davis

Jefferson Davis, President of the Confederate States of America. Brady-Handy Photograph Collection, Library of Congress, Prints and Photographs Division.

The conflict between Davis and Yancey, an Alabama senator, according to Vest, stemmed from Yancey's disappointment of not being given a cabinet position, especially after being sent to England at the beginning of the war in hopes that his eloquence as a talented orator would advance the Confederate cause. "Yancey was mortified by finding his position was not so distinguished as when delivering his wonderful orations," said Vest, who classified Yancey as "the inveterate enemy of President Davis" and was "violent in his denunciation of the manner in which the war was conducted on the Confederate side."

Yancey's exit from the Confederate Senate was more dramatic than any other. In an impassioned debate with Hill, one of Davis' steadfast supporters and the subject of Vest's 1884 comments, the Georgian Hill hurled a large glass inkstand at Yancey, striking him on the right side of the face, cutting "a fearful gash from the temple to the corner of his mouth," Vest said. "Senator Yancey was stunned by the blow and for a time almost insensible." While the injuries were unrelated to Yancey's death, Vest said the senator was never the same afterward.

When Yancey died a year later in Montgomery, Vest was there, delayed by a break in railroad communication east of the city. "Yancey passed along the deserted street followed by two or three carriages in which were his family and a few intimate friends. There was no public demonstration, and little attention was paid to the procession," Vest said. "It was a sad commentary … the Southern people had become so familiar with death and were so much engrossed in the misfortunes brought upon them by the disastrous war that the funeral of this great orator, whose burning words fired the Southern heart and done much to cause the secession of the Southern states, attracted no more attention in the community where he lived than that of the humblest and most obscure citizen."

As for Hill, the *Richmond Examiner* wrote, "He is the very picture of smooth, plausible mediocrity." While the newspaper supported the Confederacy, editor Edward Alfred Pollard (1832-1872), who promoted the idea of "The Lost Cause" as a heroic effort undertaken to preserve Southern honor and virtue, was highly critical of Davis and any legislators aligned with him.

The third barb in Davis' side was Wigfall of Texas, who joined the Senate after a brief military career. "Wigfall had great talent and good impulses, but he was an extremist in all his opinions," said Vest, who called Wigfall brilliant, aggressive, and relentless.

"He was hostile to Mr. Davis and believed his election as president was a great disaster to the Confederate cause," said Vest, referring to Wigfall as honest but unreasonable. "I remember a conversation he had with me at Richmond the day after the surrender of Norfolk [May 10, 1862], when the *Richmond Examiner*, a paper inimical to Mr. Davis, had a leading editorial stating the day before had been a most important one in the history of the Confederacy. 'It witnessed,' said *The Examiner*, 'the destruction of the *Merrimac*, the evacuation of Norfolk, and the baptism of our President.' In commenting on the editorial, Wigfall walked up and down in his committee room on military affairs and excitedly referred to the disastrous results of the War. He said it was a great misfortune that Davis defeated Toombs at Montgomery for president. 'If Toombs had been elected, the Confederates would have been in Washington City or hell within 60 days. We might have gone to the latter place, but it would have been at a great savings of money and blood.'"

Hon. Robert Toombs of Georgia. Brady-Handy Photograph Collection, Library of Congress, Prints and Photographs Division.

According to Wigfall, Davis's election meant the war would be one of endurance and exhaustion, eventually leading to its failure.

If anything, the South needed the war to end quickly. "Davis, with his West Point tactics, has ruined us," Wigfall said. "I do not accuse him of infidelity to the Southern cause nor that he lacks courage, but I do not believe he was the sort of president we ought to have chosen."

"I never believed, nor said, that one Southern man could whip 10 Yankees," Wigfall told Vest, "but I believed, and frequently declared, the Southern people were, at the beginning, superior to the North as soldiers on account of our being trained from boyhood in the use of firearms and horseback riding, while the Northern people, though equally brave, had been corrupted by greed and lacked the individuality and self-pride which characterized Southern soldiers.

"[General] Grant was right when he declared, in discussing the subject of the exchange of prisoners, that the North could lose 10 men and the South one, with mathematical certainty, that the North would eventually win," Wigfall said.

An example of Wigfall's fanatical tendencies predated the War and included a scheme that involved Davis:

"When Lincoln was elected and Davis and I were serving in the United States Senate, I asked for a conference between the Senators from the Southern states. Jesse David Bright [1812-1875], [a Confederate sympathizer] from Indiana, who was in all essentials one of our members, was invited to attend. After the caucus met, I submitted the following proposition: when the votes of the states were placed before the joint session of the Senate and House of Representatives to be counted, as the Constitution provided, five senators, myself being one, should seize the returns and carry them into an adjoining committee room, where they should be destroyed. This being done, the result of the election could not be declared, as the only copies of these returns were required to be deposited with the Secretary of State in each state, and there was no provision in the Constitution for the use of these copies if the originals sent to Washington were not produced.

Senator Jesse David Bright (1812-1875) of Indiana was the only senator from a Northern state to be expelled for being a Confederate sympathizer.

"To prevent interference by the Capitol police or any United States soldiers at Washington, I offered to bring from Baltimore, where I was well acquainted, 500 determined Southern men, well-armed and without fear, who would be present in the galleries and corridors of the House, ready for any emergency," Wigfall continued. "If this had been done, a government de facto could have been organized and proclaimed, which would have caused the recognition of the Confederacy by foreign nations. The only two senators who agreed to join me were Davis and Bright, all the others declaring the scheme impracticable and dangerous."

In Vest's view, Wigfall was a revolutionist and dismissed his plan as the desperate actions of a disappointed and hopeless man.

Vest last saw Wigfall at the 1872 Democratic National Convention in Baltimore, where Vest was a delegate. After the body nominated the ticket of Horace Greeley (1811-1872) and Missouri Governor Benjamin Gratz Brown (1826-1885), Wigfall sent Vest a card, "We ought to nominate Spotted Tail and adjourn."

Lakota chief Spotted Tail (1823-1881) was a well-known public figure after making numerous diplomatic trips to Washington in the 1870s, seeking peace and education.

James Ronald Chalmers (1831-1898) of Mississippi served as a senior officer of the Confederate States Army, and was also a state senator and United States Congressman.

In 1863, Vest traveled to Mississippi in search of Charley, his childhood friend and cousin, serving in a regiment commanded by Brigadier General James Ronald "Little Un" Chalmers (1831-1898).

Vest learned Charley was severely wounded and in critical condition.

"He's badly off, mentally and physically," said a Confederate surgeon. "Unless someone takes a special interest in him and in the right way, he will die."

Vest said it was a short walk to the hospital Charley shared with hundreds of other wounded soldiers. "The sepulchral light in the shadowy room, the half-suppressed groans of agony, the weird shapes of the Sisters of Mercy noiselessly moving from couch to couch, were not cheerful, to say the least, and when I looked down upon the poor, wan, emaciated form before me, stretched upon a cot, and realized this was what was left of the glad-hearted, robust friend of my boyhood, I was rather disposed to give up a few of my rights in the Territories if they would let me live peaceably in the States.

"'Charley,'" I said, "'old fellow, do you know me?'

"'Yes,'" he whispered, whilst a faint gleam of light came into his eyes; "I heard you were here and sent for you.'

"I sat there, and the deepening shadows came about me whilst memory went back to our boyhood—his and mine.

"Oh, how we longed then to be men! What dreams of adventure, travel, and war, flitted before us as 'seventeenthly,' 'eighteenthly' and 'in conclusion, my dear friends,' fell from those venerable lips.

"Well, we became men, and here was the end. A bed of agony and a soldier's death!

"Deeper fell the shadows, and memory lingered amidst the scenes of the far-off past. The mind is at times disposed to vagabondize and dwell upon subjects utterly at variance with our surroundings. How often in some holy place do we find unholy thoughts pressing upon us? How often with the bier and grave do we find some ludicrous idea dancing harlequin-like by our side? And so, sitting there in the gloom by the bedside of death, I laughed aloud as the image of Old Put came out on the canvas of the past.

"'Charley, do you recollect Old Put?' I asked.

"A faint ripple of laughter from the cot satisfied me there was hope for him yet.

"When the surgeon came on his nightly round, Charley was better, and in three days, he was out of danger.

"Maimed and disfigured for the land he loved, he married in Mississippi and has no doubt told his children the story of our Sunday pigeon hunt and Old Put."

Vest served on the Committee on Judiciary during the Provisional and the Second Congress. During the First Congress, he was on the Committee on Elections.

Vest's time as a legislator was not without controversy, and for a few heated moments, it bore all the excitement of the Hill-Yancey mêlée. Reports vary, but the gist of the story is that on December 3, 1864, a "demented" woman suffering from "ration madness" burst into the Confederate House and horsewhipped Vest, earning the Missourian the dubious distinction of being the only member of Congress to be publicly horsewhipped.

One account said the unnamed woman's outrage was triggered by Vest's introduction of a resolution asking for the ages of all government clerks.

In a private letter dated December 4, 1864, North Carolina representative Josiah Turner Jr. (1821-1901) wrote to his wife that Vest's attacker went to the rostrum to explain her actions. "We had a scare in the House yesterday," wrote Turner. "A pretty woman entered the Hall [in the Virginia State Capitol] just before the House was called to order and with a cowhide belabored a member—Vest from Missouri. She then took the speaker's stand and said the member traduced her character and caused her husband to leave her by saying she had been on intimate and criminal terms with him.

"She then pointed to a Georgia member and said he had said the same thing of her, but he, the Georgia member [Hill or Hershel Vespian Johnson (1812-1880)] was beneath her contempt. She was a plucky woman and should be sent to the front."

Following the attack, Mississippian Henry Cousins Chambers (1823-1871), who joined the Senate after killing his opponent in a duel, offered, and the House unanimously approved, the following resolutions in response.

> *Whereas the Honorable G.G. Vest, of Missouri, has called the attention of this House to the fact that yesterday [December 3, 1864] when the House was in the act of assembling, an attack was made upon him in the presence of many members and spectators by a woman who had intruded her presence into the Hall; and*
>
> *Whereas this House is of the opinion, from the conduct of the woman at the time, from declarations denunciatory and threatening toward other members,*

and from other facts communicated to the House, that the said woman is, as she reported to be, of unsound mind; Therefore,

Resolved, that the members of this House hereby declare their fullest confidence in the Honorable G.G. Vest, as a gentleman of honor, incapable of giving cause for the perpetration of any such outrage, and we recognize the fact that an incident of this nature so disagreeable, but involving no disgrace, might have befallen any of the many persons present at the time of the occurrence.

Resolved, That the conduct of Honorable G.G. Vest, at the time of the attack, was eminently manly and proper under the circumstances.

Resolved further, that we deem the passage of these resolutions an act of simple justice to the Honorable G.G. Vest and the other members threatened to protect him and them against the unexplained version which may go to the public of this disagreeable affair.

The incident was kept out of the newspapers except for Turner's letter; nothing much, if anything, was said or written. Within weeks Vest joined the Confederate Senate (January 12, 1865) at the urging of Davis, but by that time, Vest had lost faith in much of the Confederate leadership. He showed flirting interests in secret plots led by Kentuckian John Cabell Breckinridge (1821-1875), yet another Transylvania graduate, then Confederate Secretary of War, and Confederate House Speaker Thomas Salem Bocock (1815-1891) of Virginia, which would reform the cabinet, force Davis to reshuffle his high command and establish a general-in-chief with broad powers. The plan would create a dictatorship with General Robert Edward Lee (1807-1870) as its temporary leader.

Unlike most members of Bocock's conspiracy, Vest, as did Breckinridge, supported aggressive emergency legislation, such as the bill he introduced to conscript Marylanders living in the Confederacy. Still, unlike Breckinridge, he never considered surrender. He also remained loyal to Davis and remained in Richmond with the fleeing Confederate

***Right:** John C. Breckinridge, Senator from Kentucky. Brady-Handy Photograph Collection, Library of Congress, Prints and Photographs Division.*

***Far right:** Thomas Bocock (1815-1891) of Virginia, 1859. Photo by Julian Vannerson, Library of Congress, Prints and Photographs Division.*

forces until peace was declared. Vest maintained his friendship with Davis until Davis died in 1889, and he always referred to him as president.

While in Richmond, the 35-year-old Vest was nothing if not social. While holding an apprentice-like admiration for Davis, he was also on friendly terms with Vice President Alexander Hamilton Stephens (1812-1883), whom he called "one of the most remarkable" public men he had ever encountered. This was not the case between Davis and Stephens, whose relationship could not be classified as cordial. "The mutual confidence which ought to have been established between them never existed," Vest said.

It was a straightforward schism to understand. Davis was "an educated soldier, with all the habits, opinions, and prejudices of a soldier. He believed War to be a great science and an art," Vest said. "He regarded the doctrines and arbitration between nations as Utopian and the idle dream of optimists."

While he knew the odds against the South regarding resources, Davis believed "cotton was king," and commercial necessity would force Europe to recognize the Confederacy.

On the other hand, Stephens was "a civilian pure and simple," Vest said. "He regarded war as the greatest calamity to any people, and that defeat in a conflict between North and South was certain."

Stephens, Vest said, "predicted that the aversion of the civilized world to human slavery would override all other considerations with foreign counties and leave the Confederate States alone and unsupported, with the resources of the whole world at the command of their enemy."

Vest described Stephens as a man of positive convictions and prejudices that bordered on fanaticism. "He was an invalid from his boyhood and told me in 1865 that for more than 40 years, there was not a single day in which he had not been entirely exempt from physical suffering," Vest wrote. "His yellow, beardless, parchment-like skin and emaciated body gave him the appearance of a corpse, and his dark, piercing eyes were the only evidence of vitality."

Stephens supported Douglas for the presidency in 1860 and voted in the state convention of Georgia against secession.

Shortly after Vest's transfer to the Senate, Francis Preston Blair Sr. (1791-1876) traveled to Richmond from Washington to propose a meeting—the Conference of Hampton Roads—between the two governments to work out the terms of an honorable peace.

Representing the Confederacy were Stephens, a former U.S. congressman; Robert Mercer Taliaferro Hunter (1809-1887), a former U.S. senator, and John Archibald Campbell (1811-1889), a former associate justice of the U.S. Supreme Court. The three were selected for celebrity status, character, and conservative views.

While later reports claimed that Lincoln handed the group a blank sheet of paper headed by the words: "Restoration of the Union" and said to them, "With this one condition, you can fill up the paper with such other conditions as you think proper and the United States will accept these terms," Vest said that, from his discussions with Stephens, that was not an accurate account of the meeting.

According to Vest, Lincoln said that he would not enter into any agreement with the authorities of the Confederate States because that would require recognition of their existence as a separate power. Lincoln would not deal with the states separately for the same reasons. Still, Vest said, suppose they were to return to the Union without further bloodshed and abide by the U.S. Constitution, including the Thirteenth Amendment (emancipation). They could "rely on a very liberal use of the power confided in him to remit those pains and penalties if peace were restored."

Stephens' proposal to Lincoln called for the United and Confederate states to unite to drive Maximilian I (1832-1867) and the French from Mexico. According to the notes of Justice Campbell, Seward seemed to favor this proposal, but Lincoln would hear nothing of it.

"The last time I saw Mr. Stephens before the collapse of the Confederate Government was at a small dinner party at which James Lawrence Orr [1822-1873], a Confederate Senator from South Carolina and afterward Minister to Russia under Grant, was the host," Vest wrote. "There were present, besides Mr. Stephens, as guests, Senator Gustavus Adolphus Henry [1804-1880] of Tennessee and Senator Allen Taylor Caperton [1810-1876] of West Virginia. The menu was not extensive and consisted principally of oysters and fish.

"Mr. Stephens made his dinner exclusively on a small, rare beefsteak, which he ate without condiments or bread, not using either knife or fork. While he held the steak in his fingers and slowly nibbled at it as he drank from a glass of brandy and water, which did not affect him in the slightest degree.

"He talked freely on the war and its results and spoke in the highest terms of Mr. Lincoln," Vest wrote. "He mentioned what had passed at the Hampton Roads Conference … He expressed his regret that his proposition to unite the Union and Confederate forces against the French in Mexico had not been adopted and said that the time had now come when the Southern people must exercise the utmost fortitude and self-control to prevent utter ruin and anarchy."

Stephens said: "I anticipate the most terrible result from the collapse of the Confederacy. The talk of carrying on a guerrilla war is wicked and absurd. All we can do is to rely on the sober second thought of the Northern people and the kindly feeling of such men as Abraham Lincoln, who is too great to indulge in anything but benevolence toward a conquered and ruined people."

The next time Vest would see Stephens was after Stephens' election to the U.S. Senate in 1866, a seat he was refused. He was elected to three terms in the U.S. House of Representatives and eventually governor of Georgia.

"No matter what may be thought of his political opinions and actions," said Vest, "the story of Alexander H. Stephens and his wonderful fortitude under suffering will elicit the admiration of future generations so long as true heroism commands the honor and respect of mankind."

In the war's closing days, with only 15 senators remaining in Richmond, Vest was among six invited to a secret meeting in the Richmond hotel room of Kentuckian Henry Cornelius Burnett (1825-1866). The others were Caperton, Hunter, Wigfall, and fellow Missourian Waldo Johnson.

In the meeting, Secretary Breckinridge presented a plan to ask Lincoln for terms of surrender. "If the Confederacy goes to pieces and our armies are disbanded without any formal action on the part of the Confederate Government, the soldiers from the cotton states and that portion of our territory not occupied by the enemy will go to their homes and probably remain there unmolested," Breckinridge said. This, however, would not be the case for the Missourians and Kentuckians in uniform. Without a binding agreement with Washington before the collapse, they would meet a much more hostile reception, especially in Kentucky, where the legislature made service in the Confederate Army a felony. "What I propose," Breckinridge said, "is this: That the Confederacy should not be captured in fragments, that we should not disband like banditti, but we should surrender as a government, and we will thus maintain the dignity of our cause and secure the respect of our enemies, and the best terms for our soldiers."

There were no takers for Breckinridge's proposal, and the government soon fled Richmond by train, then by mule, then on foot. With indictments of treason awaiting Breckinridge in Kentucky and general orders calling for the execution, if captured, of Davis, Breckinridge, Secretary of State Judah Phillip Benjamin (1811-1884), and Lee, there was little choice than to escape.

Davis made it as far as Irwinville, a crossroads town in south-central Georgia, before his capture by the First Wisconsin and Fourth Michigan cavalry regiments. Breckinridge and Benjamin continued south, split up, and reunited in Havana, Cuba. Ben Hill and Vest met up in Columbus, Georgia, on the Chattahoochee River before Vest headed west into Alabama.

Hill, who tried to rally Georgia to continue fighting, "was reluctant to embrace the Confederate cause and was the last to leave it," Vest said.

Benjamin, who served with Davis in the U.S. Senate before the war, was, according to Vest, Davis' most able ally. At one time, Benjamin served as secretary of state and secretary of war. "In one respect, he was the most remarkable man I have ever known," Vest said. "He could perform the intellectual labor of a dozen ordinary men and told me once he had never known what it was to be fatigued by professional or official duties. He had a strong, massive physique, being about 5-foot-6, with broad shoulders and a well-formed head, his features being handsome and expressive; his eyes were black and piercing, and his voice had the strong, resonant tones of the bugle, with the softness of a flute."

Years later, James Murphy, who had served as an official U.S. Senate reporter for more than 40 years, told Vest that Benjamin was the ablest man he had seen in public service: "I have never met his equal as an accomplished, well-equipped, ready debater and legislator."

That declaration was no surprise to Vest, who met Benjamin shortly after arriving in Richmond. "It was universally believed President Davis was largely influenced by Benjamin [and] every unfortunate and unpopular government act was charged to Benjamin," Vest said. As the state of the Confederacy became more desperate, the attacks on Davis and Benjamin became more venomous.

"No one knew better than Mr. Benjamin that, of all the leaders in the South, he was more obnoxious to the United States authorities and their adherents in the Southern States than even President Davis himself, and he was certain that his enemies in the Confederacy would be swift to testify against him to satisfy their enmity," Vest said. "When he saw that the cause was lost beyond any hope, he embarked from the coast of Florida in an open boat and reached Nassau, whence he proceeded to England and commenced at once his study of English jurisprudence to secure admission to the English bar."

Benjamin, a Louisiana Jew, became one of England's leading attorneys before declining health forced his retirement in France. "Just before he left England for France," Vest said, "he sent me an engraved likeness of himself in his wig and gown as an English barrister or sergeant-at-law when appearing before the highest courts of the Empire."

As for Vest, he awaited amnesty in rural Louisiana and Mexico. After a brief and failed stint as a riverboat captain on the lower Mississippi River, Vest collected his family from Danville, Kentucky, where they rode out the war. They returned to Missouri in 1867, where Vest submitted to an oppressive test oath and resumed his law practice, this time in Sedalia.

In 1902, Vest was the lone surviving member of what he called "the Confederate Delegation" in Washington. "Few of the great ones in the councils of the Confederacy are living and none who has made so great a place for himself in history since the War," the *Saint Louis Post-Dispatch* wrote of Vest. "He did not remain an idle mourner over a lost cause. After the war, he went to work without whine or delay."

During his time in the U.S. Senate, he had numerous opportunities to demonstrate his conciliatory view of the war.

Among his most moving speeches was one he made in support of a bill to provide a $100-per-month pension to the widow and family of Union General James Shields (1806-1879), whom Vest succeeded in the Senate. "The general left only his glory and his sword," Vest said of Shields, the only person to serve the Senate from three different states—Illinois, Minnesota, and Missouri. "Coming from a nationality that has been unfortunate enough to pour its blood like water in defense of every country except their own, there is not an Irish heart in these free United States that will not beat with gratitude to this Congress for this sincere evidence of their appreciation of the services of their heroic countryman."

Attached to the bill was a provision of $100 per month to be paid to Caroline S. Webster, the widow of Colonel Daniel Fletcher Webster (1813-1862), a son of Secretary of State Daniel Webster (1782-1852) who was killed at the Second Battle of Bull Run.

Vest found himself in the minority when a move was made to place then-former President Grant on the retired list of the Army, making him eligible for a military pension. Vest opposed the bill vigorously, not due to animosity toward Grant but because he believed that, once Grant entered the world of partisan politics, he forfeited "the place provided for him [by military service]."

In fairness to Grant, in Vest's opinion, the great general's fame must rest on his military record alone. "His administration of the government, especially during his second term, subjected him justly to much criticism, as he permitted himself to be made an instrument of designing politicians who thought only of themselves and cared nothing for the great soldier whom they flattered and deceived," Vest said. "He [Grant] was a soldier fair and simple, and his presidential career furnishes the best possible argument against elevating to the presidency a great general who had no experience whatever in civil affairs."

Vest was also a strong proponent for pensions for Union soldiers and voted in favor of every pension bill that came before the Senate, stating that if the Confederacy had won, he would have voted that "the last dollar and the last acre within its limits to be paid the maimed, wounded and disabled soldiers of the Confederate Army and the people of the United States to whom Providence gave triumph have the same duty imposed upon them."

CHAPTER FOUR

The Attorney and the Speaker

After President Andrew Johnson pardoned Vest on December 25, 1868, Vest settled in Sedalia, Missouri. In 1869 he went into practice with Judge Russell Hicks (1799-1876) and John Finis Philips, who also attended Centre College. Like Vest, Philips married his college sweetheart (Sallie's cousin, Fleecie Batterton [1834-1920]) from Danville, Kentucky. The partnership with Philips, a Union cavalry colonel, was prescribed by the 14th Amendment provision that prohibited former Confederates from practicing law without a Union partner. The mandate lasted until May 22, 1872, when a General Amnesty Act removed the office-holding restriction. The Vest-Philips partnership lasted until Vest's 1879 election to the U.S. Senate. Their friendship lasted the rest of Vest's life.

Hon. John Finis Philips of Missouri, ca. 1865-80. Brady-Handy Photograph Collection, Library of Congress, Prints and Photographs Division.

T.T. Crittenden said Vest and Philips' Johnson County practice was "one of the strongest in this or any state."

As an attorney, Philips said, Vest "brought to the practice of law the genius of a mind grounded in jurisprudence, the personality of a man about whom gather the mystery and glamour of having been an actor in mighty affairs, a wit, and humor of purest ray, the knowledge of human nature which comes to the discriminating man of the world who has read much and thought much and seen much and suffered much, and a soul touched by the live coal from the very altar of eloquence itself."

Crittenden agreed. "He [Vest] was natural. In the days of his prime, an indefinable charm in his voice mesmerized his listeners. His mind was a 'perfect field of cloth of gold' filled with all beautiful imagery and garnished with the richest treasures of literature and history."

Philips served as a commissioner for the Supreme Court of Missouri from 1883-85 and judge of the Missouri Court of Appeals from 1885-88.

"I don't believe Vest would have made such an exceptional judge as Philips has proven, for his was not such a cool judicial mind as Judge Philips. Few indeed are so gifted as Philips in speech or with the pen, for whatever he says or writes on the bench is a perfect transcript of his mind's boundaries of the principles he discusses. He always made others understand what he said or wrote because he understood himself what he said," Crittenden said.

Warrensburg native Francis Marion Cockrell (1834-1915), who met Vest in 1860 as a Douglas elector, said Vest made a "deep impression not only on me but also on anyone who ever heard him. We often met as attorneys—sometimes on the same side of a case, sometimes on opposite sides. He was a lawyer of remarkable ability in both civil and criminal practice. His addresses before juries were always most impressive and effective."

"It is indeed difficult to describe in words Vest as he was in those days when in full health, virility, and glowing spirits," said Crittenden. "He was the most charming man I ever saw in the social circle—when he chose to be—then again, he would be the reverse, almost as suddenly.

"Almost everybody in the central part of Missouri knew him as they saw him on the streets in his daily or hunting garb, but few indeed knew the man as he was or seemed to be."

Philips said many took Vest less than seriously: "It was a common mistake in the practice of law [to believe] he was not an industrious student, relying more upon the faculty of assimilation or intuition than investigation and induction."

"As I remember, he bore an irresistible lance in a jury case. If pathos was proper, it came as if conjured up instantly by a magician's wand," said Lamm, the Missouri chief justice. "If wit was demanded, lo! It sparked in a flash. If the case allowed invective, it came to maul and destroy. If humor, there was a glow of it like heat lightning. If logic, he formulated a syllogism with mathematical precision.

"He had the intuitive knowledge of the psychological moment in a case, the turning point where and how it was won and lost. He seized by instinct the most effective weapon to demolish a witness testimony."

In an 1875 case against the City of Sedalia, Albert T. Loewer sued the city after falling off the rail-less Fourth Street footbridge. Vest countered that Loewer, a well-known tailor, was intoxicated, thus negligent.

Witnesses for the plaintiff argued that Loewer had no more than one beer on the day leading up to the accident. Vest quipped, "He [Loewer] is so slight he would get drunk sitting on a rotten apple."

Vest said of one of Loewer's character witnesses, a 300-pound policeman, "Listen when you pass him, gentlemen of the jury, and you will hear the beer slosh in his paunch like water in a shaken rain barrel."

Vest won the case, but Loewer appealed, and in 1883 the case reached the Missouri Supreme Court, where Judge Philips recused himself because of his previous involvement alongside Vest. Loewer received a $3,500 judgment, but Vest's argument stuck. The *Sedalia Weekly Bazoo* reported soon after the ruling that "Loewer goes home drunk every night, and if everything is not to his liking, woe is on the members of his family."

In 1869, Vest defended Colonel William Alfred Warner (1817-1902), a Kentucky-born goods trader, against charges that he killed his son-in-law Samuel Walter Nutter (1840-1868) on October 22, 1868, in Lexington, Missouri. The *Bazoo* reported that Nutter drank whiskey freely, making "life a burden for his wife and infant child."

When Sallie (1848-1923), who married Samuel in 1866, filed for divorce, charging Nutter with theft, incest, and other crimes, she and her young daughter, Georgie (1867-1940), moved home to Dover with Sallie's family, which included her father; her mother, Georgia Combs Warner (1827-1916); a younger brother, and two younger sisters. Nutter allegedly poisoned the family's cistern and crept around the house with his "boon companions" late at night. They stole tools and vandalized Warner's property, prompting the family to move 25 miles northeast to Carroll County, Missouri.

Nutter then printed a "mischievous, libelous, obscene and villainous" pamphlet, which he circulated in Carroll County, prompting Colonel Warner to purchase a double-barreled shotgun and return to Lexington, where he attended the county fair. The pamphlet harshly besmirched Sallie but also charged Col. Warner with murder, theft and arson.

According to the *Lexington Register*, "Nutter drove to Pigott's bookstore, and got out for a moment, leaving his sister [Elizabeth] in the buggy. Col. Warner, seeing him go in, passed down on the sidewalk to within about 40 feet of the door, carrying a double-barreled shotgun under his arm. When within the distance above named, Nutter stepped out of the store on his way to the buggy. Warner raised his gun and fired at him, filling his breast with buckshot, killing him instantly. His sister, frantic with grief and terror, and besmeared with her brother's blood, was an object of universal sympathy."

The murder was committed in front of a dozen witnesses. "The buckshot passed through several nasty pamphlets Nutter carried in his breast pocket, directly into the victim's heart," *The Bazoo* reported.

"Both parties being wealthy, and of unquestionable standing in society, the case caused considerable gossip," wrote *The Register*.

In its coverage of the seven-day trial, *The Bazoo* said the 20-year-old widow Sallie was "a pronounced brunette, with a phenomenally fine figure and gifted with more than usual conversational powers. She was endowed with more beauty and comeliness than is fair for one person to possess." Her 17-year-old sister, Mary, was described as "extremely pretty" with a "less commanding figure."

Concerning the late-night menacing, Lexington prosecutor Amos Green disputed Mrs. Nutter's testimony that she examined the tracks around her father's house one morning and swore she saw her estranged husband's tracks.

"Did you see him?" Green asked.

"No," said Sallie.

"How then did you know it was him?"

"By his footfall on the plank."

Green assailed Sallie's testimony as unreliable—that a woman could not distinguish one man's track from another and be able to swear to it.

"Yes," Vest said. "The powers of discernment and the natural acumen of women far exceed that of a man.

"Not know her husband's footfall?" Vest cried. "Why, gentlemen of the jury, my wife not only knows me when my foot strikes the walk to my house of a night, she remarkably knows where I have been and what I have been doing."

Vest's partner, Philips, made the closing argument. "Never before or since has such an able appeal or such flights of oratory been listened in Pettis County before a jury as on that occasion," *The Bazoo* reported.

The jury returned its verdict at about 10 p.m. "Most of the audience awaited the result, standing, caucusing, conjecturing, talking over the all-absorbing topic," wrote *The Bazoo*. "Colonel Warner, quite pale and anxious, kept his seat."

Silence filled the crowded courtroom until Judge Channel P. Townsley (1833-1907) asked, "Gentlemen of the jury, have you agreed on your verdict?"

Charles G. Taylor, the jury foreman, responded, "we have," and passed the verdict to the sheriff, who gave it to the clerk, who read, in a clear, distinct voice, "We, the jury, find the defendant not guilty as charged."

The silence continued except for a lone boot heel tapping on the floor.

When the verdict finally sank in, the crowd erupted in cheers and wild yells that shook the courthouse. The gentlemen waved their hats and the ladies their handkerchiefs.

Colonel Warner rose from his seat and hugged Vest and Philips. The judge and the jury soon joined the trio as "glistening tears" fell from Warner's eyes.

An interesting side note to the trial is that James Sherman Botsford (1844-1915), a young Sedalia attorney and Vest's junior counsel in the case, was less interested in the classic case as he was in Sallie, nicknamed "The Duchess of Dover," with whom he passed notes during the seven days. "The courtship was not long; after a few months, Mrs. Nutter became Mrs. Botsford," reported *The Bazoo*. They moved to Kansas City and lived happily ever after.

There was a lawyer in Sedalia of such vanity and pomposity that Vest said that if he "had a few turkey feathers stuck in the right part of his body, he would strut himself to death."

U.S. Circuit Court Judge John Forrest Dillon (1831-1914) listened on the Federal bench to a jury speech Vest presented in an insurance case claiming a man committed suicide while sane. Vest argued that suicide was conclusive proof of insanity.

"I have lived my life among lawyers and have heard the most brilliant advocates living, yet I've never heard such an eloquent plea as the one Vest made," said Dillon, a President Grant appointee best known for establishing that local government is an absolute right of the governed.

After a long, unsuccessful day of arguing bankruptcy cases before Judge Arnold Krekel (1815-1888) in the U.S. District Court in Jefferson City, Vest sat by the front-room fireplace of the McCarty House Hotel, known for its hot biscuits at breakfast and cornbread for dinner. In front of the fire, in a fitful and troubled doze, was a red-eyed, bloody-eared bulldog.

Vest spoke sympathetically with the dog, who laid his scraped nose on Vest's knee, and wagged his stumpy tail.

"I don't remember meeting you today in Krekel's court," Vest said, "but from your appearance, surely you were there."

As a delegate to the 1872 Democratic convention in Baltimore, Vest worked for the temporary Democratic Liberal Republican coalition and the nomination of Greeley for the presidency.

There he first met Thomas Francis Bayard (1828-1898), a future colleague in the U.S. Senate. "Mr. Bayard addressed the convention in opposition to the nomination of Greeley, and I sympathized with him in all he said," Vest said. "He [Greeley, who died soon after] was in poor health at the time and stated to the convention that he was on the eve of sailing for Europe in the hope that a sea voyage and absolute rest on the other side would restore his usual vigor. He [Bayard] warned his fellow Democrats that disaster would come from the nomination of a man who had been a lifelong enemy of the Democratic party and with whose principles he had not the slightest sympathy. The Southern delegates, however, and those from New York carried the convention by storm, and Mr. Bayard's eloquent appeal was without effect."

Bayard left Baltimore disappointed and depressed. Vest next saw him again in March 1879, when Vest joined the U.S. Senate.

In 1874, Vest unsuccessfully ran for Missouri governor against Cockrell and Silas Woodson (1819-1896). When asked how the campaign was going, Vest replied, "Oh, hell, I am doing no good. It seems to me half of the Confederate Army must have served in Cockrell's brigade [The Second Missouri]."

Of Cockrell and Vest, Kentucky native James Beauchamp "Champ" Clark (1850-1921) said, "[They] are as wide apart as the poles. There is nothing spectacular, humorous, sarcastic, or eloquent about Cockrell. Like Marc Antony, he is a plain, blunt man, and he pounds away in sledge-hammer style, pouring out from his wonderful memory every fact and figure tending to sustain his side of the question till he overwhelms the opposition he evidenced on a hundred fields of carnage. His speeches are rich mines of information."

Clark said this combination created the best senatorial team any state had ever seen. Cockrell and Vest served side by side for 24 years. Vest and Philips and Crittenden and Cockrell were linked by ties of friendship, religion, and the trials of war. "Vest is one of the wittiest, most sarcastic, and most eloquent of mortals and is the best man in Missouri to send into a strong Democratic community to arouse the faithful to enthusiasm, but Cockrell is far better to send among the disgruntled to soothe them and induce their return to the fold," Clark said.

Nicknamed "The Big Four," Crittenden said each was "ever ready to assist our friends as far as we could, and they ever assisted us. If we obtained office or offices, it was because our friends stood by us, giving us the advantage of their friendship."

In 1876, Vest was a candidate for the Democratic nomination for governor but was defeated by John Smith Phelps (1814-1886) of Greene County in the primary.

"Vest had no viciousness in his nature, but at times he became moody and dispirited; he sought silence and absence from the maddening crowd's ignoble strife," said Crittenden, whose relationship with Vest dated to their childhood. "I placed Vest in nomination against Phelps before one of the finest conventions ever assembled at Jefferson City. I had evidence that it was well done and was assured by the various members of the convention that Vest would win.

"From that day, for a year or more, he was distant towards me and, when meeting, would scarcely treat me with common politeness. Why, I never knew, why he never told me. I determined not to notice his coldness, believing it arose from the mortification of defeat and from the fact that he asked me to place him in nomination, and further believing these causes may have arisen from the very tenderness of his feeling, the sensitiveness of his nature and the high spirit of the man. The cloud soon passed away, and the sunshine of his nature gleamed towards me as before."

When pressed for which—Vest or Philips— was best, Crittenden again said one's strength was the other's weakness, and together they were outstanding. "If there was any difference between them as lawyers, it was shown more distinctly in examining witnesses in the cases they had before them. They seldom engaged in criminal practice, then only in defense in the last days of their partnership, and then only for large fees or for some old friend."

Each had a unique way of attacking witnesses. "Philips went after the witness, in the beginning, in what may be called a persuasive way, or like a lion softly crouching before the leap on its prey, appearing sweetly incapable of harming any creature, leading him on as if by a magician's spell," Crittenden said, whereas Vest "first bewildered, then destroyed."

"He was a terror before a jury to a liar of any kind, whether from purchase, persuasion, or weakness," Crittenden said of Vest. "He never misled a witness by trick or device unless it was plain to see that the witness had gone into the box with a falsehood on his lips or was guided by another's diagram. If so, he would crush them like a worm. He was as direct a lawyer as I saw inside a courthouse, ever deferential towards the court and fair to the litigants and his counsel."

In 1878 Vest moved from Sedalia to Kansas City and formed a brief partnership with Judge Francis Marion Black (1836-1902) until Vest's 1879 election to the U.S. Senate and Black's 1884 appointment to the Missouri Supreme Court, which he served for a decade.

As a speaker, Vest was described as lucid and limpid. "His speeches were never long—no repetitions, no dry details," Lamm said. "His language singularly pure and classic."

From most accounts, to understand Vest, you had to see him. He used smiles, elegant metaphors, telling illustrations, and apt quotations as quickly as a legal proposition, recital of facts, irony, and personification. "Every tool in the storehouse of rhetoric was at hand and delighted the listener," Lamm said.

Congressman Champ Clark said: "An orator and a debater are very different things. A man is lucky if he is either … Vest was both—and of the highest order. In debate, Vest never met his superior in the Senate or elsewhere. As an orator in many fields, he delighted all who heard him. He could be witty, humorous, eloquent, sarcastic, pathetic, gay, or serious as the spirit moved him and as the exigencies of the occasion demanded."

Vest's voice, Lamm said, had "a resonant tremor, far-reaching and effective, with powers of imitation and personification such as you hear in great actors. These parts, coupled with his abounding wit and excellent fancy, made him a raconteur and conversationalist of a high order."

Vest's handwriting, Lamm said, was like "a copper plate in neatness and legibility." His pleadings were exceedingly neat, and he had no patience with slovenliness. "After struggling with another attorney's cramped and crabbed handwriting, I heard him characterize it in open court as looking like 'a pint of fishhooks suffering with diarrhea.'"

> *"The place for man to die, is to die for man,"*
> – George Graham Vest, 1878

Between July and October 1878, a scourge hit the Mississippi Valley, which was, at that point, the worst epidemic in U.S. history: Yellow fever, also called "Yellow Jack" and "Black Vomit," the most dreadful symptom of the disease. The patient's skin and eyes turned yellow. That was followed by abdominal pain; dark, often bloody vomiting; bleeding from the nose, mouth, and eyes; liver and kidney failure, and brain dysfunction, including delirium, seizures, and comas.

It was in 1878 that T.T. Crittenden witnessed what he considered Vest's best speech, one that called for unity and praised the North for its assistance during the outbreak that killed 60,000 people, 20,000 of whom were in the Mississippi Valley, including Missouri. "Death is in the palace as well as in the hovel," began Vest's speech at Warrensburg. "The old slave and the old master are called by the sad messenger to go hand in hand to that borne from which no traveler has ever returned.

"It would be a crime for me to utter words of political criticism against the North at this time when it is sending messages of love and cargoes of supplies to those devoted people. O, God, have not the terrors of war been heavy enough, recent enough, upon the heads of those brave people, from whose eyes the tears have scarcely wiped away?"

Crittenden described Vest's voice as sweet and musical, quivering at times.

"Thank God that the war is not only over but that the wounds and scars left by it are at last healed and obliterated by the great scourge and by the administrators of such relief," Vest said. "Providence has inflicted on the South an affliction that has made the heart of the whole people, of the whole nation, beat as with one pulsation."

Personalizing his speech, Vest used First Lieutenant Hiram H. Benner of the sternwheeler relief boat *John M. Chambers* as an example of Northern chivalry. Benner, aiding the ill at Vicksburg, contracted the disease and died four days later. Vest said Benner, a 38-year-old from Woodstock, Illinois, reflected the "type of true, noble manhood that abolishes all sectional lines" and "made the whole country feel that we were indeed one blood, one kith, and one people."

The *Chambers* left Saint Louis on October 4 at 11 a.m. for the more than 600-mile journey to Vicksburg, Mississippi, but stopped only a few minutes later at the arsenal below the city to get 20 carbines and 2,000 rounds to protect the valuable cargo from river pirates.

Arming against robbers was unwarranted. There was no threat. The overwhelming fear of contact with outsiders left the river abandoned; no one ventured close, much less attempted to board or rob the boat. Along the route, the crew witnessed what newspapers described. At each stop, they got the report of the sick, dead, and dying, and the ominous warning of what to expect downriver—"fever below."

By October 13, they reached Vicksburg, having made more than 30 stops, including Cairo, Illinois; Memphis, Tennessee, which was described as a graveyard; and Greenville, Mississippi, where 70 percent of citizens were struck. In Vicksburg, the remaining cargo was delivered. That morning, Benner became sick and was confined to his quarters. Four days later, he died. He laid in state from noon until 4 p.m., followed by his funeral, which former Union and Confederate soldiers attended. Vest claimed the ceremony did more to heal the country's wounds than all the speeches, sermons, and songs combined: "Should war ever come again, against our loved flag, from a foreign foe, the brave men of the South will forget Appomattox in defeat by rallying under the standard of our united country with all the love and chivalry that made historic the armies of Lee, Jackson, and Johnston."

Of Vest's many speeches, the one of which he was most proud was delivered before the Jefferson Club in Saint Louis on October 31, 1895, at the dedication of a bust of Thomas Jefferson (1743-1826), whom Vest credited with introducing the separation of church and state and in turn, religious tolerance, freedom of conscience and freedom of religious opinion. Virginians, of which Jefferson was one, saw his actions as a sacrilege. They pursued Jefferson throughout his life and assailed his memory after death.

> *"There is not in all his speeches one which will become a classic. What he had to say was constructed in words and phrases to reach the ear of the man before him, not the distant eye of him who might read. His speeches had no literary permanence; they were of the day, the occasion; graceful, polished at points, rude and even uncouth if the occasion demanded; filled with anecdote, apt illustration, and strange bursts of passion. Stenography caught no hint of his quality; it was useless for the purpose of record when he spoke ... Yet he convinced, swayed, dominated not only the audiences at the crossroads, not only conventions, but speech-wearied legislators."*
>
> – *The Saint Louis Dispatch*, January 4, 1902

The previous statement, written without the benefit of retrospect, fails to account for Vest's "Tribute to A Dog," a favorite among dog owners more than 140 years after it was delivered. Numerous versions appear on the internet, and many weathered scrapbooks are found with the speech clipped from a yellowed newspaper. Even at the time of his death in 1904, the "Tribute" had been published in nearly every newspaper in the country.

"His address to 'twelve good men in a box'—the one describing the loyalty of a dog to his master—is one of the most beautiful, chaste, heart-melting, and tear-compelling in our vernacular," said Clark.

On March 4, 1879, Vest was elected to the U.S. Senate, and a friend dating back to his brief enlistment in the Missouri State Guard was elected to the U.S. House. Alfred M. Lay (1836-1879) dreamed of representing Missouri in Washington from childhood. Nine months later, the 43-year-old who replaced Crittenden died and was replaced by Philips.

"At last, after years of struggle, the hour came when his hand reached the prize, and even at the moment, he was stricken down," Vest said. "In all political and even personal history, I do not know a sadder page than that written of the termination of the ensuing canvass and life's ambition."

Vest traveled home to Missouri for Lay's December funeral in Jefferson City.

He said: "No life is perfect, but each has its aggregate of good or evil; and aside from empty panegyric, this, at last, must be our question as each of us drifts out upon the shoreless ocean: Was his life for good or evil, were its duties performed?"

CHAPTER FIVE

Dog's Best Friend

"Outside of a dog, books are a man's best friend. Inside of a dog, it's too dark to read."

– Groucho Marx

George Graham Vest is best known for coining the phrase "Man's best friend is his dog" or "Dog is man's best friend," which was taken from "Tribute to A Dog," "Eulogy of the Dog," or "The Dog Speech" he delivered in a September 1870 civil suit between two neighbors in war-torn western Missouri over the killing of Drum, a 5-year-old coon hound. While Vest didn't use the words "man's best friend is his dog," he did say the following, or something close to it:

> *... The best friend a man has in this world may turn against him and become his enemy. His son or daughter, that he reared with loving care, may prove ungrateful. The money he has, he may lose. It flies away from him, perhaps when he needs it most.*
>
> *A man's reputation may be sacrificed in a moment of ill-considered action. The people who are prone to fall to their knees to do us honor when success is with us may be the first to throw the stone of malice when failure settles its cloud upon our heads.*
>
> *The one absolutely unselfish friend that a man can have in this selfish world, the one that never deserts him, the one that never proves ungrateful or treacherous, is his dog.*
>
> *A man's dog stands by him in prosperity and in poverty, in health and in sickness. He will sleep on the cold ground where the wintry winds blow, and the snow drives fiercely if only he may be near his master's side. He will kiss the hand that has no food to offer. He will lick the sores and wounds that come in encounter with the roughness of the world. He guards the sleep of his pauper master as if he were a prince.*
>
> *When all other friends desert, he remains. When riches take wings and reputation falls to pieces, he is as constant in his love as the sun in its journey through the heavens. If misfortune drives the master forth an outcast in the world, friendless and homeless, the faithful dog asks no higher privilege than that of accompanying him to guard against danger, to fight against his enemies.*

And when the last scene of all comes, and death takes the master in its embrace, and his body is laid away in the cold ground, no matter if all other friends pursue their way, there by the graveside will the noble dog be found. His head between his paws, his eyes sad but open in alert watchfulness, faithful and true, even in death.

"No man can be condemned for owning a dog. If he has a dog, he has a friend; and the poorer he gets the better friend he has."

– Will Rogers

On October 28, 1869, Charles M. Burden's prize hunting dog, Drum, a black-bodied, tan-legged foxhound "with some bloodhound in him," was killed by 18-year-old farmhand Samuel "Dick" Ferguson (1852-?) on orders of Burden's neighbor and brother-in-law, Leonidas "Lon" Hornsby (1838-1904), a sheep farmer and Ferguson's uncle and guardian. Hornsby was described as a small, wiry man with flaming red hair. He lost more than 100 sheep and even some meat from his smokehouse that spring and summer, and he warned his neighbors that "he would kill the next dog he caught on his property." Dogs had stolen butter, milk, and tallow, which were used for making candles.

Charles Burden, who sued his brother-in-law for killing his dog, Old Drum, and hired George Vest during the trial.

During the day, Burden (1828-1911) traveled to Kingsville, riding through fields of ripe corn. "He passed the days with his friends and cronies, swapping yarns, and when evening came, rode back to his home through the woodlands. Drum was the first to greet him," wrote the *Saint Louis Dispatch*.

Burden's other brother-in-law, Benjamin Franklin Hornsby (1833-1871), joined Burden and his wife, Nancy (Hornsby) Burden (1838-1872), and their six children for dinner, leaving before sunset to tend to his mules. Drum followed Frank home and continued toward Lon's farm.

Near sundown, Hornsby, less than a mile away, spied the "shadowy figure of a dog under a tree on his farm"—30 paces from his backdoor—and ordered Dick to load his gun with corn and shoot. Considered litigious and "set in his ways," Hornsby was not about to back down. When he realized it was Drum, his brother-in-law's dog, he ordered Dick to take Drum's carcass to the ford on Big Creek and dump it, hoping to avoid blame.

According to testimony in the case, Burden, smoking a pipe, and Frank heard a single gunshot. The sound came from the direction of "Lon" Hornsby's farm. "I was fearful that they had killed one of my dogs. I called my dogs, and Drum didn't come up," Burden said.

"Again, and again called the old horn, walking the woodland echoes along Big Creek to the west and south and along Lost Creek to the east," wrote Walter Chaney for the *Missouri Historical Review.* "Old Drum did not answer, nor did he come. No more would Old Drum answer Burden's hunting horn."

The next morning, Burden, described in one account as being kind and gentle but "stubbornly jealous of his rights," began searching for Drum.

"I went up to Mr. [James] Hurley's the next day and inquired if he had seen my dog," Burden said. "And then I went over to Mr. [Lon] Hornsby's. He was helping grind cider. Before I got to him, he quit working and walked off. I called after him, 'Lon, have you seen anything of my dog Drum around here?'"

Burden was described as a strong character, 6 feet tall, with blue eyes. He had thick blond hair, a neatly trimmed beard and mustache, and "a magnificent physique."

Hornsby said he had not seen Burden's dog.

"What dog was it that you shot last night?" Burden asked.

Hornsby said he had not shot a dog, but Dick had; he thought it was another dog, belonging to a neighbor, David Davenport. "He said he'd been down to the lake shooting, and when he got back, Dick said a black dog was lurking around down there, and he loaded up the gun with corn and shot him," Hornsby said.

"My dog was black, yellow, and tan," Burden said.

"I'll go and see; it may not be my dog," Burden said. "If it ain't, it's all right; if it is, it's all wrong, and I'll have satisfaction at the cost of my life."

Burden's dead dog was found on October 29, a few feet above the ford on Big Creek, below Haymaker's Mill, his head in the water, his feet toward the dam, lying on his left side, filled with shot.

"He had the resemblance of being shot with mixed shot. There were different-sized holes," Burden said. "By every appearance of the dog, he had been dragged. On one side, he was muddy, and on his ear and side, the hair was ruffed the wrong way. There were sorrel hairs on him that looked like horse hairs."

Burden also found a witness—another neighbor, Mrs. Annie White (1845-1926)—who saw Dick taking a dog toward the ford on Hornsby's sorrel mule. It was easy to follow the tracks as Burden's mule was a "pacing mule," which means its right and left legs swung together. Also, Hornsby's mule was an unusual red, making his hair easy to identify.

"The dog was in the shade of a tree. I didn't see him afterward," Hornsby testified. "I did not move that dog that night. I never saw Drum after I shot until I saw him dead in the creek."

According to numerous accounts of the killing, Old Drum was a canine celebrity in Johnson, Cass and Howard counties in western Missouri. His owner called Drum "the dog that never lied" and claimed he could tell the kind of game the dog was tracking by his baying: "He could trail a man and was good for wolves and any other kind of varmint."

Burden considered him the best of his numerous dogs and had taken him on hunting trips in Arkansas and the Indian Territory, present-day Oklahoma. "He was good for wolves and such," he said. "He was as good a deer dog as I ever had. I wouldn't have taken $150 for Old Drum. Money wouldn't have bought him." Game furnished meat, making a good hunting dog indispensable. The hound dog was an essential part of the economy.

"There was weeping and wailing in homes far and near," reported the *Saint Louis Republic*, "for Drum was a friend to every man, woman, and child."

Drum was called the "fastest and least uncertain of hunting dogs." No hunt of importance in Johnson or Henry counties was held without Drum. "His bark was singularly musical," wrote *The Republic.*

Hornsby testified that he chased Old Drum away from his house more than once but did not kill the dog or have it killed. "Dogs and wolves killed more than 100 of my sheep," Hornsby said. "A dog came to my house at about 8 o'clock. Dick proposed to shoot him. I told him to load the gun with corn so it wouldn't hurt him. It was a black-looking dog, and it howled like a hound." Once shot, "it ran and jumped over the clay brick fence. It did not howl again."

Dick said the dog yelped in pain, jumped the fence, and disappeared.

Neighbors heard the howling of the wounded dog as it grew fainter until it died away.

"Burden came over October 29 angry," Hornsby said. "I told him I had not killed his dog. He said if he found his dog dead, he would take it out of my hide. I did not carry the dog down to the mill. Or drag the dog, nor did anyone else with my knowledge. If they did, I don't know it. I went to bed."

Hon. Francis Marion Cockrell of Missouri. Brady-Handy Photograph Collection, Library of Congress, Prints and Photographs Division.

Burden first sued before Justice of the Peace George Norman (1842-1896), but the November 8 trial ended in a hung jury. In January 1870, another jury found in favor of Burden in the sum of $25, thus giving Burden satisfaction and establishing that Lon Hornsby directed and caused Dick to kill Old Drum.

Hornsby appealed to the Johnson County Court of Common Appeals. The trial was slated for March, and new attorneys were on each side—Crittenden and Cockrell for

Wells H. Blodgett, 1893, Missouri History Musuem.

Hornsby and Elliot and Wells Howard Blodgett (1839-1929) for Burden. Hornsby won this round, so Burden retained Philips and Vest, who presented a motion for a new trial based on new evidence.

Nearly a year after Drum's death, the case went to trial for the fourth time in Warrensburg. During the October 1870 trial, Vest said he would "win the case or apologize to every dog in Missouri."

"The Burden and Hornsby clans were out in full force, and the most memorable dog trial proceeded," Chaney reported.

Depositions of witnesses in Kansas and Texas had been taken and read in evidence. They proved the finding of Drum's carcass on Big Creek near Haymaker's Mill and, by inference, showed that on the night he was shot, his body was carried to the creek and left there, supposedly by Ferguson. Burden's side proved that a shooting had taken place on Hornsby's property.

Hornsby's side argued that he had shot a dog, but it was not Drum. In a deposition, Charles M. "Jack" Sterling (1827-1911), who by the time of the fourth trial lived in Bourbon County, Kansas, claimed he saw Drum on the north side of Big Creek, going toward the mill at the time of the shooting at Hornsby's. He claimed Drum passed him after he crossed the ford, and soon after, he heard a pistol and a gun fired at about the same time. He heard the dog howling, and the noise grew fainter until it faded.

Sterling spent the evening of October 28 at the home of William John "Butterhead" Davis (1841-1916), and the following day, when he stopped to water his mules in the creek, he and Davis saw the same dog he had seen the night before, lying near the crossing, with his head in the creek.

Davis did not hear a shot. He was away from his house, cutting a bee tree, and when he returned home, Sterling was there.

Rev. William Walker Palmer (1848-1917) testified that he was home near Haymaker Mill and saw a dog lying on its right side with his head near the water. The dog was shot in its left side.

Hornsby produced numerous witnesses to dispute Sterling's story. Farmer Abraham Helms (1828-1886), who lived within 200 feet of the mill with his wife and six children, said 10 to 12 people were camped within 300 feet of his home in the open. All the campers were in camp before the reported time of the shooting and were awake past 10 p.m. None of the campers saw Sterling cross the ford, nor heard gunfire, nor did they hear a dog howling.

While Hornsby continued to claim in the final trial that neither he nor Ferguson shot Old Drum, he asserted his right to do so. "Is it not customary to shoot dogs when they are in the habit of prowling around after night doing mischief?" he said.

With both sides presented, Vest, who allowed his partner to offer most of the case to this point, rose from his chair to deliver the famous closing argument.

For Edwin Malcolm Chase French's 1930 book, the author interviewed members of Vest's family, which may have included his 74-year-old daughter Mollie or 71-year-old son Alexander or one of Vest's seven grandchildren.

They said Vest, a young attorney at the time of the "dog trial," was attending a session of the Circuit Court at Warrensburg, and while waiting for the trial of a case in which he was interested, a case came up for trial in which a farmer filed an action for $50 in damages against his neighbor for killing his hound dog. The lawyer, Blodgett, who represented the plaintiff, Burden, invited Vest to assist him. Vest agreed to help for $10. "During the examination and cross-examination of witnesses, both for the plaintiff and the defense, Vest kept absolutely quiet and took no part in the proceeding. When the witnesses on both sides had all been heard, and the time had arrived for arguments to the jury, the plaintiff's lawyer made the opening address to the jury, the defense lawyer [Cockrell] then spoke, and the plaintiff's lawyer then asked Vest if he did not care to address the jury. Vest said no, he thought the case had been tried as well as it could be tried, and the plaintiff's lawyer then said if he did not take some part in the proceeding, he thought that his client would object to him receiving any fee and he had better make the closing address to the jury.

Vest then arose, said Crittenden, and without notes or any preparation, 'Gentlemen of the Jury: The best friend a man has in this world ...'"

"Don't accept your dog's admiration as conclusive evidence that you are wonderful."

– Ann Landers

Several accounts of the trial reported that when Vest returned to his seat, tears were running down the faces of several of the jurors and spectators. One of Hornsby's attorneys, Crittenden, was reported to have said, "We'd better get out of here before all of us are hanged."

Crittenden confirmed the comment in an interview shortly after Vest's death. "I said to Cockrell that we were defeated, that the dog, though dead, had won," Crittenden said, "and we better get out of the courthouse with our client, else all would be hanged."

After three or four minutes of deliberation, the jury returned a verdict in favor of Burden and awarded him $50. The judge amended the judgment back to the original $25 figure.

The report of this case, *Charles Burden vs. Leonidas Hornsby*, 50 Mo. 238, is less than a page long, caption and all. There is no record of Vest's speech, except in the memory of the speaker and the courtroom witnesses.

Judge Foster P. Wright (1807-1887) presided over the final four-hour case. He allowed each side two speeches, saying, "I want this dog case fully tried and ended; it has already exhausted too much time."

In a 1901 interview, Crittenden said Blodgett gave the opening speech. "I followed next, and Cockrell followed me," Crittenden said. "I thought we had the jury on our side politically and sympathetically, and the verdict was sure to be against Drum. Blodgett had made a great speech, he being always an accomplished trial lawyer, but naturally I thought Cockrell had made a greater one."

Cockrell and Crittenden's offices were in Warrensburg, while Vest and Blodgett were from Sedalia, 30 miles to the east. "Half of the jurors were our clients who had never failed us on previous trials when we had half a chance for a verdict," said Crittenden.

As Vest prepared to take his turn, Crittenden described Vest as appearing listless and indifferent but had known Vest long enough never to underestimate the danger of his oratory, especially when he noticed a constrained smile.

"His voice was as musical as a chiming cathedral bell and as sweet as distant murmurs of flowing waters," Crittenden said.

Vest modestly claimed that his speech deserved no great place in the annals of oratory, but it has enjoyed a longer shelf life than his speeches for the establishment of Yellowstone Park in 1872 and the Pure Food Act of 1879.

Crittenden disagreed with Vest's self-deprecating opinion. "I have often heard him, but I have never heard from his lips, nor from those of any other man, so graceful, so impetuous, and so eloquent a speech as Vest's before the jury in the dog case. He seemed to recall from history all the instances where dogs displayed intelligence and fidelity to man. He quoted more lines of history and poetry about them that I supposed had been written, capping the moment he had erected by quotations from the Bible, of dogs soothing the sores of Lazarus; from Byron's ''Tis Sweet to Hear the Honest Watchdog's Bark,' and Scott's 'The Hound's Deep Hate and Huntsman's Ire;' and from Motley's graphic description of how the fidelity of a dog had prevented the capture of William of Orange by the Duke of Alva.

"It was as perfect a piece of oratory as ever was heard from the pulpit or bar," said Crittenden, who confirmed that everyone, including the jury, lawyers and audience, was entranced. "I looked over at the jury and saw that there were tears, especially the foreman, who wept copiously as one who had lost his best friend."

When Hornsby appealed to the Missouri Supreme Court, Judge Philemon Bliss (1813-1889), future law school dean at the University of Missouri, sided with Judge Wright.

The participants in the third trial on September 23, 1870, read like a Who's Who of Missouri. In addition to Vest, Vest's partner, Philips, a Union colonel during thc Civil War; George N. Elliott (1824-1899), a Union captain, and Blodgett, a Medal of Honor recipient, represented Burden. In one of the earlier hearings, *Warrensburg Journal* editor David A. Nation (1828-1903), an editor, attorney and minister who was the much-older second husband of axe-wielding prohibitionist Carry Nation (1846-1911), appeared on Burden's behalf.

Hornsby's attorneys were Crittenden, a former lieutenant colonel of the 7th Cavalry, Missouri State Militia (Federal), second in command to Philips; Cockrell, a brigadier general in control of the 1st Missouri Brigade (CSA), and Colonel A.W. Rogers.

Philips became U.S. District Court judge for the Western District of Missouri. Crittenden, elected governor in 1880, issued the $10,000 reward that led Robert Newton "Bob" Ford (1862-1892) and Charles Wilson "Charley" Ford (1857-1884) to kill Jesse James (1847-1882) in St. Joseph, Missouri, on April 3, 1882.

Blodgett, who became a state senator in Missouri and later vice president of the Wabash Railroad, told Henry Huston Crittenden (1851-1943), the governor's son, in a story for *The Annals of Kansas City*, which was reprinted in the *Missouri Historical Review*, he hired Vest.

Blodgett told Burden, "I must have some help in this case, or I will lose it," then arranged with Vest to speak before the jury for $10.

According to H.H. Crittenden, when Blodgett first approached Vest, sitting by a stove in the public part of the courtroom, Vest said, "What, that dog case?" Blodgett, who lived until 1929, told Crittenden in 1915, as the last surviving participant, that he did not think that Vest—who was in court on another matter—had paid any attention to the case during the trial, but "his masterly effort showed otherwise."

Another account says that Vest sat in on the proceedings as the second counsel but took no part in the trial until the closing arguments and only then collected his share of the fee. Unshaven and unprepared, Vest rose from his seat and made the off-the-cuff speech, said his son, Alex.

In a hyperbolic description in the June 1910 issue of *The Lotus Magazine*, travel writer and opera critic Gustov Kobbé (1857-1918) wrote, "When Vest left the courthouse, even the dogs of the village seemed to gather around him in their love and followed him, as their friend, to his hotel."

The three-minute speech has been published worldwide thousands of times. In 1927, it was used in a filibuster in the Missouri Legislature in support of a canine tax bill. After Democratic Senator Lon Slaven Haymes (1886-1977) of Springfield read the "eulogy" word for word, Senator Alfred Lackey McCawley (1876-1966) of Carthage rose from his seat and said: "And who would object to paying a tax on a friend like that?"

The brief speech brought fame to Vest and Old Drum, who lives on today via the internet, where the pair are featured on numerous sites dealing with the proper treatment of animals.

The speech is not without controversy. Former Attorney General John Tull Barker (1877-1958) long contended that Vest never made the speech. "He made some remarks during the trial, but his remarks were never recorded, and the speech we now have is simply an unknown journalist's imagination," Barker said. According to Charles O'Halloran of the Kansas City Public Library, Barker's opinion was based on his life-long acquaintance with the speech and men who knew Vest personally.

It is true that, for years, Vest's speech was referred to as "The Lost Speech." According to Judge Max D. Aber (1867-1961) in 1956, Captain William Clinton Marlatt (1841-1910), who was city clerk and in attendance for Vest's closing argument, had written it down, and for years it was in Marlatt's office. "Captain Marlatt was not a lawyer, but he was a man of uncommonly quick mental grasp and a rapid penman," Aber wrote.

Samuel Taggart White (1837-1914), a Warrensburg native and Vest's law clerk from Washington & Lee, also took notes. "He [White] used to lament that Vest's fine eulogy to the dog had not been preserved," Aber wrote. "The speech was never mentioned in and about Warrensburg legal circles, except as 'The Lost Speech.'"

Vest's "Eulogy" first appeared in print in 1890. According to Aber, in 1890, Vest's son-in-law, George P.B. Jackson (1846-1910); Jackson's law partner, John Montgomery (who also worked with White), and Vest met in Sedalia and reconstructed the speech the best they could from Vest's memory and the existing notes.

"It may be relied upon that it is probably as nearly the wording of what was said as are the words of our Devine [sic] Lord, as reported by Saint Matthew when he wrote his Gospel somewhere around 55 A.D. [20 years after Jesus' death]," Aber said. "They were in essence, the same."

"I am Mog. Half man, half dog. I'm my own best friend"

– Comedic actor John Candy in the movie "Spaceballs"

The feuding brothers-in-law eventually reconciled. Both are buried in the Hornsby Cemetery, south of Holden, Missouri.

Fate was cruel to several of the participants. In an interview with the *Saint Louis Republic*, Alonzo Sterling, a minister who knew all the participants, said, "The costs on both sides were hefty. This dog case crippled both men financially, even breaking up Hornsby's property."

Dick Ferguson, the reported shooter of Old Drum, was killed by gunshot wounds months after leaving Missouri to start a new life in Anadarko, Oklahoma. According to Sterling, Burden moved west to Washington, where he died at an old age. Hornsby was reduced to a day laborer and reviled as a dog killer in his community.

The story was retold many times on film and stage.

In 1958, Central Missouri State College presented "Old Drum," a play by Professor Ruth Kline and directed by her husband, Charles. CMSC revisited the trial in "Drum" by Jack Butler in 1970. In 1993, the Johnson County Historical Society and Old Drum Festival Committee presented "Who Shot Old Drum?" by John Horner.

Missouri-born actor Scott Bakula portrayed Vest in the 2000 made-for-television film, "The Trial of Old Drum." Set in the 1950s, country music legend Randy Travis plays a modernized version of Charles Burden.

Future President Ronald Reagan (1911-2004) played Vest in an episode of the "Death Valley Days" TV series in 1964.

The lamented Old Drum certainly had his post-mortem day in the sun. In 1948, Fred Allen Ford (1891-1976) of Blue Springs, Missouri, Harry Williams of Holden, Missouri, and Richard Raker of Warrensburg erected a granite stone at the crossing of Big Creek, where the dog's body was found. A statue of Drum, sculpted by Saint Louis sculptor Reno Gastaldi (1918-2007), stands outside the Johnson County Courthouse in Warrensburg, erected on September 23, 1958, the 88th anniversary of the trial; more than 3,000 spectators attended the dedication.

This bronze statue in front of the Johnson County Courthouse in Warrensburg, Missouri, was placed in honor of Old Drum, the faithful dog of Charles Burden made famous by George Vest.

Vest's great-granddaughter, Mary Vest Dunham Colt, was one of the attendees. His granddaughter Sally Vest Jackson Harnsberger (Mary Jane's daughter) sent a letter on behalf of the surviving grandchildren and great-grandchildren.

The historical society maintains other statues of Drum inside and outside the original courthouse. A bust of Drum stands inside the Missouri Supreme Court Building in Jefferson City.

Drum's reach extends far beyond Missouri. The stained-glass window welcoming visitors to Columbus, Ohio's animal shelter depicts the Johnson County statue.

In 1991, Old Drum was No. 6 overall on *National Lampoon*'s Roadside America listings of a dozen "True-Blue Dead Dogs." In 2017, then-Missouri Governor Eric Greitens (1974-) signed Senate Bill 376, naming Old Drum Missouri's State Historical Dog.

Conservators treated original records related to the case, ensuring their preservation.

The *1870 Burden v. Hornsby* case file from the Johnson County Court of Common Pleas was sent to the State of Missouri Archives' conservation lab for analysis and treatment. Conservators mended torn pages, removed adhesives, and used humidification to flatten folded and wrinkled pages.

After treatment, the documents were utilized to create an interactive lesson plan, *Man's Best Friend: The Old Drum Story*, for grades 9 to 12. In addition to sharing a vital part of Missouri's past with students, the educational resource uses the case's journey from a justice of the peace to the Missouri Supreme Court to teach students how the judicial system operates, exposing them to several original historical documents. The documents were then presented to the Johnson County Historical Society, which returned the records to the Old Courthouse, where the trial was held, for public display.

> *"If you pick up a starving dog and make him prosperous, he will not bite you; that is the principal difference between a dog and a man."*
>
> – Mark Twain

One of Twain's most adored quotes was, "If a man could be crossed with the cat, it would improve man, but it would deteriorate the cat." Twain was a cat person whose love of felines pervaded his literature and writing habits. Regardless, when he presented a paper to the New York and London Anti-Vivisection Societies in 1899, he prefaced it with Vest's "Eulogy on the Dog." Vivisection is performing operations on live animals for experimentation or scientific research, supporting Twain's claim: "The more I learn about people, the more I like my dog."

[WARNING: If shooting dogs wasn't bad enough, readers, especially animal lovers, should know that the following section contains disturbing material one editor described as "awful."]

Mark Twain on Vivisection

I believe I am not interested to know whether vivisection produces results that are profitable to the human race or doesn't.

To know the results are profitable to the race would not remove my hostility to it. The pains which it inflicts upon unconsenting animals is the basis of my enmity towards it, and it is to me sufficient justification of the enmity without looking further.

It is so distinctly a matter of feeling with me and is so strong and so deeply rooted in my make and constitution, I am sure I could not even see a vivisector vivisected with anything more than a sort of qualified satisfaction.

I do not say I should not go and look on; I only mean that I should almost surely fail to get out of it the degree of contentment which it ought, of course, to be expected to furnish.

I find some very impressive paragraphs in a paper which was read before the National Individualists Club (1898) by a medical man … and have tried to understand why it should be considered a handsome thing to belong to a human race that has vivisectors in it.

Vivisectors possess a drug called curare, which effectually prevents any struggle or cry when given to an animal. A horrible feature of curare is that it has no anesthetic effect; but on the contrary, it intensifies the sensibility to pain. The animal is perfectly conscious, suffers doubly.

Twain hammers his point by using graphically descriptive examples of atrocities performed on sensitive animals, including cats, dogs, frogs, and rabbits. "They have been boiled, baked, scalded, burnt, frozen, and repeatedly drowned, brought back to consciousness and drowned again."

It's not your typical Twain story, but for one of the great writers of the 19th and 20th centuries and proclaimed cat lover to front his paper with Vest's enduring work is a testament to its effectiveness.

Samuel Langhorne Clemens, aka Mark Twain, 1907. Photo by A.F. Bradley.

CHAPTER SIX

Jesse, Frank, and George

On July 7, 1876, two weeks after "Custer's Last Stand," the James-Younger Gang robbed the Missouri-Pacific Railroad at Rocky Cut, near Otterville, Missouri, east of Sedalia. Jesse Woodson James and Thomas Coleman "Cole" Younger (1844-1916), the gang's leaders, treated Vest to breakfast in Sedalia the Friday morning of the robbery. They told Vest their plans and asked what he would charge to defend them if caught. Vest paused and replied, "Half of anything you get."

Like Vest, Jesse was a Democrat. He was simultaneously intimidating, reckless, serene, rational, and a lunatic. His high, thin contralto voice "twanged like a catgut guitar whenever he got excited," wrote the *Kansas City Star*. Also, like Vest, Jesse knew the books of the Bible and could recite psalms and poems. Much of Jesse's story is a myth based on fact. So entangled is his story that fiction and reality are impossible to separate.

Jesse's eyes were "clear steel-blue" with a slight green tint. He was left-handed and cut off the nub of his middle-left finger while cleaning a gun. When he entered a room, heads turned; in stores, clerks backed away. Animals cowered.

Cole was described as looking like a bishop but fighting like a Bengal tiger. Cole was "quiet," "deeply religious," and a man any congregation would welcome. Unlike Jesse, he was articulate, personable, and likable.

Vest was an excellent choice to represent the gang. He came with the recommendation of his long-time friend General Shelby—Cole and Jesse's commanding officer, mentor, and confidant. Those who followed Missouri law knew Colonel Warner (see page 52) was guilty of murdering his estranged son-in-law in 1868, but Vest knew precisely which heartstrings to pull to sway a Missouri jury. Vest won far more cases than he lost, regardless of his clients' guilt or innocence.

His clients were not just outlaws; they represented Missouri's complex personas—the conflict between slavery and opposition to it, houses divided, emancipation, what the Jameses considered "heavy-handed reconstruction," greed, the expansion and corruption of the railroads—progress, the dawn of a new age and the loss of an old one.

That night, the gang grabbed $15,000 ($428,000 in today's value), but the trial for which Jesse and Cole asked for Vest's representation never materialized.

The Rocky Cut cash was earmarked to finance the robbers' trip to Minnesota, the home of recently added gang member William "Bill" Chadwell (1853-1876), who allegedly used the alias Bill Stiles. If successful, it would be the gang's finale. A sizable northern bank in the correct frontier town could set them up for life and recoup the financial losses the Youngers' father unjustly endured. Once completed, they would navigate south to Missouri, where Vest would save them from any charges that might follow.

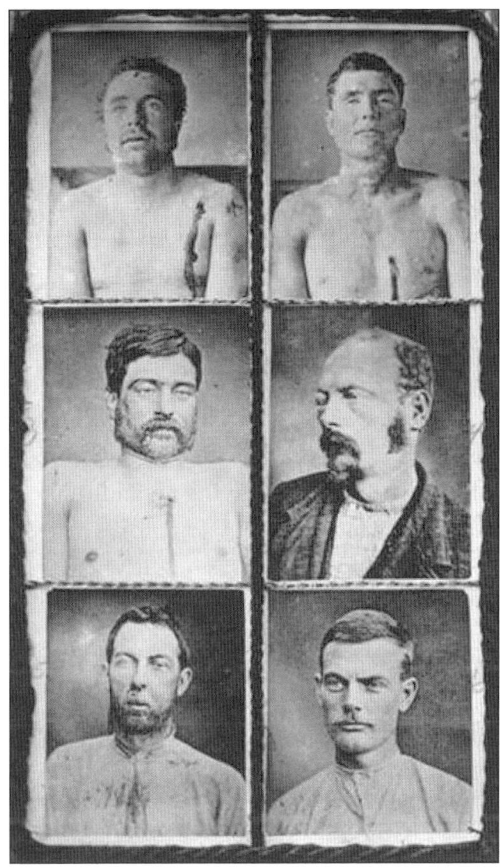

Dead and captured Northfield Raid gang members, produced by Sumner Studio, 1876. Left to right from top: Clell Miller, Bill Chadwell (misidentified by authorities as Bill Stiles), Charlie Pitts, Cole Younger, Jim Younger, and Bob Younger. Minnesota Historical Society photo.

Around sundown, Jesse and Cole, Frank James (1843-1915), Robert Ewing "Bob" Younger (1853-1889), William McClelland "Clell" Miller (1850-1876), Samuel George Wells (alias Charlie Pitts) (1844-1876), Bill and another newcomer, Hobbs Kerry, rendezvoused. The first six moved on to apprehend the night watchman while Bill and Hobbs were lookouts, holding the horses.

As a precaution, the gang stacked ties on the track, and when the eastbound train from Kansas City to Saint Louis appeared around 10:30 p.m., they had the watchman flag it down. When the train stopped, they boarded, emptied two safes, quickly mounted their horses, and disappeared into the night.

A nervous 23-year-old Kerry was arrested on July 31 in Joplin after flashing cash, what was left of his cut, and bragging about being a member of the James-Younger Gang. The simpleton enjoyed talking and promptly gave up the names of his accomplices. He also revealed what he thought accurate: that the gang was headed south to Texas.

For his cooperation, Kerry's sentence was shortened to four years. What became of him after his prison stay is unknown.

Bill pitched the idea of striking a northern bank, a plan Jesse and Bob loved. Cole and Frank tried to talk them out of venturing so far north. They entered a game of outlaw chicken when they couldn't dissuade them. Clell, Jesse's most devoted disciple, had little choice. James Hardin "Jim" Younger (1848-1902), enjoying a peaceful life in California, met the brothers in Council Bluffs, Iowa. Cole hoped Jim, the most persuasive of the brothers, would talk some sense into Bob. "I never saw him [Bob] so blindly enthused," said Jim. "Neither Cole nor I could reach him."

Cole then urged Jim to rejoin the group to keep their baby brother safe. Soon Charlie was in, too, also reluctantly.

The eight split up to reach Minnesota and boarded a train to Saint Paul. Jesse, Frank, Clell, and Jim went first, and Cole, Bob, Charlie, and Bill followed. By mid-August, they were scouting Minnesota.

The gang initially planned to rob the First National Bank of Mankato on September 4. Novelist and playwright Sinclair Lewis (1885-1951) wrote of Mankato, "in its garden-sheltered streets and aisles of elms of white and green New England is reborn."

That plan was scrapped because of the crowded downtown streets. The First National Bank of Northfield, more off the beaten path, was next on the list.

Northfield was a thriving agricultural center focused on wheat and corn and rich in mills. Located on the Cannon River in southeastern Minnesota, 40 miles south of Saint Paul, Northfield was not on the way to anywhere. Bill knew the roads well and could easily guide them around and out of Minnesota.

General Adelbert Ames, ca. 1860-65, who later served as the governor of Mississippi. National Archives photo.

Cole and Bob later said the gang also selected the bank because they believed Union Major General Benjamin Franklin Butler (1818-1893), whom they called "Silver Spoons Butler," had $75,000 in ill-gotten gains invested in the bank, and Butler's son-in-law, Union General Adelbert Ames (1835-1933), Mississippi's Reconstruction governor, with whom they "had a spite against," had recently deposited $50,000 in the bank. To Jesse, the money was secondary. He wanted to bring down Ames, whom he called "a villainous Yankee" and "the carpet-bag governor of Mississippi." An aggressive supporter of civil rights for freedmen, Ames returned to Northfield after resigning as governor.

"They wanted to rob a bank full of Yankee gold," said historian and author John J. Koblas (1942-2013), who perpetuated the theory that Bill Stiles was an actual person rather than Bill Chadwell's alias. "It was a North-South thing. ... Some people called the raid on Northfield the last battle of the Civil War. The War had been over for 11 years.

"I say there's a strong possibility of a ninth man [Stiles] waiting on the edge of town, probably with fresh horses, guarding the escape route," wrote Koblas in *The Jesse James Northfield Raid: Confessions of the Ninth Man*. In Koblas' theory, Stiles spent months plotting escape routes and getting familiar with each prospective bank. According to Stiles, the farmers in the rich Minnesota countryside were "easy pickings" and "couldn't identify an outlaw band if it surrounded them."

After arriving in Minnesota, the group spent a week in Saint Paul, seeing the sights, playing poker, and shopping for matching linen duster coats, top-of-the-line hats, and jewelry. There, they met up with Stiles, a career criminal in and around the Twin Cities and the Dakotas.

Half the group then went to Red Wing and the other to Mankato, east and southwest of Northfield, respectively. They also scouted Faribault, Owatonna, Millersburg, and Lake Crystal. In Chaska, they played poker with Carver County Sheriff Frederick "F.E." DuToit (1844-1922), a journalist and later state senator, at the Brinkhaus Saloon Livery Barn.

They bought fine horses and saddles and explored, agreeing to meet near Dundas, south of Northfield, on the morning of September 7. They told people they were surveyors studying Minnesota's topography or Kentucky explorers bound for Dakota's Black Hills.

They wanted to appear as two or three separate groups of travelers, so the matching dusters were probably not the best idea.

Three pieces of intel would have proven handy to the gang. First, September 7 was the first day of Minnesota's hunting season, so most men were close to their guns. Second, Northfield's gentleman farmers, whom they saw as easy marks, had migrated from Vermont, where they had served in the Union cavalry. They were not, as the mysterious Stiles claimed, "rubes." Many were witnesses to the Saint Albans Raid, the northernmost land action of the Civil War, in which Kentuckian Bennett Henderson Young (1843-1919) led 22 Confederate soldiers across the Canadian border on October 21, 1864, seeking money to fund their failing army and draw attention away from the southern battlefront. Third, by chance, an Indian circus (Wild West Show) was planned that evening in Northfield, and many of the citizens expected a "staged" shootout promoting the event. The evening show was arranged by Mayor Hiram Scriver (1830-1890), who built the city's first large stone building, which housed the First National Bank, the Lee & Hitchcock dry goods store, and a hardware store, J.S. Allen & Sons.

The original plan was to break into groups. Jesse and Bob would go into the bank. Frank, Cole, and Clell would stand watch outside, and Jim, Charlie, and Bill would guard the Cannon River Bridge.

The group met in Dundas early that Thursday morning and revised the plan. Frank now wanted to go into the bank, leaving Cole and Clell as lookouts. The group's goal was to appear unrelated, so they traveled various routes to Northfield, meeting up again in the woods north of town, where most of the gang consumed copious amounts of whiskey.

At one o'clock, Jesse, Bob, and Frank would cross the bridge and the large Bridge Square. Cole and Clell would follow an hour later and take positions as the trio entered the bank. Jim, Charlie, and Bill would hang back. Under no circumstances would citizens be killed. If fired upon, the group would shoot to wound or scare, not kill. Cole or Clell would fire a shot if anything went wrong, calling the reserves to advance. After the robbery, they would reunite at the bridge. Bill, Clell, and Bob would cut the telegraph lines, and Bill, the well-traveled Minnesotan, would lead them to safety.

According to Robert Allan Pinkerton (1848-1907), founder of the famed Pinkerton Detective Agency, Jesse was "the worst man, without any exception, in America." Described as a slender 5-foot-8, Jesse was a vain health nut. Worried about his ever-thinning chestnut brown hair, he kept it well-trimmed and tried various cures for his growing baldness. Jesse drank vegetable juices and potions and worked out with weighted pins. "He is utterly devoid of fear and has no more compunction about cold-blooded murder than he has about eating his breakfast," Pinkerton said.

Of Pinkerton, Vest said, "Time and time again, these men, said to have been Mr. Pinkerton's detectives, have come into the State of Missouri without consultation with state authorities, and ignoring the laws and autonomy of the state government, have undertaken for their purposes to make arrests."

In 2013, historian James Allder compiled the available sources into an exhaustive timeline of the afternoon's events. The witnesses who shared memories over the years agree on most of Allder's points, but not all. Historians disagree on who was in the bank and outside.

In the hundreds of books written about the raid, most agree the gang entered Northfield from different directions, and at least five of the gang members met across the Cannon River Bridge at a restaurant owned by Vermonter John Girden Jeft (1838-1908), near Ames Mill (owned by General Ames' father, Jesse). They enjoyed a 50-minute breakfast of fried eggs, ham, and more whiskey, finishing shortly after noon.

At one o'clock, Jesse, Bob, and Charlie headed for Bridge Square, a mud-and-dirt, horseshoe-shaped bend of Division and Fourth streets. Their horses cantered past Ames Mill and crossed the bridge. They tied their horses to nearby hitching posts and strolled several yards along the large Scriver Building to the Lee & Hitchcock dry goods store, at the opposite end of the building as the bank. Charlie sat atop a box, and Jesse (or possibly Frank) and Bob leaned against the banister and ran up the side of the building facing Division to the south.

The trio drew the attention of the townspeople, who noted their "marvelous" appearance. In a 1966 interview with the *Saint Paul Sunday Pioneer*, 100-year-old Maude Adelle Ordway (1866-1970) remembered seeing them as she crossed the square with her father, Edward Swift Bill (1833-1919), from the hardware store owned by Anselm R. Manning (1833-1909) to the grocery owned by her disabled uncle, Frederick "Fred" Shatto (1833-1907). Born in Vermont, Bill was a private in the 8th Minnesota Infantry and participated in Sherman's March to the Sea. Maude was impressed with the strangers' big hats, clean linen duster coats, and silver horse bridles. "The horses were beautiful animals," she said.

John Archer (1838-1920) said of the horses, "they were all first-class animals and would attract attention anywhere."

Former Union cavalryman Francis Howard (1838-1901), who pursued the Saint Albans Raiders in 1864, passed Cole and Clell on the far side of the Cannon River Bridge. He met up with his friend, Elias T. Stacy (1843-1882), in front of the Scriver Building, and both took notice of the other strangers—Bob, Jesse, and Charlie—around the corner.

"Stacy, those gentlemen bear watching."

"I think so, too," Stacy said.

Hardware store owner James Sim Allen (1825-) remarked aloud, "Who are these men? I don't like the looks of them."

Howard and Stacy, standing nearby, agreed.

George Chapman Bates (1839-1901), a Vermont infantryman, and C.O. Waldo, a "commercial traveler" from Council Bluffs, Iowa, stood in the Bates store doorway. The robbers unknowingly drew attention, and the prevailing scuttlebutt tagged them as well-to-do cattle buyers.

Danforth John "D.J." Whiting (1844-1920), a dentist, was up the steel staircase of the Scriver Building. He saw the men loitering below and was suspicious but shrugged it off and returned to work.

Back across the square, Cole and Clell were still across the Cannon River Bridge. Cole closed his pocket watch and nodded to Clell, and the two casually crossed the bridge. Cole realized the situation wasn't right. He saw that the corner of the Scriver Building and Division Street was crowded. "Surely the boys will not go into the bank with so many people about; I wonder why they did not ride on through town?" Cole pondered.

Allen walked down the sidewalk in front of Lee & Hitchcock's, eyeing the men on the boxes beyond the corner, when he heard horses.

Cole and Clell crossed the square toward the bank.

Allen quietly remarked, "They are here to rob the bank."

Cole and Clell slowed their horses.

Never a fan of the plan, Cole hoped the trio had seen the crowd and nixed the scheme for a better day. The trio slid off the boxes and started toward the bank.

"They're going in," Cole said with surprise.

Bob, Charlie, and Jesse entered the bank, leaving the large wooden folding doors ajar.

Nonchalantly, Clell smoked his pipe. "An alarm will be given as sure as there's a hell," Cole muttered. "Take that damned pipe out of your mouth."

Clell sported a white linen handkerchief around his neck, a new shirt with gold sleeve buttons, a matching gold ring, and a John Hancock chapeau over his curly black hair. He dumped his pipe, as Cole suggested.

Unaware that they were the center of attention, Cole and Clell dismounted and tethered their horses. Cole took a seat on the same dry-good boxes the others vacated. Clell relit his pipe and struck a pose against a hitching post.

Coming up the street from the opposite direction was Adelbert Ames, the former governor of Reconstruction-era Mississippi. "Look, it's the governor himself," Cole said, loudly enough for Ames to hear it, tipping his hat and tipping Ames off that Southerners were loitering outside the bank. "Howdy, governor," said Clell, who smelled of alcohol and was noticeably intoxicated. Ames and his family continued south on Division.

Watching the strangers' maneuvers, Howard, the Vermont cavalryman, told Stacy and Allen, "There is a Saint Albans Raid."

Having been in Vermont on October 21, 1864, Howard knew first-hand what such a raid looked like. He was there when Kentuckian Young led his Confederate compatriots into Vermont from Canada.

Like most of his men, Young served in the Second Kentucky Cavalry under General John Hunt Morgan (1825-1864) and on his 1,000-mile raid into Indiana and Ohio. Young planned to rob banks to raise money and to trick the Union Army into diverting troops to defend its northern border against further raids. They got the money, killed at least one local, and escaped back across the border.

The similarities between the raids are striking. Young arrived in Saint Albans a week before the Vermont raid. He scouted the city, particularly the First National, Saint Albans, and Franklin County banks. The Saint Albans raiders reached the town in pairs after Young, who posed as part of a hunting and fishing club. Young postponed the raid, initially set for October 18, because the town was too busy, waiting until October 19, a Wednesday, as it would be "the dullest [day] of the week."

It began after noon with Young firing a synchronizing shot.

When they robbed the Saint Albans Bank, they took cash from people making deposits. When one of the raiders announced, "We are Confederate soldiers, and you are our prisoners," the townspeople believed it was an elaborate prank. Within 12 minutes, the raiders were gone.

It took a second for Howard's comment to sink in. Once it did, Allen slowly moved past the corner of the dry goods store and began walking toward the bank. His breathing quickened, and incrementally, step by step, his pace quickened.

Meanwhile, Howard went to the roof to observe the impending events. Beneath him, Whiting watched from his second-floor window. When Whiting saw Cole and Clell round the corner of the Scriver Building, he grew suspicious. Cole looked over his shoulder, and Howard could see the last detachment—Bill, Frank, and Jim—take position at the foot of the bridge.

Inside the bank, Jesse, Bob, and Charlie rushed to the bank counter. Charlie leaped through the two-foot teller's window while Jesse and Bob climbed onto the countertop to the far left, squatting between the teller's window and the cashier's desk. In tandem, the robbers aimed at the men behind the counter: bank teller Alonzo Enos Bunker (1849-1929) and assistant bookkeeper Frank James Wilcox (1848-1921). A third banker, acting bookkeeper Joseph Lee Heywood (1837-1876), sat in the cashier's seat to the far right but hidden by the high front of the desk.

"If you holler, we'll blow your brains out," Charlie barked.

Bob discovered Heywood and asked if he was the cashier. "No. He's not in," Heywood said, which was technically accurate.

Bunker and Wilcox were asked the same, each denying being the cashier. Bob looked back to Heywood and told him he knew he was the cashier. He ordered Heywood, who was city treasurer and the treasurer of Carleton College, to unlock the safe in the vault "damned quick."

Heywood said he could not.

The robbers, reeking of alcohol, ordered the bankers to their knees, with Bob boasting, "We have 40 men outside, so there's no need to resist."

Outside, Cole fiddled with his saddle girth out on the noisy street, watching traffic in the 80-foot-wide thoroughfare. The unconcerned and oblivious Clell re-packed his pipe. No one seemed to sense anything was amiss. When Cole saw the folding doors were still open, he knew it was only a matter of time before someone overheard what was happening inside. He told Clell to close the doors again.

Clell lit his pipe, walked up, and stepped inside the bank, telling the men they had left the doors open. He shut the doors, stepped off the walk, and restruck his pose against the hitching post.

Across the street, opposite the bank, was the hardware store owned by William "W.H." Riddell (1800-1878). The Scottish merchant was working inside when a customer said, "Something suspicious is going on over at the bank." Riddell paid no mind.

But then, Mrs. John (Mary Mosan) Handy (1828-1923), a visitor from Saint Albans, exclaimed, "They are robbing the bank; I saw revolvers!"

Next door, Henry Mason Wheeler (1854-1930), on break from medical school at the University of Michigan, rocked in a chair outside Wheeler & Blackman's, his father's apothecary, chatting with passersby. He thought the strangers were cattlemen until a passing farmer mentioned seeing eight men on saddled horses coming out of the woods north of town.

In 1876, seeing a man mounted on a saddled horse, let alone eight, wearing matching coats was unusual. Most people traveled by wagon or walked. Horses were expensive. A strong horse was generally pulling wagons of goods.

Inside the bank, the robbers pulled the bankers back to their feet and searched their pockets for weapons and wallets. Charlie found a large knife in Wilcox's pocket and asked, "What's this?"

Wilcox, a recent college graduate with an impressively long, thick beard, said, "a jackknife." Bob ordered him back on his knees and under the counter. Bob rifled around, finding a roll of nickels. "Where is the till?"

Bunker showed Bob an open box on the counter. Bob pulled a two-bushel flour sack from his coat pocket, removing maybe $12 from the box and into the bag.

Bunker reached for a Derringer on a shelf below the teller's window—but Bob snatched and pocketed it. "Keep still!" Bob scoffed, "You couldn't do anything with that little Derringer anyway."

Back outside, Allen moved slowly, glaring at Cole. When Cole turned his back, Allen focused on Clell, who he said badly needed a shave. Despite his fine clothes, Clell's boots were mismatched—one of fine leather, the other of scraps.

As Allen reached the bank's folding doors, Clell's gloved hand pulled him back and pulled him close by his collar.

"What's happening here?" Allen demanded.

Hidden from view by the horses, Clell drew his .44 caliber pistol and put it between Allen's upper lip and nose. "Keep your goddamned mouth shut."

Instead of shoving Allen into the bank to be guarded, Clell pushed him away, assuming from Allen's frightened expression he would go on his way and remain silent. Allen walked, then ran, yelling, "Get your guns, boys! They're robbing the bank."

Wheeler ran down a back alley toward the Dampier House hotel. Clell mounted his horse and joined Cole in charging up and down Division warning citizens to get inside. "Get off the street, or I'll kill you!" said Cole, who fired a full volley, shattering more windows.

For a minute, the street went silent as people gathered their weapons—pistols, shotguns, rifles, and rocks. Bill, Bob, and Frank heard the gunshots and galloped their horses across the Square.

At the top of the staircase, Whiting saw the three round the corner onto Division. The five robbers fired in the air and at the ground, zigzagging up and down Division and Fourth, shouting variations of: "Get inside, sonsabitches!"

Since they were firing shots in the air, some still thought it was part of the show and were more concerned by the foul language than the gunplay.

In his hardware store, Allen loaded and handed out guns. People took positions on rooftops, porches, windows, and sidewalks. They opened fire on the outlaws. Bullets flew from every direction. No one was hit. It had to be a show.

Wheeler reached the Dampier House, across from the bank. He grabbed Charles Edward Dampier's old .50-caliber Smith Carbine rifle from the lobby and three slugs and went to a third-story bedroom window. The senior Dampier (1829-1889) had been a lieutenant in the Union Army. His son, Charlie (1854-1923), was one of Wheeler's medical school classmates.

Bates was talking business with Waldo in the back of his store when they heard the shots. "Those men mean to rob the bank!" Bates cried out, running to and through the open doorway onto the street. Cole and Clell rode up to him, shouting.

Bates retreated, returning with a shotgun, which misfired. He rushed back inside, reappearing quickly with an old, empty 6-shooter. As a ruse, Bates aimed the pistol at the men as they passed, shouting, "Now I've got you!"

In response, Bill shot out Bates' glass window.

Clell slid from his horse and ran to the bank, pleading, "Hurry up, boys—they've given the alarm!"

Inside the bank, the robbers focused on Haywood, screaming, "You are the cashier. Open the safe!"

"It's a time-lock and cannot be unlocked," Haywood claimed.

It was true; the safe was mounted with a Yale Chronometer Time-Lock. The safe could not be unlocked because it wasn't locked. More than $18,000 was in the unlocked safe, but the robbers never tried the door.

Jesse opened the vault door and stepped inside while Bob trained his guns on Bunker and Wilcox. As Jesse entered the vault, Heywood dashed by Bob and threw his weight into the safe door, trying to lock Jesse inside. Jesse forced his way out, but his arm and hand were smashed and bruised. Jesse knocked Haywood to the floor with his pistol, stepped over him, and pulled the banker's head back hard. He placed a knife to Heywood's throat, drawing blood.

Heywood pleaded, "Go ahead and slit my throat; I can't open the safe."

"Damned liar!" Jesse said, "You'll open that safe, or I'll cut your throat ear to ear! You understand me?"

Jesse fired a shot past Heywood's head into the floor, hoping fear would motivate the 39-year husband and father.

When Cole heard the pistol shot, he rode toward the bank.

Still, no one was hit.

On the street, the robbers continued galloping up and down Division, around the corner, and back. Ex-Marshal Elias Hobbs (1830-1895) threw rocks each time they passed.

Manning grabbed a breech-loading Remington rolling-block rifle from his window display and filled his pockets with cartridges. Aiming hastily, his shot went wild. He fired again but his rifle jammed. As he fiddled with it, Bates called, "Jump back now, or they'll get you!"

The sound of constant, overlapping gunfire echoed in the square. Northfield's prominent citizens took cover. Others watched helplessly behind broken windows as their neighbors scattered, shouting and screaming.

Little Maude's father found a pistol and stepped out of Shatto's store as the glass above his head shattered. Maude was sprinkled with glass and huddled close to her sister, Luna Elizabeth (1860-1962), and her mother, Theresa A. (1839-1928), terrified. Maude cried, "Father, please, I want to go home!"

With one hand, Charlie weighed the $15 worth of silver within the vault and shook his head in belligerence. His attention was drawn to a locked tin box on a lower shelf. He shot the box open. Inside were a few land deeds.

Quickly stumbling around the corner into the narrow hallway adjoining the lobby, Bunker raced to the rear exit. He struggled to open the door. A second later, armed with a cap-and-ball 1851 Navy Colt, Charlie appeared at the end of the hallway, shot at Bunker, and missed.

On the other side of the door, Mr. Miller, a deaf furniture store owner, was on the steps, trying to see through the blinds. When Bunker forced the door open, Miller tumbled down the steps. Bunker vaulted over him onto Water Street.

Charlie fired again, hitting Bunker's upper shoulder above the clavicle. Shocked and terrified, Bunker fled out of sight; the onlookers on the square did not know the banker had been wounded.

Heywood desperately tried to escape Jesse's grip. Charlie came to Jesse's aid, but Heywood got free and ran toward the entrance, screaming, "Murder!" Jesse grabbed Heywood and slammed his pistol over the banker's lower neck. Stunned, Heywood fell again, and Jesse dragged him toward the vault.

"Open it!" he shouted.

Dazed, Heywood was silent.

Cole shouted through the window, "Game's up, boys; we're beaten!"

Bob exited the bank first and heard Cole say to grab Charlie's horse, tied at the foot of the stairway. Cole dismounted and returned fire. Seeing Bob, Cole returned on his horse, intending to ride around the corner and launch across the square and over the bridge. He galloped a few yards, spotted Manning, and shot a pane of glass out over Manning's head.

Cole turned back, searching for Jesse and Charlie, who he assumed would follow Bob, but they were still inside. Cole rode to the bank's open door and shouted, "For God's sake, come out! They're shootin' us to pieces!"

Not true. None of the robbers had yet to be hit.

Allen passed out shotguns with price tags still attached. Rev. Ross Clinton Phillips (1853-1932) laid out rifles and revolvers on a counter inside Manning's hardware store.

Joseph Bell "J.B." Hyde (1843-1890) and James Shields Gregg (1845-1909) both fired ineffective shotgun blasts, but Stacy scored the first hit. As Clell remounted his horse, Stacy fired with a shotgun loaded with birdshot, peppering Clell's face, puncturing his left eye, pieces of skin and blood streaming onto his linen outfit. The force knocked Clell back in his saddle. Screaming and moaning, he blindly reached for his reins and charged, shooting his pistols.

Cole took a slug in his left shoulder from Manning's rifle but continued to ride. As Clell's horse circled round and round, Stacy fired again, hitting Clell in the back. Clell called out, "Cole, I'm shot."

Bates was moving past Dampier House when he heard a shot overhead; he flinched, seeing Clell hit a third time, just below the left shoulder, severing his subclavian artery.

The blast knocked Clell off his horse. He landed face-first in the mud. With blood gushing from his eye, face, and shoulder, he lifted himself on his arms but, after about three seconds, toppled over. Cole raced to him, dismounted, and, using his horse for cover, knelt to see if Clell was dead. Cole grabbed Clell's pistols and cartridge belts and struggled to remount. As he did, a bullet tore through his left thigh. Cole winced but pulled himself up on his horse and made another charge. As he passed the bank door, he yelled again. "They're killing us out here!"

South on Division, 20 feet past the corner of Fifth, Nicolaus Gustafson (1846-1876) exited a store and found himself in the middle of the bangarang, oblivious to the danger. Gustafson, a recent Swedish immigrant, came into town to sell vegetables and barter for goods. According to witnesses, the robbers shouted at Gustafson to get out of the way, but Nicolaus didn't understand. He was hit by a glancing shot above the eye, which exited the top of his head but was not immediately fatal.

Gustafson ran past carpenter John Olson (1833-1913), another Swede working on a nearby cellar door. The two tripped over each other. When Olson reached the door, it was locked. He crouched for a few seconds and started back up to help Gustafson. A robber spotted Olson and told him to stop. "Sit where you are, or I'll kill you, too."

Witnesses said Gustafson staggered to the nearby Cannon River and bathed his wound. Olson tried to keep him comfortable and arranged his burial when he died four days later.

In an interview, Cole maintained that Gustafson, on the south end of town, could only have been hit by a ricocheted shot. He said if a member of the gang was responsible, he could only attribute that shot to "Woods," who, in this case, was probably Frank.

The attorney who prosecuted the Younger brothers wrote a letter in 1897 to the parole board claiming he traveled to Northfield in 1876 to interview eyewitnesses and could find none who could identify the "Swede's" shooter. He said the residents concurred with Cole that Gustafson was probably hit by stray gunfire.

However, John Morton (1836-1923), a jeweler and watchmaker whose store was located on Fifth Street, watched from a nook "beside the door of his store" and saw "the Swede" come around the corner just as one of the robbers rode up to him, and shouted, "Get back." Getting only a confused response, the robber fired. Morton reported that the robber who shot Gustafson went to the body of a dead Clell, taking his pistols, which matches Cole's actions. Morton visited the prison and identified Cole as Gustafson's killer.

Ellen M. Ames (1833-1913), the general's sister, backed Morton's claim.

Back in the bank, Charlie re-emerged from the hallway to the front entrance, exiting through the folding doors onto the sidewalk. The robbers were surrounded by the mob.

Behind him, Jesse peripherally saw Heywood returning to the cashier's desk, sitting down, and opening a drawer. Jesse may have believed Heywood was looking for a gun, or he was angry about his bruised hand. Whatever the reason, Jesse leaned across the teller's window, placed his pistol to Heywood's temple, and fired.

Wilcox darted down the hallway, out the back door, and into the rear entrance of Manning's store.

Heywood lived a few moments, breathing easily but unable to speak.

The robbers left behind a linen duster and the grain sack containing $12.

On Division, Hyde emptied both barrels, striking Charlie in the shoulder and wrist before retreating to reload.

Manning's aim found Bob, who dismounted and used Charlie's horse as cover. Bob dove behind the crates stacked underneath the steel staircase. Unarmed, Whiting, in his office above Bob at the top of the stairs, bounced from an open doorway to an open window, excitedly observing the fracas. In Cole's recollection, Whiting was armed, and when he saw the dentist hovering over them, he shouted, "Shoot that man up in the window!"

A volley of shots peppered Whiting's window and doorway.

Cole shouted, "Kill the white-livered son of a bitch on the corner!"

Cole called for Bob to "charge up" on Manning, who took cover at the corner and returned fire. Cole shouted, "Shoot through the stairs!"

Bob re-positioned himself beneath the staircase. Due to the angle, witnesses said neither could get a clear shot. Bob used the crates and steel girders for cover, and Manning used the corner of the building.

Bob charged again, and Manning retreated around the corner into Lee and Hitchcock's store. Manning went to an open window, hoping to get a shot at Bob as he rounded the corner. Bob retreated under the stairs, leaving him vulnerable to Wheeler on the third floor of the Dampier House. Wheeler's third shot shattered Bob's elbow.

Bob scrambled, looking for another hiding place, and realized he was surrounded—and worse, separated. Cole looked over and saw Bob change his pistol from his right to his left hand. Bob's right arm hung limp. Bob fired two, maybe three, bullets through the staircase girders, and the unabated gunfire continued.

Wounded, Cole struggled to mount his horse. Cole told Charlie to run across the square toward the bridge, and he would catch up to him.

Charlie took off, running.

"Let's head out!" Cole shouted.

Cole mounted and was simultaneously fired upon from both sides of the street. Someone, possibly Manning, fired a shot into Cole's shoulder. From the hotel window, Wheeler shot off Cole's hat.

As Bill rounded the corner of the Scriver Building onto Division, Manning revolved the corner with him and took a shot. Manning missed. So again, Manning climbed the staircase. This time, he went halfway up. From there, he carefully aimed his rifle, hitting Bill, 70 yards away, through the heart.

Bill's horse galloped in Manning's direction. As a reflex, Bill stood in his saddle and gasped for air before tumbling dead to the dirt street.

Frank, shot in the calf, also struggled to mount his horse, so Frank and Jesse shared a ride.

Seeing the gang fleeing, Bob limped from under the stairs. He saw Bates taking aim and fired, grazing Bates' cheek and the bridge of his nose. The bullet was later found in a collar box in Bates' store.

Bob shouted, "My God, boys! Hold on! Don't leave me—I'm shot!"

As the others fled to the square beyond Division, Jim was the last man on horseback, still on Division. Holding the reins of Clell's horse, Jim raced to catch the others when he heard Bob. He rode back and pulled Bob onto Clell's horse.

Hyde fired a reloaded shotgun, blasting off Bob's thumb.

Armed with a long-barreled Colt .45 Army "peacemaker," Cole covered Charlie's escape. Somewhere between 40 and 100 yards later, Cole rode alongside Charlie, who climbed onto a barrel on the sidewalk to the square's right. Cole strained, pulling him onto the horse, and Charlie said jokingly, "What kept you so long?"

Holding the reins of the second horse, Jim was shot, first in the back of his right leg, then his shoulder. Cole shouted, "Lead on," and Jim crossed the square, chased by several townspeople.

Each gang member was wounded. Frank and Charlie were both shot in their right legs. Jesse, the last one shot, took a bullet in the upper thigh. The survivors rode out of town on Dundas Road toward Millersburg.

The Minnesota legislature passed a joint resolution honoring the citizens of Northfield for defending their city. Sheriff Frank P. Martin (1851-1931) was not mentioned, probably because he spent the ordeal hidden in a large wooden box behind Allen's store.

Cole confirmed in a hand-written letter that whiskey was to blame for the unprofessional way the bank robbery was handled. Cole didn't drink. Jesse, who rarely drank anything more substantial than beer, and the rest consumed more than was wise in the wooded area north of town and again over breakfast. Cole said they were drunk, which accounted for their lack of judgment on the crowded street, and explained why they left the bank's folding door open. Cole said he would never have gone into town if he had known they were sauced.

Minutes after the gang's departure, Clell, left for dead, rose on his hands and knees, rolled over, and died.

The remaining men fled out of town to the southwest instead of back across the Cannon River Bridge. As a result, their plan to escape across the bridge, stopping at the railroad depot west of the river to cut the telegraph wires, was neglected. Now, on the run, the surviving members of the gang left behind two dead. Drifting gun smoke filled the Square. The town resembled a war zone up and down Division and Fourth.

Seven minutes, a mere 420 seconds, passed between the trio entering the bank and the last man exiting the square.

No identification was found on Bill or Clell's bodies. On Bill was a slip of paper torn from a two-week-old edition of the *Rice County Journal*, detailing the new burglar-proof safe and its chronometer time-lock. Also on his body were a fine Waltham gold watch, 10 cents, unspent cartridges in his belt, and many more in his pockets.

Clell's effects were a Howard gold watch, worth at least $175; a Minnesota map purchased from Williams Bros., Minneapolis; a compass, and $5.75. A paper was found with "A.S. Coywood"—or Haywood—"1129 Eleventh N.W." written in pencil on one side and a ballot from Vest's failed run for governor in the last Missouri election printed on the other.

Bill's corpse was displayed to discourage children from a life of crime. According to the Northfield Historical Society, Wheeler dug up the two outlaws, put them in barrels marked "mixed paint," and shipped them to Ann Arbor for medical study. After graduating from medical school, Wheeler returned to Minnesota before moving to Grand Forks in the Dakota Territory. Clell's skeleton adorned the corner of Wheeler's office for the rest of his career.

As news of the incident spread, Minnesota Governor John Sargent Pillsbury (1827-1901), who co-founded the world's largest cake mix company, offered a $1,000 reward for each surviving man. The First National Bank of Northfield added $500. In an interview, Cole said if they'd "wrecked" the telegraph lines as planned, their trauma inflicted by the chasing glory seekers would have been cut by two-thirds.

Cole was shot five times: in his left thigh, left hip, right arm, right side, and left shoulder. Jim was shot thrice, in each shoulder and the back of his right leg. Frank and Charlie were shot once each, Frank in the right leg, above the knee, and Charlie in the upper left arm. Beyond the thigh wound, Jesse's arm and hand, pinched in the vault door, hurt for weeks.

Bob was in the worst shape. He had been shot twice, in the left leg and right elbow, which bled profusely.

The take was $26.70, hardly worth the onslaught they endured. To make matters worse, the six outlaws rode on four horses: Frank and Jesse shared one, and Bob and Cole rode on another.

The Minnesota expedition depended on Bill's knowledge of the layout of the back roads. It was the others' first time in Minnesota. Without Bill, they were without their trail guide, and not only did he have the map, but he also had the compass. Minnesota also lacked the hundreds of friends and sympathizers to shelter and hide them from the pursuing posse. The gang could not afford to stop and rest.

In short, the gang couldn't have been in worse shape.

Or so you might think.

Shortly after the gang exited Northfield, the telegraph wires were abuzz, sending messages across the Gopher State. By day's end, more than 500 men were on the gang's trail. Within days, several thousand joined the hunt.

The gang members bandaged wounds over the first 24 hours and looked for horses. They planned to travel west to the Dakotas, then south. On September 8, torrential rains began and continued for two weeks. The downpour helped cover their tracks but slowed them even more.

Drenched, they struggled to find shelter, stole chickens, and dressed wounds.

On the 14th, Jim and Cole took turns holding Bob on the horse. Bob asked to be left behind. Jesse agreed, saying a blind man could follow the "blood trail," and they should dispose of Bob and end his suffering.

Cole called Jesse a cold-hearted villain and said he would stay with his brother until he died and "carry his body as far as I have the strength."

Cole suggested the gang split up, allowing the lesser-wounded outlaws to travel faster while the more-wounded could take their time. He reasoned that the posse would likely pursue the faster group and overlook the tattered group's trail. Charlie insisted on staying with the Youngers, so Jesse and Frank traveled west while the Youngers and Charlie went south.

For 48 hours, Jesse and Frank rode nonstop. On the 17th, they entered the Dakotas, abandoned their horses, and stole new ones. The first horse was blind in one eye, the other in both. According to the ninth-man theory, Frank and Jesse met up with Stiles and rested on his family's Grand Forks farm.

The Youngers and Charlie limped south. Cole's wounds made riding torture, so he walked, assisted by a walking stick. On the 19th, near Linden, Minnesota, they stole more chickens, a turkey, a watermelon, and corn. Before enjoying it, they heard voices and fled. The posse discovered their camp, two coats, a blood-soaked handkerchief, two leather bridles, and two torn, bloody shirts.

On the 21st, near Lake Linden, they exchanged greetings with 17-year-old Asle Oscar Sorbel (1859-1930), who was milking cows. When Asle told his father, Ole Olson Sorbel (1824-1879), the men might be the infamous Northfield robbers, the Norwegian immigrant told him to stop being imaginative and return to work.

Charlie and Jim returned to buy some bread. After they wandered back into the woods, Asle and Ole examined their footprints. Their toes were clearly seen, showing they walked the soles out of their boots. Ole told Asle to ride to Madelia to alert the sheriff. "We were imprudent in going to the house for food," Jim said later, "but we were so hungry."

In Madelia, Asle found former Colonel Thomas Lent Vought (1833-1917), who quickly assembled a group of former soldiers later known as the "Madelia Seven." William Wallace Murphy (1839-1904) was a captain, as was Sheriff James M. Glispin (1846-1890). The others were George Alphonso Branford (1847-1935), sharpshooter Benjamin M. Rice (1851-1889), powerfully built Charles Melvin Pomeroy Jr. (1848-1914), and store clerk S. Jim "Slim" Severson (1855-?).

Newspaper editor William R. Estes (1852-1905) was sent to gather reserves, eventually reaching more than 200, nearly the town's entire male population.

Following Asle, the posse spotted the outlaws in Hanska Slough, near the Watawon River. Glispin yelled for them to halt, and the outlaws scattered. Murphy ordered his men to open fire, but the robbers were out of range and hidden by the trees. The gang went deeper into the bog. Exhausted, the four nestled behind a large deadfall of brush. Bob, too weak and disoriented to aim, reloaded the others' guns.

The outlaws focused on Murphy, the apparent leader, believing killing him was the only escape.

The posse's plan was for the seven former soldiers to flush them out, hopefully alive. They advanced through the marsh in line formation, six to seven feet apart.

Cole fired his pistol through the brush pile, splintering the large briarwood pipe in Murphy's coat pocket.

On a ridge, the reserves fired over the advancing seven. Cole, Jim, and Charlie fired rapidly through the deadfall. In the ensuing free-for-all, Cole was shot three more times. Slim was grazed in the side and Vought above the hip.

Charlie was wounded four more times. As Jim turned his back to the deadfall, possibly to reload, a slug hit him in the back, near his spine, but he continued fighting. Seeing the hopeless situation, Charlie said, "We better surrender."

Cole refused. "Charlie, if you want to surrender, go, but this is where Cole Younger dies."

Charlie shrugged. "All right, captain, I can die as game as you can."

Charlie jumped up, a Colt .45 in each hand. Glispin kneeled. Simultaneously, each fired. Charlie's bullet grazed Bradford's hand. Glispin's slug pierced Charlie's heart, killing him.

The posse called out to the outlaws to surrender. The response was more gunfire. A bullet hit Cole's right hand, knocking his gun over the deadfall, out of reach. He reached down, grabbed one of Charlie's pistols, and continued firing. In the next volley, Cole took a bullet in the chest. Jim was hit in the upper jaw, between the lip and nose, as he peered over the deadfall. The bullet shattered his jaw, knocking out several teeth. Jim fell, holding his gaping jaw with both hands. A slug hit Cole behind his right ear as Cole turned to look at Jim. The slug traveled upwards and lodged over Cole's right eye.

Glispin ordered "cease fire" and yelled, "Do you mean to surrender?"

Bob faintly said, "Yes, I surrender! Don't shoot anymore … the boys are all riddled. For God's sake, don't shoot me!"

Glispin ordered Bob to his feet. As he stood, waving a bloody white cloth in his left hand, a reserve, Willis M. Bundy (1849-1950), fired a shot into Bob's right lung, dropping him to his knees. "Damnit, I was surrendering," Bob muttered.

Behind the brush, Jim moaned. Belligerently, Cole staggered to his knees. "Come on," he sputtered, "I'll fight any two of you bastards in a fair fight!"

The Youngers were escorted to a wagon. Charlie's body was tossed in the wagon, and the group returned to Madelia. Cole stood and tipped his hat to some young women on the sidewalk. Jim hung his head over the side, blood gushing from his jaw. Cole joked and talked with his captors.

Taken to the Flanders House, the Youngers rested. Waterlogged, Cole's toenails fell off when his boots were removed. After a few days, Cole talked to the press. He said the circumstances of the war as Confederate warriors motivated the Northfield Raid. He cited the unmerciful treatment of his father, Judge Henry Washington Younger (1810-1862), by Union forces, who killed him and forced his wife, Bursheba Leighton Fristoe (1816-1870), to burn down her home. As an obvious sympathy play, the *Saint Paul Dispatch* said Cole "used his charm and intelligence consistently and effectively."

Bob had three bullet wounds, Jim five, and Cole 11.

Doctors cauterized Jim's jaw three times over the next few weeks. Sections of his upper jaw were removed, and Jim never again ate solid food.

On November 18, 1876, with their wounds healed, the brothers entered the Minnesota State Penitentiary at Stillwater. To escape hanging, the Youngers pled guilty to the Northfield robbery, the assault of Bunker, and the murders of Gustafson and Heywood.

Each was given a life sentence. Bob died in 1889 of tuberculosis, which many attributed to his lung wound. Bob lived with the guilt for insisting on going to Northfield and thereby getting himself and his brothers imprisoned. "Bob asked so many times if we forgave him for being so headstrong," Cole said. "We assured him we were more at fault; being older, we should have found a way to prevent the whole thing."

After serving 25 years, Cole and Jim were paroled on July 14, 1901. The Youngers never revealed the names of the robbers who escaped. When asked, they would say (B.J.) Woodson and (Thomas) Howard (Frank's and Jesse's aliases, respectively, although unknown at the time).

The existence of a ninth member is not mentioned in Cole's interviews or autobiography. Many researchers scoff at the idea, but Koblas uncovered a report that Stiles' father (or brother), Elisha Stiles, traveled from Grand Forks to Northfield to identify his son's body and left town, relieved his son was not among the dead. Koblas' book is based on a 1931 interview of Koblas' Bill Stiles (1850-1937) by Ed Earl Repp (1901-1979), a science fiction and Wild West writer.

If true, Stiles' life of crime continued until a religious conversion in Los Angeles in 1913. To complicate matters, yet another Bill, "Billy" Stiles (William Larkin Stiles [1871-1908]), led a small gang of train robbers in Arizona before dropping the Stiles name and becoming a deputy sheriff.

After resting in the Dakotas, Jesse, and Frank headed south. They were seen in Sioux City, Iowa, on September 25. From there, they vanished.

Stories placed the James brothers in Mexico or Nebraska, where they married a pair of Arapaho or Sioux women and fathered children. What the brothers did during this time will likely remain a mystery.

In 1877, Jesse and Frank surfaced in Nashville, Tennessee, where they went by Howard and Woodson, respectively. Jesse recruited a new gang in 1879 and returned to crime, holding up a train at Glendale, Missouri, on October 8. The robbery began a spree of crimes, including two more train robberies and the holdup of the federal paymaster in Killen, Alabama.

The new gang consisted of a rotation of young cousins prone to turn on each other rather than battle-hardened guerrillas.

In 1879, the gang robbed two stores in Mississippi.

On July 15, 1881, Frank and Jesse, Clarence B. Hite (1861-1883), Robert Woodson "Wood" Hite (1850-1881), and James Andrew "Dick" Liddell (1852-1901) robbed the Rock Island Railroad near Winston, Missouri, killing two employees.

On September 7, 1881, Jesse and five others held up the Chicago and Alton Railroad near Blue Cut, and on October 8, a train near Glendale, both in Saint Louis County. Another source says the same gang robbed the Rock Island on July 15, along with newcomer Charles Wilson "Charley" Ford.

Jesse never regretted his robberies or many killings—at least 17—but would obsessively pout about slanders or slights. He greatly needed attention and could be overly genteel and polite to disguise what he considered his "too-humble origins."

They returned to Tennessee between crimes, but by November 1881, authorities grew suspicious, so the brothers returned to Missouri's safer environs. With the gang again reduced to two, both intended to retire. Jesse moved his family to St. Joseph, Missouri, near where he was born and reared.

Following the 1881 bank robberies, Crittenden, whom Vest helped get elected, said bringing in Frank and Jesse was his top priority. His inaugural address declared that no political motives could keep the brothers from justice. Barred by law from offering more than a $300 award, Crittenden urged railroad executives and bankers to put up a $5,000 bounty for their killing and $5,000 more for their conviction. A "kitty" totaling $50,000 was raised during the Saint Louis meeting—enough to bring in any affiliated criminals.

Crittenden's proclamation noted the 1879 Glendale and 1881 Rock Island train robberies and the outstanding indictment for the 1869 murder of bank owner and cashier John W. Sheets (1818-1869).

Besides his young cousins, Charley Ford and Robert Newton "Bob" Ford, Jesse's trusted circle was dwindling.

By then, Bob Ford had met with Crittenden, planning to bring Jesse in peacefully. Charley had been on a few raids with the Jameses, and Bob Ford was an eager recruit. Jesse asked the Fords to move in with him and his family for protection. Jesse often stayed with their sister, Martha Elizabeth "Mattie" Bolton (1849-1925), and, according to rumor, Jesse was "smitten" with her.

In December 1881, Dick killed Wood in a Mattie-centered gunfight, and Bob assisted. With Mattie serving as an intermediary, the Fords met again with Crittenden.

On February 11, 1882, Federal Marshall James Timberlake (1846-1891) was appointed the chief investigator into the James Gang. A second lieutenant under General Shelby and one of the 1,000 men who went with him to Mexico at the end of the war, Timberlake arrested Clarence Hite, who quickly confessed to his role in the train robbery but died of tuberculosis in prison before he could testify.

On April 3, 1882, Jesse and the Fords planned to travel 32 miles south to Platte City for a robbery.

After breakfast, Jesse and the Fords went into the living room. Jesse had read in the newspaper that Dick confessed to participating in Wood's murder. Jesse, growing paranoid, suspected the Fords knew about Dick's confession but kept it to themselves. Bob Ford believed Jesse knew they were about to betray him. Jesse laid his revolvers on a sofa, noticed a dusty picture above the mantel, and stood on a chair to straighten and clean it.

Bob Ford, "the coward who shot Mr. Howard," drew his gun and shot unarmed Jesse twice in the back of the head, leaving him challenging to identify. His missing fingertip and other wounds confirmed his identity.

The Fords wired Crittenden to claim the reward. Fearing that Frank was gunning for them, both left Missouri. They surrendered themselves and were charged with first-degree murder. Within 24 hours, they were indicted, pled guilty, sentenced to hang, and, two hours later, were pardoned.

In Jesse's obituary in *The Sedalia Democrat*, editor John Newman Edwards (1839-1889) wrote, "We called him an outlaw, and he was—but fate made him so. Jesse James had no home. He was hunted, shot, and driven away … a price on his head. What else could the man do?"

Edwards, General Shelby's adjutant, created the Jesse James legend. The founder of the *Kansas City Times*, Edwards was a pro-Confederate journalist whose wedding was held on Shelby's well-known and often-visited farm.

Using his connection with Shelby, Edwards met with Frank and Jesse after the 1869 Daviess County Savings Association robbery in Gallatin, Missouri. He painted the pair as ex-Confederates "striking back" against Northern corruption, graft, and oppression. Edwards' connection to Vest was cemented after Edwards moved to Sedalia to edit *The Democrat*. In 1877, he wrote "Noted Guerrillas," which included Frank and Jesse alongside bushwhackers William Clark Quantrill (1837-1865) and William T. "Bloody Bill" Anderson (1840-1864), with whom the brothers served in the Civil War.

On April 9, 1882, the *Saint Louis Globe-Democrat* ran a front-page story on Jesse, which included comments from Vest about the first time he met the James Brothers, eight years before the Northfield Raid.

Vest was entertaining a party one evening in Washington with the memories of his Missouri law practice when the conversation drifted to the James boys. Someone asked Vest if he had met the bandits, and he said he would tell them the tale if they promised not to repeat it.

"He [Shelby] is an old friend of mine," Vest said of his Transylvania classmate. "He urged me for a long time to come down to his splendid place in Lafayette County [Missouri] and spend a few days hunting and fishing."

Vest took Shelby up on his offer a few days after the 1874 Gads Hill Train Robbery (where the gang had pocketed $12,000 in cash).

"I was completely worn out by close attention to business in the Sedalia courts and needed some time away," said Vest, who took the Lexington Branch of the Missouri Pacific Railroad to a little station in Page City.

"It was a beautiful moonlit night, and as the house was a little over a mile distant, I shouldered my double-barreled shotgun, which I had taken along for some sport, and trudged over the white [snow-covered] lane leading to the homestead. Tall forest trees surrounded the house, and as I emerged from their shadow into the moonlight, 20 steps from the house, a clear ringing voice cried, 'halt!'"

Vest saw a polished rifle barrel protruding from a partially raised window. "I intuitively felt that the man on the other end of the barrel had a bead on me, and I halted. I became a statue. My blood seemed to chill. In a moment—it seemed hours to me—I heard Old Jo's voice ring out, "Who are you?"

With trembling lips, Vest answered, "G-g-g-George Vest, come down to see you."

"Wait a minute," was the reply.

After about five minutes, Vest heard the rattling of bars and chains, and the front door opened. He was told to put down his gun and approach slowly. When he drew near the door, Shelby announced, "It's all right, boys, I vouch for him."

Lafayette County, 40 miles east of Kansas City, was settled primarily by Kentuckians in a region known as "Little Dixie." The settlers brought their slaves with them and cultivated hemp and tobacco and bred horses.

Vest and Shelby were born six days and 20 miles apart. Shelby arrived in Missouri at 21, and Vest followed two years later. Both participated in "The Battle of the Hemp Bales."

Vest and Shelby's friendship was long, but it had been years since Vest's last visit. "The cozy little sitting room had been converted into a fortress," Vest said. "The windows were barricaded securely with the furniture moved up against the door. On the table in the corner lay a collection of revolvers and repeating rifles that would have excited a pirate's admiration."

Around the room were five silent men—Frank and Jesse and three of the Youngers—all wearing small firearms.

"These are some friends of mine," Shelby said.

Vest said he and Shelby spent hours catching up, and the other guests remained silent, never expressing any interest in the conversation. "Eventually, I was shown to bed, where I tossed and turned until daylight in a troubled sleep. When I came down to breakfast, the curtains were drawn. Old Jo sat in an easy chair, smoking his pipe and playing with a couple of youngsters."

The arsenal was gone, and so were the visitors.

"They had departed so quietly as to not break my light sleep," Vest said. "I did not know whether they would return that night, so I pleaded the pressure of business and limited my visit to one day."

On October 5, 1882, five months after his brother's death, with Vest in the U.S. Senate, Frank surrendered to Crittenden in Jefferson City. The night before, Frank stayed at the McCarthy House, one of Vest's favorite hotels. It had been pre-arranged that Frank would not be extradited to Minnesota if he surrendered.

Like a war hero, Frank walked through people-lined streets to the Capitol to turn over his gun, a Remington 1875 nickel-plated .44-40 caliber pistol. "Governor, I have been hunted for 21 years and have literally lived in the saddle, having never known a day of perfect peace," James said. "It was one long, anxious, eternal vigil.

"Governor, I have not let any man touch my guns since 1861."

Frank was linked to two dozen murders between 1865 and 1882, but only two cases came to trial.

The first was for the July 15, 1881, robbery of the Rock Island Line at Winston, Missouri, in which Frank McMillan (1854-1881) and conductor William Harrison Westfall (1843-1881) were killed. The gang held up the passengers when the express safe contained only $900.

Some believed Westfall was involved in the Pinkertons' 1875 slash-and-dash raid on the James Farm, wounding the Jameses' mother and stepfather and disemboweling Archie, their 9-year-old stepbrother. "You're the one I want," Jesse sneered at Westfall. Frank drew his pistol, hitting Westfall in the upper arm. As Westfall ran toward the back door of the train, Frank fired again, missing. Jesse did not, striking Westfall twice in the back of the head. McMillan was collateral damage.

Vest was familiar with the Pinkertons and no fan of their tactics. As the James Gang's clandestine attorney, he prepped a civil case following the January 26 attack on the James farm.

"A train was chartered upon the Hannibal to St. Joseph Railroad to convey from Chicago to a depot in Clay County, Missouri, some of Pinkerton's men, and at midnight a private dwelling in that county was surrounded by this gang of marauders," Vest recalled to the Senate in 1892. "A battle occurred in the darkness between these people, who mistook each other for the men they had come to capture. In the most cowardly and cruel way they threw hand grenades into the homestead where there was a sleeping family of women and children. One of them exploded in the sleeping room of the mother [Zerelda Elizabeth (1825-1911)] of these James boys, killed a child [Archie], and tore off the mother's arm, and she is now an old, decrepit, mutilated woman.

"The Pinkertons were not punished for this crime. They escaped in the night, caring for their wounded for they had fired upon each other," said Vest, who struggled to gather enough evidence to bring suit.

"It was impossible to make the Hannibal and St. Joseph Railroad Company responsible," Vest continued, "because they disclaimed any knowledge of the purpose or to whom they had chartered the train of cars. It was impossible in the City of Chicago, with all the adverse interests and circumstances which prevailed there, to obtain proof that Mr. Pinkerton authorized the forage and raid into a peaceable community."

Vest disputed Pinkerton's claim that his company was focused on protecting private property. "In the unfortunate affair at the James Homestead, his detectives were there without any authority of law. There is no defense for the Pinkertons when we consider the absolute truth of the statement that they went there not as deputy sheriffs, not clothed in any legal authority, but simply employed for acts of violence by a corporation."

In defending Frank for the Westfall-McMillan murders, Shelby stepped forward as a character witness and was fined $10 for contempt for testifying while intoxicated.

The second trial centered on the March 11, 1881, payroll robbery in Muscle Shoals, Alabama. Vest's former partner, Philips, won Frank's acquittal on both. As promised, Missouri kept the jurisdiction of Frank, keeping him from extradition to Minnesota and guaranteeing Frank's freedom from numerous charges lodged against him.

As Vest predicted, a friendly Missouri jury would only convict Robin Hood and his Merry Men with overwhelming, rock-solid evidence, of which there was none.

"Frank James was tried by a jury of his countrymen, defended by counsel, and prosecuted by the ablest lawyers in the state, and acquitted," Vest said in 1892. "If he had been dyed with blood, incarnadined from head to foot, he had that right to be tried by a jury of his peers, and when acquitted under the glorious institutions and traditions that our fathers have left us, he could not again be put in peril for that offense."

In the only known civil suit against the James brothers, Daniel Smoote (1816-1880) sought $223.50 from the James brothers for a horse, saddle, and bridle stolen as they fled the Daviess County Savings Association robbery in Gallatin, Missouri, on December 7, 1869. During the holdup, Jesse murdered Sheets, shooting the former Union captain in the head and heart, thinking Sheets was Major Samuel P. Cox (1828-1913), the commander responsible for the 1864 death of "Bloody Bill" Anderson, the Jameses' commanding officer.

Frank and Jesse responded that they were not in Daviess County on the day of the robbery, but when they failed to appear in court, Smoote won. There is no record of Smoote being paid, but one account claims his horse was later returned.

It was the death of Jesse that, according to the Missouri Historical Society, sparked the earliest documented example of public interest in the preservation of historic sites. Sightseers were willing to pay a quarter to tour James' home in St. Joseph and the family farm near Kearney. His mother, Zerelda, sold rocks from the farm as souvenirs.

The first "tourists" to the Saint Joseph residence, a 24- by 30-foot house, were financier and railroad magnate Jay Gould (1836-1892), poet and humorous Eugene Field (1850-1895), Crittenden, Cockrell, and Vest.

Both locations are listed on the National Register of Historic Places.

The Youngers were model prisoners, once saving others from a fire. They remained loyal and never admitted to Frank and Jesse (nor Stiles) being part of the Northfield Raid.

During Cole's stay in Stillwater, he founded *The Prison Mirror*, the longest-running prison newspaper in the United States. After many appeals, Cole and Jim were paroled in 1901 on the condition they remain in Minnesota. Jim, 54, committed suicide on October 19, 1902.

In February 1903, Cole was pardoned if he never returned to Minnesota. Within a month, Cole finished his autobiography. When book sales tanked, he joined a Wild West show with Frank, which was also a disaster. In November, Cole pulled his pistol on one of the show owners to get the two of them released from the tour.

Frank returned to the family homestead. Cole became a preacher, an occupation he long desired as he told author James William "J.W." Buel (1849-1920) in 1880. Buel wrote more than 50 books, including *The Border Bandits: An Authentic and Thrilling History of the Noted Outlaws, Jesse and Frank James, and Their Bands of Highwaymen*. Buel asked Cole about his prison duties. "I occupy much of my time in theological studies for which I have a natural inclination," Cole said. "It was the earliest desire of my parents to prepare me for the ministry, but the horrors of war, the murder of my father, and the outrages perpetrated upon my poor old mother, my sisters, and brothers destroyed our hopes so effectually that none of us could be prepared for any duty in life except revenge."

In 1909, Cole began a lecture tour sharing *What My Life Has Taught Me.*

"A man may be an outlaw and yet a patriot," he said. "There is the outlaw with a heart of velvet and a hand of steel; there is the outlaw who never molested the sacred sanctity of any man's home; there is the outlaw who never dethroned a woman's honor or assailed her heritage; and there is the outlaw who has never robbed the honest poor."

CHAPTER SEVEN

Wasp of the Senate

In 1877, Vest moved to Kansas City. A year and a half later, in the election of 1879, Vest defeated fellow Democrats Samuel Taylor Glover (1813-1884) and railroad magnate Thomas Allen (1813-1882) with the support of young journalist Joseph Pulitzer (1847-1911), who became co-owner and editor of the *Saint Louis Post-Dispatch* on December 12, 1878. A *Post-Dispatch* reporter described Pulitzer as "more than 6 feet tall. He wore rimless glasses, a soft hat and a blue chinchilla overcoat obviously tailored in New York."

Joseph Pulitzer, ca. 1900, American politician and newspaper publisher.

Pulitzer, the namesake of journalism's highest honor, began his reign by announcing that the *Post-Dispatch* would be "the organ of truth; will follow no caucuses but its own convictions; will not support the 'Administration,' but criticize it; will oppose all frauds and shams wherever and whatever they are; will advocate principles and ideas rather than prejudices and partisanship. These ideas and principles are precisely the same as those upon which our government was originally founded."

Three weeks later, in the December 30 edition, Pulitzer endorsed Vest over Allen, whom he portrayed as fronting for big-money interests. "If it is a crime to sympathize with the struggle of the poor but brilliant man like Vest against the combined power of money, offices, patronage, newspaper influence, and slander, we plead guilty," Pulitzer wrote.

When the Missouri *Republican*, with its circulation of 20,000—several times that of the *Post-Dispatch*—called Vest "corrupt," Pulitzer labeled it "an unmitigated lie." When The *Republican* implied that Vest was a boozer, Pulitzer called it "a gross slander" used to defame "nearly every prominent man in the history of the state."

While Pulitzer's defense may have been true, the accusations, at least regarding alcohol, may have been valid. Marian Elaine Dawes (1911-1995), who wrote a successful dissertation on Vest in 1932, said Vest was "generally sober, but at times, otherwise." In either condition, he spoke eloquently on the issues of the day. "Vest would probably agree that his greatest enemy was John Barleycorn [whiskey]," Dawes said.

Pulitzer's January 10, 1879, editorial stated: "Democracy means opposition to all special privileges. Republicanism means favoritism to corporations. The tremendous power and influence of nearly all corporations and favored classes are notoriously on the Republican side. Money is the great power today. Men sell their souls for it. Women sell their bodies for it. Others worship it. The money power has grown so great that the issue of all issues is whether the corporations shall rule this country or the country again rule the corporations. [Corporate influence] reaches the Supreme Court and the White House itself! Yet it is seriously proposed by purchased papers and political prostitutes to send the most conspicuous creature of 'capital and privilege' in this State [Allen] to the Senate of the United States as a representative of the Missouri Democracy."

Vest began his campaign early and covered the state thoroughly. One issue he became known for was free coinage of silver, which the Republicans had ended in 1873. Vest blamed the move for an economic depression and attacked the Greenback-Labor Party, calling it the "Coyote Party"—notable only for its noise.

Gen. James Shields. Brady-Handy Photograph Collection, Library of Congress, Prints and Photographs Division.

"It's like the first night out on the plains," he said. "You lie awake with your gun cocked ready for wolves barking around you in every direction. When you wake, you nervously look around for acres of wolves and see only a poor little devil looking at you over a sand hill."

Vest's predecessor in the Senate was James Shields (1806-1879), a brigadier general in the Mexican-American War, who once challenged a young Abraham Lincoln to a duel and is the only person in U.S. history to serve as senator from three states—Illinois from 1849 to 1855, Minnesota from 1858 to 1859, and Missouri in 1879.

Once in office—thanks in significant part to Pulitzer—Vest stayed there until March 3, 1903, running unopposed in 1885, 1891 and 1897.

"Let others do as they may, for myself I shall remain with the party to which I have given the best years of my life, and in whose ranks, God willing, I expect to die."

- George Graham Vest speech to the Macon County, Missouri, Democrats, April 3, 1878

Vest said that, when he took the oath of office as United States senator on March 18, 1879, the Senate comprised many able and distinguished men. On the Republican side were Roscoe Conkling (1829-1888), whom Vest called "a most picturesque and attractive figure;" James Gillespie Blaine (1830-1893) of Maine, Matthew Hale Carpenter (1824-1881) of Wisconsin, George Franklin Edmunds (1828-1919) of Vermont, George Frisbie Hoar (1826-1904) of Massachusetts, John James Ingalls (1833-1900) of Kansas, John Alexander Logan (1826-1886) of Illinois, and William Boyd Allison (1829-1908) of Iowa. The Democratic leaders were Allen Granberry Thurman (1813-1895) and George Hunt Pendleton (1825-1889) of Ohio, Thomas Francis Bayard (1828-1898) of Delaware, Daniel Wolsey Voorhees (1827-1897) and Joseph Ewing McDonald (1819-1891) of Indiana, James Burnie Beck (1822-1890) of Kentucky, Benjamin Harvey Hill (1823-1882) of Georgia, Lucius Quintus Cincinnatus Lamar of Mississippi, and the wildly racist John Tyler Morgan (1824-1907) of Alabama.

Lucius Quintus Cincinnatus Lamar of Mississippi served as a Supreme Court justice and secretary of interior for President Grover Cleveland. Brady-Handy Photograph Collection, Library of Congress, Prints and Photographs Division.

Vest had served briefly with Lamar in the Confederate Senate. "When I entered the [U.S.] Senate in the spring of 1879, Lamar suffered a succession of nervous attacks, which depressed him greatly and caused him to take little interest in public business," Vest noted. "It was obvious that he lived in constant apprehension of complete paralysis."

Of Conkling, Vest said, "Nature had been prodigal in dealing with this remarkable man. Tall, graceful, with a perfectly healthy body, classic features and head denoting great intellect, he had also a splendid voice and great command of the language. He was not a self-made man, in the ordinary meaning of the term, but came from a distinguished family and received the best education available."

Roscoe Conkling cartoon

Despite Vest's praise, he did not consider Conkling much of a leader or person.

"He was haughty, imperious, and often insulting with his social equals who differed from him, but soft and gentle as a summer breeze to subordinates and inferiors. My impression was that he ought to have been born a king and the head of a government exercising absolute power."

After Vest took the oath of office, General Cockrell introduced him to Conkling, but the two never spoke again, even when both were members of the Committee on Commerce in 1881. "Our intercourse was limited to my addressing him as Mr. Chairman and his recognition of me as the Senator from Missouri.

"There was never any antagonism between us except general disagreements on political questions, but an incident occurred on the day after I entered the Senate which fixed my relations with Senator Conkling."

Vest and Senator Benjamin Franklin Jonas (1834-1911) of Louisiana were in the Democratic cloakroom, listening to war stories from Kentuckian John Stuart "Cerro Gordo" Williams (so nicknamed for his distinguished service at the Battle of Cerro Gordo during the Mexican-American War), when Conkling entered the room on his way to the Senate chambers. Williams (1818-1898), who had also been introduced to Conkling the previous day, said, "Good morning, Senator Conkling," and extended his right hand.

Confederate General John Stuart Williams (1818-1898), ca. 1880. Library of Congress photo.

"Instead of accepting his hand or making any reply, Conkling slightly inclined his head and, waving Williams aside, strode into the Senate, leaving all of us in a state of profound astonishment," Vest said.

"What was the meaning of that?" asked Williams in puzzled amazement. "Do you suppose that man intended to insult me?"

Vest, who had known Williams since childhood, called Williams one of the kindest and most courteous gentlemen he had ever known and tried to pass off Conkling's behavior as a strange custom afforded to freshmen senators. "I felt indignant at the treatment he [Williams] received from Conkling and determined that I would not subject myself to any similar indignity by making any advances toward the New York Senator."

Vest's disdain for Conkling was confirmed on April 24, 1879, when Conkling addressed the Senate on a Legislative, Executive, and Judicial Appropriations Bill. "Although the Civil War had terminated 14 years before, the country was still afflicted with its aftermath," Vest said. "It was the first time I had ever heard Mr. Conkling speak, and I listened to him with the closest attention. He had before him on his desk, when he commenced speaking, several sheets of notepaper on which were memoranda that were used and then thrown on the floor. After he had spoken for half an hour, General

[William Tecumseh] Sherman [1820-1891], who was then Commanding General of the Army, appeared on the door of the Senate in full uniform and, on seeing him, Conkling said, 'Good morning, General Sherman. I am glad to see you here. Take that seat' [pointing to an empty chair in the front on the Democratic side]. This incident is not found in the Congressional Record, but it occurred exactly as I have stated and was a striking illustration of Conkling's imperious nature."

Vest described Conkling's speech as exceedingly bitter and partisan. "He made frequent allusions to the outrages committed on the Negroes in Southern states and waved the 'bloody shirt' with great dramatic effect. His delivery was perfect, but there was an absence of the first requisite of oratory—the magnetic touch which controls the audience. He appeared to be a great actor but not a great orator."

In 1879, Conkling and Lamar had a dust-up that anyone who knew the two men should have seen coming. "Lamar and Conkling couldn't be personal friends," said Vest. "They were entirely unlike in every respect. Conkling treated all but a few of his colleagues with arrogance or contemptuous indifference."

An all-night "acrimonious debate" session left the senators tired and irritated. "The air was charged with electricity which required only a spark to create an explosion," Vest recalled.

At dawn, Conkling moved for adjournment. When the Democrats resisted the motion, the Republicans questioned their integrity. Lamar returned fire and said he held the motion in contempt equal to that he felt for Conkling.

Conkling said that, if Lamar intended to charge him with falsehood, he would, but for the rules of the Senate, pronounce Lamar a black-guard liar and coward.

Lamar responded with the 19th-century version of "if the shoe fits, wear it," ending the exchange.

What Vest didn't like about Conkling was his pretentiousness, which is something Vest was never called. When he first came to Washington, he lived in a small cottage next to the engine house on Capitol Hill, near the Senate stables. He shared the space with the sergeant of arms of the Senate (former Confederate Richard Jesse Bright [1833-1920]). Vest took his meals at the Senate restaurant or ate downtown at Chamberlain's Restaurant, whose chef, Emeline Jones (1832-1932), an emancipated slave, was considered one of the best chefs of the day and purportedly the inventor of potato chips (Saratoga Chips). Presidents Cleveland and Chester Alan Arthur (1829-1886) were both big fans of her cooking.

When Missourians visited Washington, they were amazed at the modesty of Vest's living quarters. When Sallie visited Washington, the temporary bachelor quarters were abandoned, and a house or rooms more to her liking were rented.

On June 25, 1879, Vest introduced a resolution for the free coinage of silver. It was referred to the Finance Committee, which Vest called the "tomb of the Capulets," and never resurfaced.

"An amusing incident occurred between two of my best friends in the Democratic cloakroom of the Senate," said Vest, recalling a conversation he had with an Englishman while visiting Carlsbad, Austria, where the Englishman said Americans were "idolaters" for their worship of George Washington, saying, "You actually teach your children that he was without sin and could not tell a lie even if he wished to do so."

The friends were Senators Blackburn and John Warwick Daniel (1842-1910) of Virginia. "Senator Daniel was dozing on a sofa in the cloakroom, and I called his attention to what Blackburn had said about our first President. 'Oh,' replied Daniel, 'Blackburn has a personal grievance against Washington.' Senator Blackburn, who talks exceedingly well, both publicly and privately, was discussing the relative merits of great military commanders and declared that, though Washington was, all in all, the most admirable character in history, he was not a great general," Vest said.

"'What grievance have I against him?' exclaimed Blackburn hotly.

"'Well,' Senator Daniel said, 'Washington couldn't tell a lie.'"

While Vest's kinship with Blackburn predated his election to the Senate, his association with Blaine extended to his teenage years in Kentucky.

Senator James G. Blaine of Maine, ca. 1865-80. Brady-Handy Photograph Collection, Library of Congress, Prints and Photographs Division.

"I first heard of James G. Blaine in about 1850 when there was a riot or mutiny among the cadets at the Western Military Institute, then located at Blue Lick Springs in [Nicholas County] Kentucky," Vest said. "This was a military school established [in 1847] by Colonel Thornton Fitzhugh Johnson [1805-1851], a graduate of West Point and a retired Army officer who belonged to one of the most distinguished families in Kentucky. Richard Mentor Johnson [1780-1850], once Vice President of the United States, and Robert Ward Johnson [1814-1879], a U.S. Senator from Arkansas and afterward a Confederate Senator, were members of this family.

"In the trouble at Blue Lick Springs, there was a serious collision between the faculty, in which Blaine was a professor of mathematics, and the cadets—knives and pistols being freely used by the latter.

"There was a great deal of comment in the newspapers upon the affair, one account being that Major Blaine, as he was termed, distinguished himself in suppressing the disturbance, although he used only the weapons given him by nature, while the cadets, who were all from Southern states, were armed with pistols and knives," Vest said. "Another account was that Major Blaine fought gallantly until the appearance of the pistols and knives when he retreated from the conflict. From what I subsequently knew of Blaine, it is impossible for me to believe that he was deficient in personal courage, for I have never known a more aggressive and fearless man in public or private life."

Blaine, who also taught Greek and Latin, remained at the school through 1851. "He was a trusted and valued assistant of Col. T.F. Johnson, who, under no circumstances, would have tolerated anything like cowardice, or even timidity, on the part of anyone connected with the institution of which he was principal," Vest said.

The Western Military Institute, which Vest's father constructed, later moved to Nashville, and it is estimated that more than 1,000 of its graduates—drawn from 18 states—served in the Confederate army.

"Blaine was, at the time, a handsome and attractive young man, about 21, and was exceedingly popular with the Kentuckians, in whose homes he was a welcome guest," Vest said. "He adapted himself readily to the habits of the people generally and, although a Pennsylvanian by birth, was in taste and feeling a Kentuckian.

"He very often came over to the Democratic side of the Senate chamber and talked freely with those of us who were familiar with the history of Kentucky," Vest said. "He knew all about the state and its public men and was never tired of discussing the striking characteristics of the Kentuckians."

According to Vest, Blaine fashioned himself as a modern-day Henry Clay. "Nothing pleased him so much as the institution of a parallel between his career and that of the great Kentuckian," Vest said.

William Lowndes Yancey (1814-63), member of the U.S. Congress from 1844-46 and a Confederate senator during the American Civil War. Library of Congress photo.

Vest's first association with Blaine as a senator came during the called session of 1879, when Blaine spoke in response to an amendment proposed by Senator Ben Hill of Georgia—the same Hill who had hurled a glass inkstand at Confederate Congressman William L. Yancey, effectively ending Yancey's career. "Blaine was not an orator, but a strong, incisive, and attractive speaker, who prepared himself thoroughly and was quick to see the most vulnerable point of attack in the enemy's lines," Vest said.

"The seat of Roscoe Conkling, Blaine's most inveterate enemy, who was always ready to make any sacrifice necessary to defeat Blaine's ambition, was on the Republican side of the aisle in the Senate chamber, while Blaine occupied a seat on the same row but some distance east of that occupied by Conkling. The debate became heated, and Blaine, in his excitement, advanced toward Conkling and the Democratic side of the chamber, shaking his fist defiantly at his opponents and hurling invectives at the Confederate Brigadiers, as he called them."

Conkling, forgetting for an instant the long-running feud between the two, suggested a point to be made, which Blaine grabbed up with eagerness. "It was the only time in 15 years that the two had spoken to each other," Vest said.

Hill responded to Blaine's attack on the Confederate government for its treatment of Federal prisoners eloquently and logically. "His 1879 speech on the amendments to the military appropriations bill prohibiting the use of troops at the polls, after three and a quarter hours, I was so wholly hypnotized as to make it necessary for me to use some exertion when he quit speaking to throw off the spell that was upon me.

"I had heard Senator Hill speak frequently but never as eloquently as on this occasion."

Also taking his seat during the called session of 1879 was former Confederate General Wade Hampton III (1818-1902) of South Carolina, who would soon be one of Vest's closest associates. For 12 years, the two sat next to each other and shared many tales.

While Hampton felt it was his duty to serve his home state, he considered secession neither wise nor necessary. Like Vest and General Robert E. Lee, Hampton held slaves but was not, like Jefferson Davis, as hard-core a proponent of the institution. Hampton angered pro-slavery extremists by speaking before the war against the further trafficking of slaves but afterward did his best to suppress Blacks from voting.

"When General Hampton spoke of the war, which was not often, he dwelt more on the humorous incidents of his military life than on any service he rendered to the Confederate cause," Vest said.

One of the funnier of Hampton's stories involved his capture of a naked Union soldier whom "Hampton's Legion" happened upon bathing in a Virginia creek.

"He begged to be released and said that only the night before, he had obtained a furlough to visit his sweetheart and was washing off the camp dirt before starting his journey home. He seemed surprised when I told him he was my prisoner," Hampton said. "He told me that he was a clerk in the commissary service and on duty with a detachment of Federal troops, whose pickets were nearby.

"He did not want to be sent to a Southern prison, and, as I thought his case a rather hard one, I finally told him that I had made up my mind not to keep him, which seemed to give him the greatest possible satisfaction. When he came out of the water, however, and started to put on his clothes, I gravely told him that I would release him but could not let him take his clothes, as my men were much in need of them. He started off in a perfectly nude condition, thankful to get away without any clothing. Still, after allowing him to go a short distance, I called him back and told him to dress and to take better care of himself in the future," Hampton continued.

According to Hampton, the soldier praised and thanked him and said that, if he ever had a son, he'd name him in Hampton's honor.

"Last evening," Hampton said, "when I started up on the elevator at my hotel, a well-dressed young fellow spoke to me and inquired if I was not Senator Wade Hampton. When I answered in the affirmative, he said, 'Do you remember, Senator, having captured a naked Federal soldier?'

"I told him that I remembered the incident perfectly.

"He said, 'Well, that soldier was my father, and my name is Wade Hampton. Good evening, sir,' he said as he stepped from the elevator and disappeared."

Hampton was best known for being wrongly accused of setting his hometown of Columbia, South Carolina, ablaze while protecting the Confederate rear against the onslaught of Sherman's advancing Federal forces.

In his memoirs, Sherman said that the charges against Hampton were false. "I distinctly charged it to General Wade Hampton to shake the faith of his people in him, for he was, in my opinion, a braggart and professed to be the special champion of South Carolina."

In a conversation with Vest, Hampton said that, while he would not make himself seem ridiculous by seeking any personal satisfaction from Sherman, "I hope that we may never meet, for I distrust my self-control if face to face with a man who has wronged me so foully."

In Hampton's belief, he suffered enough actual outrages without dealing with fictional ones. "During the whole war, I never committed an act violating the rules of civilized warfare and never permitted my soldiers to do so," Hampton said. "I was second in command when the cavalry raid was made into Pennsylvania in October 1862, and Colonel Alexander Kelly McClure [1828-1909], the well-known editor of the *Philadelphia Times* and Lincoln biographer, testified in his memoirs how scrupulously I caused the rights of private citizens and non-combatants to be respected by my men when we captured Chambersburg.

"Yet when I returned home after the War, I found my residence burned, two miles from Columbia, and Millwood, the home of my grandfather and father, around which clustered the most sacred memories of my life. I lost in the War all my estate and had seen my brother and youngest son shot down upon the battlefield, but General Sherman was not satisfied … and attempted to place upon me the terrible stigma of having burned the houses of my friends and neighbors in Columbia."

In 1902, Vest spoke to the Senate in honor of his friend's memory. "I knew him well and loved him sincerely," Vest said. "He was the highest type of a Christian gentleman: patient, brave, honest, and unselfish. He was not depressed by adversity or unduly elated by prosperity. Having lost all except life and honor, he bowed submissively to the result of a great war, in which he shared the fortunes of his people."

During that called session of 1879, Vest also had his first of numerous run-ins with Senator Ingalls. "In an eloquent and vigorous speech, Senator Ingalls bitterly assailed the Southern whites for having caused the Negro exodus from the South to Kansas in the preceding year by their outrages upon the Negroes who had been emancipated during the war," Vest wrote. "In concluding his address, he paid a glowing tribute to the people of Kansas who had received with open arms the Negroes fleeing to an asylum in his home state and declared that his constituents were glad to have them as citizens and neighbors.

"I was at that time a resident of Kansas City, Missouri, and lived in sight of Wyandotte, Kansas, where the first consignment of Negroes from the South landed under the promise that they should be taken to Elysium, where they would have happy homes and both political and social equality," Vest wrote. "I felt it my duty to answer the assertion of Senator Ingalls regarding the exodus and stated in the Senate that I had visited Wyandotte to ascertain the real facts and had found about 200 of the poor deluded Negroes living in holes dug in the bank of the Missouri River—one-tenth of their number having died from exposure and resulting disease, the citizens of Wyandotte refusing them shelter, food or necessary clothing."

During Vest's visit two boxes of clothing arrived from charitable citizens of Boston and Chicago. "I have seen in my Western life upon the plains the coyotes as they tore each other in attempting to get at the carcass of a freshly slaughtered buffalo: I have heard the shrieks of famished wolves, but I've never heard anything like when the government deprived those gathered that to which they were entitled."

Vest presented a circular purportedly sent to thousands of Southern Blacks, urging them to come to Kansas, where they could live comfortably and escape the oppression of their former enslavers.

Senator John James Ingalls of Kansas, March 12, 1873. Brady-Handy Photograph Collection, Library of Congress, Prints and Photographs Division.

"The Negro who gave me the circular said he received it at his home in Mississippi," Vest said. "Senator Ingalls interrupted me to declare this circular was a forgery."

Vest replied that the man in Wyandotte who had given it to him had no reason to lie about when and where he obtained the advertisement.

"I also read to the Senate an address to the people of the United States by the mayor and principal citizens of Wyandotte, a majority of whom I knew were Republicans protesting the coming to Kansas of Southern Negroes and stating that the citizens of Wyandotte and the entire state would resist the influx of these unfortunate creatures in the future. Senator Ingalls interrupted me again to say that the signers of this address were Democrats. After denying his statement from personal knowledge, I asked him the direct question, if the Mayor of Wyandotte, who appeared as the first in the list of signers, was not, and had not always been, a staunch Republican."

Ingalls, who Vest said would go to any length to win an argument, did not answer.

"It was impossible that Senator Ingalls, who lived in Atchison, a short distance from Wyandotte, did not know that my statement regarding the exodus was true," Vest said.

When Senator William Windom (1827-1891) spoke on the topic, Vest responded: "I am a better friend to the Negroes than the gentleman from Minnesota. I was born with them, nursed by them."

When the Senate's Claim Committee approved a $4,750 claim by former Kansas Territorial Clerk Samuel A. Lowe (1825-1879) for copying the territory's laws, Ingalls argued it was an attempt to induce the Senate to pay for the compilation of its infamous slave code.

Vest, who said he wasn't familiar with the details of Lowe's claim, seized the opportunity to prolong the Kansas-Missouri dispute. "I have no disposition to go back to the history of that terrible and unfortunate border war; great outrages were perpetrated by both sides. The original crime cannot be fastened and never will, if the pages of history are just to the living and the dead, upon the people of Missouri.

"The institution of slavery has ceased to exist and for myself I have no disposition to palliate or excuse any outrage that may have been committed. I desire that the recollection of them shall pass away, but I know, and hundreds now living know, the unparalleled outrages perpetrated upon the people of my state by the men who are claimed today to have been martyrs in the cause of liberty and freedom on the soil of Kansas. The institution of slavery was with us by no violation of our own, and we were unable to get rid of it by lawful means at the time," Vest said.

In March 1879, Senator Hoar moved an amendment granting pensions to the soldiers of the Mexican-American War, but Jefferson Davis (a first lieutenant colonel who fought at the battles of Monterrey and Buena Vista) did not receive any such funds. Thurman argued that Hoar's Massachusetts was "the state in which treason has been published and preached longer and more violently than in any other." Hoar, Thurman said, never denounced Lloyd Garrison (1805-1879), journalist and anti-slavery crusader, for saying the Constitution of the United States was "a compact with hell."

In his speech, Hoar denounced Davis as an unrepentant traitor. Lamar responded: "Sir, it required no courage to do that; it required no magnanimity; no courtesy.

It only required hate, bitter, malignant, sectional feeling, and a sense of personal impunity."

In contrast, Vest presented a bill granting the continuance of pension payments to the family of General Shields, who faced General Thomas J. "Stonewall" Jackson at the Battle of Kernstown (Virginia) in 1862, handing Jackson his only tactical defeat. In death, Shields' most valuable possession was the ceremonial swords given at the end of the Mexican-American War. Vest said of Shields, an Irish-American Democrat, "Coming from a nationality which has been unfortunate enough to pour its blood like water in defense of every country except their own, there is not an Irish heart in these free United States that will not beat in gratitude to this Congress for this sincere evidence of appreciation for the services of their heroic countryman."

Attached to the Shields Bill was a provision that $100 per month be paid to Caroline Story White Webster (1811-1886), the widow of Union Colonel Daniel Fletcher Webster (1813-1862). Killed at the Second Battle of Bull Run on August 30, 1862, the colonel was the son of the legendary Daniel Webster (1782-1852), who represented New Hampshire and Massachusetts in the U.S. Senate and was the 14th and 19th U.S. secretary of state.

Vest claimed to have voted in favor of every pension bill that came before the Senate and said he would have done so if the Confederacy had prevailed. He said he would have voted the last dollar and acre be paid to the maimed, wounded and disabled soldiers of the Confederate Army and "the people of the United States to whom Providence gave triumph in the conflict, have the same right, and not only the same right but the same duty imposed upon them."

On April 17, 1879, Vest heard Senator Voorhees of Indiana speak for the first time. The speech opened a debate on amendments to a bill prohibiting the appropriation of public money from paying U.S. marshals for services at the polls. "It was a great speech—eloquent, logical, and comprehensive," Vest said. "Conkling, Blaine, Edmunds, Hoar, and Ingalls replied to Voorhees, but, in my judgment, his argument was never successfully answered."

Vest was astonished when he realized Voorhees read his speech. "He was unquestionably one of the most fluent extemporaneous speakers in political life," Vest said. "Afterward, I inquired of Voorhees why he read his speeches in the Senate, and he told me that one of his defects as a speaker was a tendency to say things on the impulse of the moment, which he subsequently regretted; and, as his addresses in the Senate were principally intended for his constituents and were published in The Congressional Record, he had fallen into the habit of writing out all of his prepared speeches."

Political Cartoons Featuring Vest and Other National Figures of the Era

From 1876-1918, *Puck* magazine was well-known for its coverage of political and social events of the time, primarily through colorful cartoons, caricatures and political satire. Originally published by Joseph Keppler and Adolph Schwarzmann, it is known as the first successful humor magazine in the United States. As a national political figure, George Vest was featured quite frequently, as can be seen in the following reproductions.

The 1883 political cartoon, "A Dreadful Attack of Presidential Fever," by Frederick Burr Opper (1857-1937), appeared in Puck *magazine and included George Graham Vest as a U.S. senator (holding a thermometer). The illustration shows Puck in the Senate chamber, among many senators sick with "Presidential Fever;" Puck is offering a spoonful of "Anti-Presidential Quinine"*

to John Sherman. The other senators present are Wade Hampton, George F. Hoar, James D. Cameron, William Mahone, Warner Miller, Daniel Wolsey Voorhees, John Logan, George Edmunds, Thomas Bayard, John Percival Jones, and Judge David Davis. George M. Robeson, Jay Gould, and Roscoe Conkling are peering over the chamber walls. (Courtesy of the Library of Congress)

"They can't hold up this train" shows President Cleveland as a railroad engineer is driving a locomotvie labeled "Administration R.R." that is roaring out of a tunnel labeled "Business Depression Tunnel," and knocking out of the way legislators who are placing "Dilitary Amendments" and "Teller's Dilatory Tactics" on the tracks, trying to derail the train; the legislators include

Francis M. Cockrell, James Z. George, James L. Pugh, William A. Peffer, George G. Vest, James D. Cameron, William M. Stewart, Henry M. Teller, John P. Jones, and Edward O. Wolcott. This print by Charles J. Taylor was published by Keppler & Schwarzmann, October 11, 1893. (Courtesy of the Library of Congress.)

Vest was quoted (page 147) calling the Southern Democrats akin to "a council of monkeys," which may have been the inspiration for "Through the Jungle" by Udo J. Keppler (1872-1956). The cartoon shows President Grover Cleveland as an explorer, with cabinet members John G. Carlisle and Walter Q. Gresham, in a jungle, where they have come across a band

of monkeys labeled D. Hill, C. Dana, W. Reid, Blackburn, Vest, Jones, Pugh, Foraker, Wolcott, Teller, Morgan, Peffer, [and] Stewart. Published by Keppler & Schwarzmann, November 22, 1893. (Courtesy of the Library of Congress)

Vest is among a menacing pack of dogs in the January 31, 1894, centerfold, "The National Honor and Credit is in Good Hands," by Louis Dalrymple (1866-1905). It features President Grover Cleveland, Pulitzer (as a donkey), members of the

media and the Democratic side of the Senate. Published by Keppler & Schwarzmann, January 31, 1894. (Courtesy of the Library of Congress)

Louis Dalrymple's "Shade of General Hancock" shows a group of senators gathered around a table with the ghost of Winfield Scott Hancock (1824-1886) hovering above. Senator David B. Hill screams at Vest, "They laughed at me when I said the tariff is a local issue; but I was right, after all." Published by Keppler & Schwarzmann, May 2, 1894. (Courtesy of the Library of Congress)

"May the Country Be Spared This Pitiful Sight!" by Louis Dalrymple, shows a group of Democrats wearing fezzes, turbans and other articles of Middle Eastern dress, at a bier to burn the Democrat Free Coinage Platform. Published by Keppler & Schwarzmann, July 8, 1896. (Courtesy of the Library of Congress)

"Last ghost-dance of the free silver tribe - just before being sent to the Salt River Reservation," by Louis Dalrymple, shows a Native American encampment of the Democrat/Populist presidential candidate and his followers dancing around a campfire

BEING SENT TO THE SALT RIVER RESERVATION.

labeled "Repudiation"; depicted from left are Peffer, Jerry Simpson, Teller, Vest, Watson, Bryan, Sewall, J.P. Jones, Altgeld, Bland, and Stewart. Published by Keppler & Schwarzmann, November 4, 1896. (Courtesy of the Library of Congress.)

"A Very Sick Patient ... He Pays Well, But the Senatorial Quacks Can't Save Him" by F.M. Hutchins (1867-1896) shows several legislators as quack physicians trying to cure a large sick man labeled "Protection" with various pseudo cures. Published by Keppler & Schwarzmann, July 18, 1894. (Courtesy of the Library of Congress)

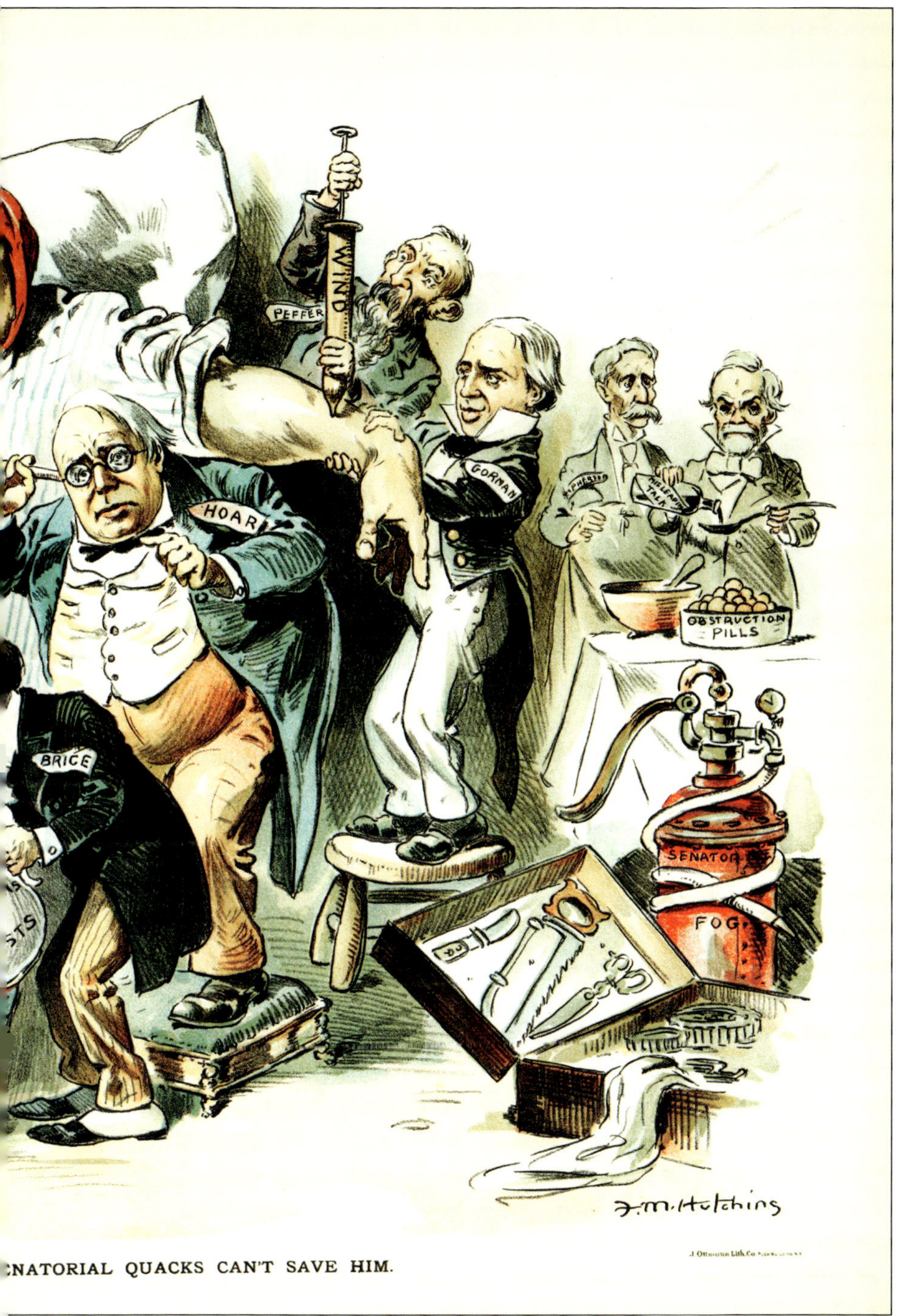

NATORIAL QUACKS CAN'T SAVE HIM.

The June 9, 1897, Puck *centerfold shows former president Grover Cleveland and his wife, Frances, playing with their children, Ruth, Esther, and Marion, in the backyard of their residence, and several men labeled "Morgan, Daniel, Pugh, Faulkner, Vest, Dana, [and] Gorman" spying on them from behind a fence, bushes, and over a hedge. "He Keeps Them*

Worried" was the work of Charles Jay Taylor (1855-1929), a landscape artist who illustrated for Harpers *and the* New York Daily Graphic. *Published by Keppler & Schwarzmann, June 9, 1897. (Courtesy of the Library of Congress)*

The January 1899 centerfold of Puck, *"Who Will Haul It Down," was penned by Louis Dalrymple. Vest has a resignation in his pocket as he battles against annexation, with President McKinley standing on a road leading to the White House. Published by Keppler & Schwarzmann, January 11, 1899. (Courtesy of the Library of Congress)*

PHILIPPINE ISLDS
HAWAII
OTTENDORFER
PULITZER
so, by the fortunes of war
government, to chaos after
have had? After destroying
Government to provide for
hall we proclaim to the world
d peoples whose future by the
were otherwise, but who will
NNAH BANQUET.
BRYAN'S
ANTI-ANNEXATION ISSUE
FOR 1900
HALF
SPEECHES
Dalrymple,
J. OTTMANN LITH.

T DOWN?”

In the March 22, 1899, issue of Puck, *Vest and his compatriots try to topple the administration, with Joseph Pulitzer of* The New York World *defacing an 1898 monument. Published by Keppler & Schwarzmann, March 22, 1899. (Courtesy of the Library of Congress)*

"Democracy's Plight" by J.S. Pughe (1870-1909), depicts William Jennings Bryan, John P. Jones, and Arthur P. Gorman mesmerized by a large genie carrying a sword labeled "Free Silver," while George Vest has his ear to the ground, unaware of the genie. Published by Keppler & Schwarzmann, October 11, 1899. (Courtesy of the Library of Congress)

The May 10, 1899, Puck *centerfold, "The Idol of the Aunties" shows Vest on his knees across a mound from his long-time friend and supporter Joseph Pulitzer. Drawn by Louis Dalrymple, it depicts influential Americans bowing before Emilio*

AUNTIES.

Aguinaldo (1869-1964), commander-in-chief and first president of the Philippines. Published by Keppler & Schwarzmann, May 10, 1899. (Courtesy of the Library of Congress)

"The Dogs and the Moon" by Udo J. Keppler shows a pack of dogs, with their tails between their legs, howling at a full moon labeled "Prosperity" outside the U.S. Capitol, featuring Tillman, Vest, Jones, Bryan, Altgeld, Gore, and Hogg. Published by Keppler & Schwarzmann, October 25, 1899. (Courtesy of the Library of Congress)

Over the next 18 years, Vest's association with Voorhees, as he would describe it, was "an oasis in the desert of political life where the Dead Sea apples of selfish ambition turn to ashes on the lips that touch them."

Hon. Thomas Andrews Hendricks of Indiana, ca. 1860-65. Brady-Handy Photograph Collection, Library of Congress, Prints and Photographs Division.

Major General Winfield S. Hancock (1824-86). Library of Congress photo.

James O. Broadhead, U.S. Congressman from Missouri (1882-85), U.S. Minister to Switzerland (1893-97), and first president of the American Bar Association.

Unless prevented by health, Vest participated in all presidential campaigns, beginning with 1880, when he was a delegate at large to the Democratic National Convention in Cincinnati.

Prior to the convention, in New York, Vest and Colonel James Overton Broadhead (1819-1898) visited Samuel Jones Tilden (1814-1886), a potential candidate, at his home in Gramercy Park. Judging him to be physically unfit, Vest urged Thomas Andrews Hendricks (1819-1885) to run. Hendricks, who was also in poor health, also declined. Eventually, the party settled on Civil War hero Winfield Scott Hancock (1824-1886) and William Hayden English (1822-1896) to challenge Arthur and James Garfield (1831-1881).

Citing the "Great Fraud of 1876"—a reference to the hotly contested presidential election that Tilden lost to Rutherford B. Hayes—Vest stumped in Missouri, Indiana, Ohio and West Virginia.

Shortly after joining the Senate, Vest renewed his friendship with Bayard, whom he first met during the National Democratic Convention of 1872. "I remember being a guest at his residence in Washington when he invited a few of us to meet his lifelong friend, William Riggins Travers [1819-1887], whose reputation as a wit and humorist extended to two continents," Vest said.

Right: *Senator Thomas F. Bayard of Delaware, ca. 1870-80. Brady-Handy Photograph Collection, Library of Congress, Prints and Photographs Division.*

Far right: *Attorney William Riggins Travers, 1905.*

During an after-dinner conversation, someone suggested that the Democrats' choice to push amendments to the general appropriation bills would put the party on the defensive and would probably cause them to lose their majority in both houses of Congress.

"Stuttering Travers," who *The New York Times* wrote "was the most popular man in the country," said the Democrats would be as surprised as he and Bayard were when they tried to buy a rat terrier in New York for Bayard's rat-infested home in Wilmington, Delaware. "We picked out a very handsome, active little dog, and the proprietor dropped him in the pit, took a gray-whiskered rat out of a box, and placed him in front of the terrier," Travers said. "After looking at each other for half a second, the dog turned tail and ran at full speed around the pit with the rat in hot pursuit. 'Buy the rat, Tom,' I shouted, 'buy the rat.'"

In relaying this story years later, Vest conditionally apologized. "This story is now an ancient chestnut, but it amused me when I heard it told by Travers, and it is good enough to bear repetition," Vest said. Travers, the first president of Saratoga Racetrack, is satirized as character Sillerton Jackson in *The Age of Innocence* by Pulitzer Prize-winning author Edith Wharton (1862-1937).

Vest described Bayard, who unsuccessfully ran for president and served as secretary of state under Cleveland, as singularly independent and true to his honest convictions, two extremely rare traits for any politician, especially a long-term one. Vest said: "He refused to be governed by any convention or caucus and declared that he would not sacrifice his self-respect by surrendering what he believed was right and best for the country. He also claimed he did not vote for any riders or amendments to appropriation bills that contained general legislation. Bayard considered such bills a violation of Senate rules and against the spirit and letter of the Constitution.

"He could not be classed as an orator," Vest said, "but he was a fluent, logical speaker who commanded at all times the closest attention of the Senate." A strict adherent to the rule of law, Bayard was tall and powerfully built. "He had the most winning smile I have ever known."

None of the senators whom Vest knew loved Senate life more than Bayard: "He delighted in praising the dignity of the Senate and said it had no equal in the world," Vest said.

An amusing story about Bayard occurred at a March 2, 1885, dinner party hosted by Senators Beck, an 1846 Transylvania graduate, and Williams. Because of seniority rules, Williams, who wanted badly to be chairman of the Committee on Agriculture, was passed over in favor of Senator Henry Gassaway Davis (1823-1916) of West Virginia. The slight did not sit well with Williams, who was suffering from an inflamed eye. He could not stomach Bayard's praise of the Senate any longer.

"Senator Bayard, I am tired of hearing about the dignity of the Senate," Williams interjected. "It has more dignity, frigidity, stupidity, and antiquity than any body of men I have ever seen. Everything goes by seniority, and if a new Senator makes a good speech, the old Senators become resentful and retire to the cloakroom, where they comment on the newcomer. If any Senator makes a good point and is applauded by the galleries, the presiding officer declares that no applause will be permitted. If the offense is repeated, he orders the sergeant-at-arms to clear the galleries."

Williams espoused the glories of Kentucky politics compared to those in Washington. "I speak to acres of people while the men cheer and the women wave their handkerchiefs and clap in approval," Williams said. "If I remain in this Senate, I shall soon become as much of an idiot as the rest of you. I am going home tonight, and if you come out next summer, Senator Bayard, I will give you a burgoo that will discount all the clambakes on the Atlantic Coast with the United States Senate thrown in."

While Bayard joined in the laughter Williams' outburst drew, the next day, Bayard came to Vest's office, asking about the word "burgoo" and its meaning.

"I explained to Mr. Bayard that the burgoo was a Kentucky institution, a necessary adjunct to all political campaigns, and that it occupied a position relative to that of clambakes in the seaboard states. 'It is,' I said, 'prepared with much care and skill by experts, who claim to have some secret process in its preparation, unknown to the public.'" Quoting the English poet John Keats (1795-1821), Vest explained that it was a game or gypsy stew akin to one prepared by Old Meg.

"'A burgoo,' I continued, 'is usually near some famous spring. The best time for such an event is in the middle or latter part of August or September when vegetables are abundant, especially young corn, tomatoes, and potatoes. The farmers bring young chickens, squirrels, apples, watermelons, and cider. Of course, eloquent speakers are advertised to be present, and barrels of spring water mixed with whisky, mint, and sugar are placed on the grounds with the heads knocked out so that everyone can drink all he wants without paying for it.'"

Vest's friendship with Bayard continued after Bayard joined Cleveland's administration and later became Ambassador to the Court of St. James. "In both positions, he sustained his high reputation for ability and patriotism," Vest said. "I greatly respected his character and attributes and loved him sincerely."

As for Williams, his exit from the Senate was as memorable as his entrance.

"Cerro Gordo Williams was a typical Kentucky gentleman of the olden time," Vest said. "Though his maiden speech in the Senate was not ornate or a polished effort, it was frank, manly, and most attractive. I had not heard such a speech since my boyhood and could almost smell the barbecued meat, which I enjoyed so much while listening to Clay, Crittenden, and the other famous orators of my native state.

"While Williams was speaking, Blaine entered the chamber and, obviously intending to disconcert the new Senator, asked him in a sneering tone why he had taken up arms in the Civil War against the Union when his State had not passed an ordinance of secession," Vest said. "Senator Williams, without a moment's hesitation, replied, with flashing eyes and a voice that rang through the chamber like a trumpet, that he believed the Southern cause to be just and had gone to the front at the beginning of the War without hiring a substitute."

Blaine had been drafted and had sent a substitute to the Union Army. "The retort took Blaine by surprise," Vest said, "and for the first and only time in his career, he took his seat without reply while laughter rippled throughout the entire chamber."

Reflecting on Blaine's legacy, Vest speculated it would be linked to his memorial address given at the funeral of President Garfield in September 1881. "It was a wonderful oration worthy of the best day's oratory," Vest said. "Nothing in the English language is more beautiful than the closing words of this great tribute to the murdered President."

James Abram Garfield (1831-1881), 20th president of the United States. Brady-Handy Photograph Collection, Library of Congress, Prints and Photographs Division.

With wan, fevered face tenderly lifted to the cooling breeze, he looked out wistfully upon the ocean's changing waters; on its fair sails whitening in the morning light; on its restless waves rolling shoreward to break and die beneath the noonday sun; on the red clouds of evening arched low to the horizon; on the serene and shining pathway of the stars. His dying eyes read a mystic meaning that only the rapt and parting soul should know. Let us believe that in the silence of the receding world, he heard the great waves breaking on a farther shore and felt the breath of the eternal morning upon his wasted brow. Gently, silently, the love of a great people bore the pale sufferer to the longed-for healing of the sea, to live or die as God should, within sight of its heaving billows, within the sound of its manifold voices.

His phenomenal memory and ability to maintain grudges diminished the rest of Blaine's career, including his failed 1884 presidential run. "He seemed to know something about everything, and could be an entertaining conversationist," Vest said. "Blaine was a good hater and never made attempts to compromise with those who had offended him," exhibited in Blaine's refusal to shake hands with Edmunds at President Arthur's New York funeral in 1886.

❖ ❖ ❖

Far left: *General William T. Sherman, Photo by Mathew Brady, National Archives.*

Left: *John Sherman of Ohio, ca. 1865-80, who served in both houses of the U.S. Congress, Secretary of the Treasury, and Secretary of State. Brady-Handy Photograph Collection, Library of Congress, Prints and Photographs Division.*

In 1881, General Sherman's brother John (1823-1900) joined the Senate, representing Ohio. Sherman served in both houses of Congress, as secretary of the Treasury, and as secretary of state. In Vest's opinion, John Sherman was the most distinguished and valuable Republican leader since the Civil War.

"He had none of the qualities that make a popular idol, but men followed him because he was bold, aggressive and had great ability," Vest wrote. "He was not brilliant. He had no personal magnetism, but his mind acted systematically and logically, like a machine, undistracted by impulse or passion."

Vest was not alone in his opinion of Sherman. In 1881, when Garfield lay dying in the White House in the hot Washington summer, Ohio humorist Donn Piatt (1819-1891) said the doctors could, with the use of electric fans and ice in the president's sick room, put Sherman in the basement, which would lower the temperature through the entire building.

"Mr. Sherman had no sense of humor and was never known to laugh at a story no matter how humorous it might be or how well it was told," Vest said.

North Carolina Senator Zebulon Baird Vance (1830-1894) once told Sherman and Vest he had recently purchased a team of oxen. "I had some difficulty," Vance said. "After purchasing the matching pair, I asked the seller their names. 'The off ox,' he said, 'is Pete, and I never named his brother because he does whatever his brother does.' But I decided to call them Pete and Repeat."

Senator Zebulon Baird Vance of North Carolina, later governor of that state. Brady-Handy Photograph Collection, Library of Congress, Prints and Photographs Division.

Sherman looked seriously at Vance and said: "You have made a mistake. Those names are too similar, and the oxen will be confused by the similarity of the sound."

Vest held strong prejudices against Sherman when he first joined the Senate and viewed him as tricky and unscrupulous. "He was a strong partisan and always ready to fight his political opponents without asking or giving quarter," Vest said.

Sherman once told Vest that, when Southern Democrats repealed the Missouri Compromise, he became a Republican because he not only felt it to be a breach of faith but a determination on their part to extend slavery to all the territories and thus control national politics.

Over time, Vest grew to respect Sherman as a statesman with opposite but understandable views. "He was an extreme Federalist," Vest said, "believing—like Alexander Hamilton—in a strong central government with little sympathy for the masses, who, in his opinion, should be governed by the wealthy and educated."

Vest's time in the Senate was often marginalized; many considered him one-dimensional and reactionary. Still, historian M. Paul Holsinger credits Vest as one of his day's leading constitutionalists, a dedicated spokesman for personal liberties. Throughout the 1880s, Vest waged a losing battle to protect the rights of members of the Church of Jesus Christ of Latter-Day Saints, the Mormons, whose ideals, especially polygamy, he opposed.

In 1880, Senator Edmunds introduced legislation that would replace territorial courts and judges with a five-man Utah Commission with the power to investigate any supposed incidence of plural marriage and to bar from voting all persons found guilty of the crime. Any Mormon who refused to submit to the commission's findings and dissolve his multiple marriages was subject to federal charges and long-term imprisonment.

Vest argued that, if enacted, it would create a "star chamber of five men, responsible to nobody, governed alone by their own prejudices."

On February 15, 1882, Vest rose to show that he was, in fact, an aggressive antagonist, a quick, intense, and resourceful debater capable of holding his own with the giants of the Senate. His "wasp" nickname came from his feisty ability to sting his political opponents when provoked, using his sharp tongue, clever rejoinders, and acerbic wit.

He argued that the bill's supporters believed that Congress had the power to enact any legislation it saw fit for federally controlled territories. The idea, Vest said, "that the territories are absolute creatures to be governed by the Congress as they please, without reference to the Constitution or law or right, is, in my judgment, abhorrent to every principle of American freedom."

Vest first cited *Baker v. the People*, an obscure New York case in which the state Supreme Court ruled a man not convicted of a crime could not be barred from voting or holding office. He then quoted Chief Justice Roger Brooke Taney (1777-1864) from the infamous *Dred Scott v. Sandford* case, that limiting the federal government's powers contained "letters of gold, letters which declare the essence of the Constitution and rights of every American citizen." Vest argued that the arbitrary punishment of hundreds of Mormons for devoutly carrying out their religious beliefs was an unprecedented wrong.

Vest continued that Taney decreed that "the citizen and the Constitution walked side by side into the territories of the West," thus making it impossible for the federal government to assume discretionary and despotic powers denied in the Constitution.

Vest offered an amendment that no bigamist or polygamist could be barred from voting or holding office unless duly convicted "in a court of competent jurisdiction."

Vest's amendment was voted down 33-11 with 32 not voting.

"As much as I detest polygamy, much as I believe to be utterly subversive of all pure society and good morals, I shall never vote for a provision which, in my judgment, subverts the highest and dearest rights of every American citizen," Vest said.

Edmunds and supporters of his bill spent the rest of the day and the following morning attacking Vest's assertions. When Vest's turn came, he delivered emotionally that Congress, by substituting a commission for the regular court system, was passing a bill of attainder—a law that punishes a person or a group of people without trial—contrary to the nation's accepted norms. "If this be not a bill of attainder under the theory of the Constitution of the United States, there never has been a bill of attainder proposed in all history. Never in the darkest days of the Stuarts or the Tudors, never in the darkest days of despotism, I undertake to say here, weighing my words deliberately, was there ever enacted a statute more exactly within the meaning of a bill of attainder."

Vest knew his opposition to the language of the act would label him as favoring Mormonism and plural marriage, neither of which was true. "I am not here to defend polygamy; I would resent the imputation, a personal insult from any man at any time or any place; but where I abhor polygamy . . . I revere the Constitution of my country and the rights of personal liberty, guaranteed to every American citizen. I tell you now, Senators of the United States: Pass this bill, and you will establish a precedent that will come home to plague you for all time to come. The feeling that today exists against polygamy may exist tomorrow against any Church, against any class in this broad land."

While Vest could often be highly emotional in his speeches, he was coldly logical and analytical at his core. "I am prepared for the abuse and calumny that will follow any man who dares to oppose a bill against polygamy; and yet, so help me God, if my official life should terminate tomorrow, I would not give my vote for the principles contained in this measure," he said.

As expected, the bill overwhelmingly passed, drawing sustained applause. House approval came quickly, as did President Arthur's signature. Vest's fears were rapidly realized as commissioners moved with abandon to break off polygamous families, denying them fundamental rights. John Taylor (1808-1887), president of the Latter-Day Saints, and other Mormon leaders went into hiding to escape imprisonment.

The legislation did little to curb polygamy, which Mormons considered divinely inspired. They believed their leaders were martyrs and became more convicted in their opinions, leading President Cleveland to plead for "discreet legislation."

On December 8, 1885, Edmunds, with renewed bipartisan support, introduced Senate Bill 10 to turn up the heat on the Mormons. The Edmunds-Tucker Act expanded the commission to 15 members and gave it the power to require, without a subpoena, anyone to appear in court. While Mormon men were not forced into self-incrimination, a man's wife was compelled to testify. Homes could be searched without cause. Criminal statutes were expanded to include anything found. The long-established woman's suffrage approved in the Utah Territory would be abolished, "sparing women the shameful fate of voting as their husbands wished," Vest said.

Most disturbing to Vest was a provision that would seize the property of the Church of Jesus Christ of Latter-Day Saints and return it to its original owners, where possible. The rest would be controlled by the federal government and used to fund schools in the Utah Territory. Vest argued that it was unconstitutional for Congress to appropriate Mormon church monies for any purpose, even one as laudatory as education. "If there is any parallel to this legislation on the statute books of the United States, I am utterly ignorant of it.

"How a lawyer can look upon [this bill] with anything else than distrust is beyond my comprehension," Vest continued, asserting the separation of church and state. "Seizing church property is nothing else but arbitrary—naked, simple, bold confiscation and nothing else. If it can be done in this case, it can be done to any Baptist, Methodist, or Presbyterian church in any of the territories. This is not the law of the land as I understand it."

The bill passed decisively, 38-7, on January 8, 1886. Despite his opposition, Vest was not among the official minority as he was absent for each roll-call vote on the Mormon question. The bill never received presidential approval, but without veto, it passed into law on March 2, 1887.

Mormon leaders immediately challenged the constitutionality of the Edmunds-Tucker Act and met overwhelming opposition. The federal government, acting through Congress, could, as Vest feared, revoke formerly held vested rights when dealing with territories. The court and the new commissioners moved quickly to eradicate Utah of polygamy. By 1890, Wilford Woodruff (1807-1898), who succeeded Taylor after he died in 1887 as president of the Latter-Day Saints, announced the church would obey the law. At its October general conference, the body reluctantly adopted the "Woodruff Manifesto," agreeing to try to accept federal power. Utah was admitted to the Union six years later as the 45th state.

In April 1882, 17 years after the war, a bill was introduced to repeal a statute restricting former Confederate soldiers from serving in the U.S. military. Edmunds objected. Vest responded, "Your flag, our flag, waves in triumph in every township of this broad Union. Your taxes are collected; your national name is respected. Sir, do the people need anything else to recollect that war except the graves of our common dead?"

Vest asked that Edmunds and his ilk should recognize that the South was honest when swearing and accepting the results of defeat.

"The people of the United States want peace, not in terms, but in fact," Vest said. "They want the material prosperity of the country advanced. They want the past put behind them."

In 1884, with a lifetime of public service nationally and at home in Indiana, Hendricks was nominated by acclamation and elected the 21st Vice President of the United States.

In 1880, Governor Hendricks and his wife went to Hot Springs, Arkansas, where Governor Hendricks was attacked by paralysis, which was kept secret. Two years later, he was seriously ill with lameness in one of his feet and was told the disease was incurable. "He calmly resigned himself to the inevitable and considered his career closed," Vest said, "but to his own surprise, his health improved, and he again devoted himself to his profession.

"He knew, however, that he might be stricken down again at any time, and he walked in the shadow of death until the final summons came."

Vest was a busy campaigner. He denounced the Republicans' record at gala affairs and torch-led parades across Missouri. The Democrats prevailed by a narrow margin, and Vice President Hendricks presided over the Senate beginning in March 1885.

"He was not the active, cheerful man I remembered," Vest recalled. "In April, after the close of the session, I met him at the Post Office Department and drove with him to his rooms at the Willard Hotel. He told me he and Mrs. Hendricks would go to Atlantic City that afternoon and asked me to accompany them."

Vest told Hendricks he could not get away as he was trying to become acquainted with President Cleveland and his cabinet. "He said the new administration had little use for Democrats like us," Vest said.

Hendricks said, "I am, under the new regime, an old fossil," but he could find honest and competent men to head the departments filled with appointees during the Reconstruction era.

"When I next looked upon his face there was no friendly recognition from his kindly eyes, and his eloquent lips were silent," said Vest, who traveled to Indianapolis for Hendricks' funeral, which drew several thousand people. "Faithful to every trust, stainless in private life and with implicit reliance upon the Christian faith, which he always avowed and illustrated, his death inflicted an irreparable loss upon his country."

Vest's memories of Hendricks were associated with "The Old Roman" Thurman, one of the key Democratic leaders when Vest reached the Senate. "They differed in many respects," Vest said, "but both belonged to that highest class of statesmen who subordinated all personal considerations to public duty."

Thurman was not an orator and didn't pretend to be. "He often said, 'If not logical, I am nothing,'" Vest said. His desk was adorned with a snuffbox, and his red bandanna was the battle flag around which the Democrats rallied.

Upon Hendricks' death, Vest said, "He was the noblest type of American manhood, self-reliant and self-made. Incorruptible in public life and pure in private conduct, asking and giving no quarter. He did not sprinkle rosewater over his party's enemies or give sweetmeats to the political wolves and tigers ready to spring at his throat. He died suddenly as a chieftain on some stricken field, and it was well. Better one pang, one throb, than weeks of pain and slow decay. Better to fall like the struck eagle whose full stretched wings droop in mid-heaven above the mountain top, than to writhe through the weary days and sleepless nights waiting the inevitable hour."

Senator Henry W. Blair of New Hampshire, ca. 1865-80. Brady-Handy Photograph Collection, Library of Congress, Prints and Photographs Division.

New Hampshire Republican Henry William Blair (1834-1920) proposed Congress give $105 million to the states to fight illiteracy, especially in the South, sparking a three-week Constitutional debate in 1883. Most Republicans opposed the bill, believing it would not be fairly administered, and it was amended, guaranteeing there would be no discrimination between white and Black schools. Vest, an opponent of Blair on many other issues, favored this bill but believed it need additional modifications.

When Republicans tried to limit further debate and any further mention of the Constitution, Vest sarcastically asked, "Why talk about the Constitution? Why sing hymns to it when we have had a Constitutional funeral throughout this debate?"

Vest called Southern Democrats, of which he was one, a "council of monkeys that gravely deliberated matters of state until some mischievous joker threw a handful of nuts in their midst, breaking them up in most admired disorder. One hundred and five million has been thrown, and the monkeys are grabbing in every direction."

Frustrated, Vest closed by saying, "I will never again undertake to stand here and make a Constitutional argument and appeal to this side of the chamber to sustain it," a vow he repeatedly broke over the next 20 years.

In 1885, President Cleveland appointed Lamar Secretary of the Interior and in 1887 named him an associate justice of the U.S. Supreme Court. "I called on him on a matter of routine business, and he asked me if I had heard about his appointment," Vest said. "I told him frankly that I was sorry he mentioned the matter because I was afraid my reply might not be agreeable."

Lamar asked Vest's opinion because he knew his response would be honest.

"I said to him, 'You ought never, in my opinion, have left the Senate, but your administration of the Interior Department has been in every way commendable. But you are now 62 years old, and your health is precarious. You have not been engaged in the practice of law for more than 15 years and have not even enrolled as a member of the Supreme Court bar. The law is, as you know, a jealous mistress. When you take your seat on the Supreme Bench, you will find yourself associated with old, experienced judges, familiar with precedents, and able to dispose of many cases without much exertion. I know you well enough to be certain that you will do your share of the necessary work at the risk of your health, life, and your ability and integrity; there cannot be the slightest doubt."

Dr. Willam Pepper, 1864

Vest said he would support his confirmation and reach out to others who might help but advised against moving forward. "My apprehensions were unfortunately realized," Vest said. "After two years on the bench, his health failed." William Pepper (1843-1898), an eminent Philadelphia physician, said Lamar was suffering from a disorder of the arterial system and kidney trouble, both made worse by his overwork on the bench.

In 1887, Vest fought against a popular movement to annul two Utah corporations, the Mormon Church and the Immigration Society. Against the public opinion of the time, Vest contended that the proposed law violated the fundamental principles of the Constitution and property rights. He particularly opposed the proposition section that would seize the corporations' funds to fund common schools in Utah. "[This is a] naked, simple, bold confiscation and nothing else," Vest argued.

"He knew every nook and corner of a Missourian's heart and could touch every nerve of impulse and emotion at will," Lamm said of Vest. "No one in his day dared to contest with him his political supremacy, and the state had a loyal pride in his honesty in a venal age, in the gallant way he bore his lance in a political joust and had a keen sympathy with his likes and dislikes."

Cockrell, who served 24 years in the Senate with Vest, said the "Little Giant" had a reputation for being incorruptible and conscientious. "I regard him as one of the strong men in the Senate during his long term of service," Cockrell said. "He was the most eloquent man in that body."

As for his own body, he was, according to the Boonville *Weekly Advertiser*, a few inches more than 5 feet tall: "He was small when born and has never quite been able to catch up with his growth."

Vest was known for wearing an old-style black frock coat, a broad slouch hat, a black tie, and a white shirt. "It appears he has obeyed the injunction, 'pull down your vest,' thus leaving his shirt to roam at will," wrote the *Advertiser*. "Around his short neck, he wore an old-time watch chain, one strand of which showed over the expanse of his white shirt."

In 1887, Minnesota Governor Cushman Kellogg Davis (1838-1900) joined Vest in the Senate. While they differed on nearly every issue, they appreciated Shakespeare. Cushman was also an admirer of Napoleon Bonaparte (1769-1821), who supported America becoming an imperial power. Vest believed the United States' annexation attempts in the Philippines were unconstitutional and an affront to the country's founding principles: "All governments derive their just powers from the consent of the governed."

Cushman Kellogg Davis, U.S. Senator and seventh Governor of Minnesota. Library of Congress photo.

During debates in 1887 over a proposed constitutional amendment to give voting rights to women, Vest said women were too emotional and susceptible to corruption. He added that women's voting rights would undermine families by disrupting God's arrangement of the sexes. Other politicians opposed to women's suffrage made similar assertions in the last quarter of the 19th century and even up to the ratification of the 19th amendment that granted women's suffrage in 1920.

During Vest's time in the Senate, he continued to practice law and appeared numerous times before the U.S. Supreme Court. In April 1887, Vest and Joseph Hodges Choate Sr. (1832-1917) represented the brewing industry, including his Saint Louis friend Adolphus Busch (1839-1913). The bones of the argument were that it was unconstitutional for a state—in this case, Kansas—to prohibit the manufacture and sale of intoxicating liquors without compensating existing owners for their diminished property. Between October 1886 and December 1887, three justices radically reversed their positions in Vest's favor.

U.S. Representative and Senator Joseph Hodges Choate, January 1, 1898. Library of Congress photo.

In his oral argument and written brief, Vest denounced the Kansas Prohibitory Act, comparing it with a decree of the French Commune (an overreaching government action, bordering on dictatorship).

Vest and Choate's efforts helped delay Prohibition, which began in 1920 and continued until its repeal in 1933.

"I do not choose to be placed in the category of advocating intemperance, and I do not choose to be placed in the category of opposing temperance, but I do not believe in the Federal Government, either by investigation or otherwise, invading what I suppose to be the constitutional province of the states," said Vest.

Prominent Men and Women of the Day, published in 1888, described Vest as a man with many marked peculiarities. "He is a rapid and vigorous talker, seemingly never at a loss for a word, and while never ornate or flowery in his remarks, he observes a nicety of expression and discrimination in the use of effective words that is the great feature of his addresses," the publication wrote. "The only drawback to his manner of speech is a certain nervousness of manner indicated by the frequent jerking of his head when excited, which is further accentuated by the high key in which his voice is pitched."

The 1888 report went on to describe Vest's aggressive disposition and his love of oratory: "He enjoys the heat of debate but never needlessly prolongs one after all hands have had a chance to announce their sentiments and conviction."

In 1888, Vest was credited with bringing the Democratic Convention to Saint Louis, where the now-infirm Thurman was nominated for vice president but was defeated.

George F. Edmunds of Vermont, ca. 1865-80. Brady-Handy Photograph Collection, Library of Congress, Prints and Photographs Division.

Thurman's most bitter political rival was Senator Edmunds of Vermont, who was also his closest friend, proving a Garfield quote that the "sweetest fruit often hung over the party wall."

"They differed widely on all political questions, but Thurman and Edmunds were devoted friends, and whenever luncheon time came, they could be seen arm in arm on their way to a committee room, where they spent an hour taking refreshments and enjoying genial companionship," Vest said. "They were both great lawyers, although their intellectual methods differed. Thurman did not pay much attention for technicalities and details, but Edmunds, though thoroughly versed in all branches of law, greatly enjoyed technical objections to bills offered in the Senate of which he was not the author."

In convention coverage, Vest was described as a typical Western politician, not above doing favors for his supporters. "He serves his constituents not only by throwing light upon economic questions but helping them to get any offices that may be lying around loose," reported the Saint Louis *Republic*, published daily from 1888-1919. "Consequently, the Senator is not a civil service reformer and does not hesitate to admit he is not. He has a powerful influence in his own State, but he does not assume the attitude of a political boss."

There was, however, a Vest Club that met the senator at the train when he arrived. According to The *Globe Democrat*, "At 8 o'clock, 135 members formed in line ... headed by a band, and the carriage in which Vest rode marched to each of the club rooms."

Vest was the primary speaker. His comments received wild applause as he reviewed the history of the Democratic Party from Jefferson to Cleveland. He denounced the Republicans' tariff policies and the encroachment of corporate wealth. The Republicans, he said, "have gathered, as a solid phalanx, around monopolies and corporate wealth, and the Democrat who abandons Cleveland in his efforts to overthrow it is a traitor to his party and an enemy to this country."

Despite Vest's efforts, Republican Benjamin Harrison (1833-1901) won.

Back in the Senate, Vest found himself unintentionally the cause of a squabble between his antagonist, Senator Ingalls, and his friends Blackburn and Voorhees.

"Just before the Presidential election [of 1888], I alluded in a general political discussion to a resolution adopted at a meeting of the citizens of Washington declaring in favor of Senator Ingalls, who was then chairman of the Committee on the District of Columbia, for the Presidency, and I expressed regret that the compliment was an empty one, as the gentlemen tendering it could not vote and were possibly influenced by their desire to obtain large appropriations in Congress for the improvement of Washington City," Vest said. "Being informed the next day that Ingalls was irritated by what I had said, I requested Kansas Senator Preston Bierce Plumb [1837-1891] to ask his colleague if he intended to make any reply, and if he did, to say that I should be glad to know on what day he would do so, as I expected to leave the city on important business the next morning, to be absent some four or five days. I wished to be present when he addressed the Senate.

"Senator Plumb returned to me in a few moments with the statement that Senator Ingalls had assured him he had no intention of speaking and that I could govern my actions accordingly. I left Washington the next morning and was surprised to read in the New York papers two days afterward that Ingalls had delivered a bitter speech in the Senate in which he sneeringly alluded to Blackburn and myself and attacked the Democratic Party generally, with special attention to General John Charles Black [1839-1915], General Winfield Scott Hancock, and President Cleveland. He declared sarcastically that Black was a total wreck, physically and mentally, and ridiculed Hancock and declared the election of Cleveland made respectable the aspirations of the most degraded wretch to the Presidency."

With Vest absent, Blackburn responded on his behalf, drawing from Ingalls' amended biography, "wherein he stated that he had served during the Civil War as a judge advocate in the Kansas Home Guards, and [Blackburn] reminded him that, when Black lay desperately wounded upon the battlefield of Pea Ridge and Hancock was spilling his blood at Gettysburg, the Kansas Senator was serving with the red-legs and jayhawkers, which principal occupation was that of stealing chickens and robbing widows and orphans."

If Vest had been present, he wouldn't have been as kind.

"Blackburn was unfamiliar with Kansas politics and did not know that, during the Civil War, Senator Ingalls had been twice nominated and defeated for the office of lieutenant governor on the anti-Lane or 'Peace Party' ticket," Vest recalled. "When elected to the U. S. Senate, Ingalls furnished the Clerk of The Congressional Directory with his biography and stated his candidacy on the Peace Party ticket for the lieutenant governorship, omitting all reference to his military service. After coming to the Senate and finding the 'bloody shirt' was the most effective instrument to secure the soldier vote, which was largely increasing in his State because of immigration, Ingalls changed his biography in the directory" and substituted his military service in place of his failed candidacies.

Voorhees, also a warm friend of Cleveland, Hancock and Black, was so irritated by Ingalls' continued attacks on his friends that, coupled with the loss of his devoted wife, Anna Hardesty, in 1887, his health began to suffer. He became irritable and impatient.

Several days later, when Voorhees replied to Ingalls' attacks, Ingalls, president pro tempore of the Senate, listened "attentively and then prepared a parliamentary trap, which he constructed with full knowledge of the temperament and physical condition of the Indiana Senator," Vest said. "Some 10 days after Voorhees had spoken, Ingalls addressed the Senate without giving previous notice, and for about half an hour indulged in innuendos, obviously directed at Voorhees, based upon charges of disloyal correspondence with the enemy during the War, but making no specific accusations. While Ingalls was speaking, Voorhees entered the chamber and impulsively sprang to his feet with an exciting denial of the statement or imputation that he had been guilty of any disloyal act or word. If he had not noticed what Ingalls had said, the latter's speech would have had no effect. Still, it would have passed into *The Congressional Record* as a collection of platitudes containing nothing of special interest. Unfortunately, Voorhees, by his passionate reply, gave Ingalls the opportunity he desired, and he immediately proceeded to read from documents before him specific charges of disloyalty against Voorhees and stated that these proofs were undeniable, having been found in the law office of Senator Voorhees at Terre Haute, Indiana, by government officials. Voorhees, known as 'The Tall Sycamore of the Wabash,' interrupted him by denouncing this documentary proof as a forgery. When Ingalls repeated the charge, he declared the Senator from Kansas an infamous liar. Ingalls, who had the most wonderful self-control and never became excited, coolly replied, 'The citizen from Indiana was disorderly and should be sent to the rock pile.' The incident was painful and did not add to the reputation of the Senate as the most dignified deliberative assembly in the world."

While, in Vest's opinion, Ingalls would bend any truth to his purposes, he was not so quick to forgive others for doing the same.

Ingalls' truth bending was illustrated in a Senate floor colloquy with Vest in March 1888. "He stated that General Lee surrendered at Appomattox Courthouse with 73,911 men fit for duty; an assertion I denied at the time, saying in reply that General Lee surrendered with less than 8,000 men with muskets in their hands, my declaration being based upon information given me by the highest authority on the Confederate side," Vest said.

On March 16, 1888, Vest received a letter from General John Brown Gordon (1832-1904), Lee's second in command and a U.S. senator from 1873-1880 and 1891-1897.

> *My dear Vest: You were correct in your statement. There can be no successful contradiction of the statement. General Lee had a little less than 8,000 muskets available for battle at Appomattox. A considerably larger number were surrendered, but the greater proportion of men were sick from the hospitals in Richmond and other points; the disabled men from hunger and exhaustion from the incessant marching by night and fighting by day, and the teamsters, etc.*
>
> *Sincerely yours, J.B. Gordon.*

"Senator Ingalls was unable to resist the temptation to attack any of his colleagues, even those of his party, whose record or character presented a vulnerable point for assault," Vest said. "On one occasion, when president pro tempore of the Senate, [Ingalls] called another Senator to the chair and, going down on the floor, made a vicious personal attack upon Senator Joseph Emerson Brown [1821-1894] of Georgia, one of the most amiable and courteous members of the Senate. The venerable Georgian was sitting quietly looking over a committee report when a cyclone of satire and vituperation burst upon him without the slightest notice of its coming. The look of astonishment on the amiable countenance of the victim, as verbs, nouns, pronouns, adjectives, and epithets filled the air, caused a ripple of amusement through the Senate. Still, the climax was reached when Ingalls alluded to a habit Senator Brown had, when speaking, of gently rubbing one hand over the other by quoting Hood's lines:

Joseph Emerson Brown served as a U.S. Senator, Chief Justice of the Georgia Supreme Court, and four-term Governor of Georgia. Library of Congress photo.

'And then in the fullness of joy and hope,
'Seemed to be washing his hands with invisible soap,
In imperceptible water.'

"At this critical moment, Senator Brown looked down at the offending members as if inquiring why they had brought on the volcanic eruption which was blazing about him," Vest said.

A couple of weeks later, when Vest was walking down from the Capitol with Ingalls, curiosity got the best of him, and he asked why he had assailed Brown. Ingalls responded that he didn't like Brown, for the same reasons that Vest didn't care for Ingalls—that Brown reminded Ingalls of the character Uriah Heep (a falsely humble hypocrite) in Charles Dickens' 1850 novel *David Copperfield*.

Ingalls told Vest, "I have no ill-feeling toward the Confederates who fought for the Southern cause and did not shirk the result, but that Brown had done all he could as Governor of Georgia during the War to cripple the Confederate authorities at Richmond and refused to allow the Georgia militia to leave the State, although the Confederate armies were depleted and there were not enough men on the lines before Richmond to defend from a general assault; that Governor Brown, after the War, had joined the Republican party and voted for Grant in the National Republican Convention and at the polls.

"Now," said Ingalls, "he is a red-hot Democrat because the Democrats are in power all over the South."

Vest did not think much of Ingalls' politics and methods. However, he did admire Ingalls' many skills. "He was a master of satire and invective," Vest said. "I do not believe Ingalls was malicious or bad-hearted. He was an expert in denunciation and could not resist the temptation of exhibiting his wonderful capability in that regard. He loved poetry, music, painting, sculpture, and the beautiful in nature."

To Vest's credit, while he was critical of his adversaries, he would defend them when he felt they were unjustly attacked. Even Ingalls.

Soon after Ingalls delivered his eulogy upon the death of Senator James Nelson Burnes (1827-1889) of Missouri, an article appeared charging that part of Ingalls' address had been plagiarized from Jean Baptiste Massillon's 1824 sermon on immortality. "This report was untrue, as I have compared the speech of Ingalls with the sermon, and, though there is some similarity in thought and language, there is no evidence that Ingalls was guilty of plagiarism," Vest said. "Indeed, it would be impossible for me to believe any man with the marvelous talent of Ingalls, both as to thought and diction, could be guilty of copying from even so great an orator as Massillon."

Governor Crittenden said that, as a senator, Vest ranked evenly with the best in ability and outranked most, if not all, in oratory. "He was placed on the Judiciary Committee because he was a great lawyer and on the Finance Committee because he studied that intricate question very closely," and on the Commerce Committee because Missouri was on the great highway of commerce, Crittenden said. "He commanded the undivided attentional of that generally lifeless body, especially those on tariffs and ship subsidies, because he discussed both of those leading questions with signal ability and learning, adding the splendid phraseology and actions of the great orator before a listening country."

In June 1889, Vest wrote from Sweet Springs to James Wellington "Duke" Draffen (1826-1896), his former law partner in Boonville, whom he planned to visit on his way to a committee meeting in Chicago. Four years earlier, Vest assisted Draffen by putting in a good word so he could land a district judgeship. No mention was made of the favor. Instead, Vest expressed his displeasure with the quickened pace of community life. "I can't help but think that this new and fast world is not an improvement on that when we were young men," Vest wrote. "Money is now the end and object. It is above everything else, and the cancer of greed is eating away at our country."

On December 18, 1889, Vest, a member of the Senate Judiciary Committee, and James Lawrence Pugh (1820-1907), a former Confederate congressman from Alabama and critic of Jefferson Davis, were invited to a dinner party following the Supreme Court seating of Associate Justice David Josiah Brewer (1837-1910) at the home of Chief Justice Melville Weston Fuller (1833-1910). "The dinner was most enjoyable, and as I was leaving at a late hour, in the same carriage as Pugh, he said, 'Do you know, Vest, that we are two of the most remarkable men now living? Here we are, members of the United States Senate, guests of the chief justice, and rolling along asphalt pavements after a splendid banquet in the country's capital, which we tried for four years to destroy."

While Vest may have chuckled at Pugh's carriage comment, it didn't go over as well when it came from Ingalls during a March 26, 1890, discussion to regulate trusts, where Vest raised several constitutional questions.

"I do not propose to detain the Senate at this time in the afternoon by making even a brief reply to what was said by the Senator from Kansas [Ingalls] regarding the impropriety of those of us who, as he says, tried to destroy the Constitution during the late war and the immodesty and hardihood to ask that the provisions of the Constitution be honestly and faithfully carried out. Suppose the result of the war, as claimed by the Senator from Kansas—for it is the legitimate consequence of his argument—was to put the entire Southern people outside of the pale of constitutional obligations and to put upon them the ban that they should never have after being permitted to question the violation of that instrument. His conclusion is correct, and we are liable to its criticisms. That great struggle, as I understand it and as the world understands it, was concerning the construction of the Constitution, and when the force against arms brought about a result when the arbitrament of battle decided against the Southern people, then has never been with any honorable man since but one single question, and that was whether the South accepted honestly that result and intended to abide by it."

"Will the Senator allow me a question?" asked Ingalls.

"Certainly," said Vest.

"Does the Senator believe that the constitutional construction for which the South contended was right or wrong?"

"I believed at the time it was right."

"Well, but now?" asked Ingalls.

"I believed that it was right, but I accepted the result, and I accepted the result to be that I was honestly to abide by the construction of the Constitution of the United States put upon it by the Supreme Court, the highest judicial tribunal in this country, and made the arbiter as to what the meaning for the Constitution was.

"I did not accept as the result of that struggle all the Constitutional views presented by the Republican Party or the Kansas Senator. I deny that the war put me in a position where I was bound to take, for all time to come, what he or his associates might say this instrument meant. Sir, if I came to the Senate representing a sovereign state in this Union under the prescription that the Senator from Kansas has announced here today, my State might as well, for all intents and purposes, be out of the Union with rights and guarantees of the Constitution nullified as to it and its people. I am here, as I understand my obligation, to obey the Constitution of the United States as the result of the war and not to take the construction put upon it by the Senator from Kansas."

CHAPTER EIGHT

Champion of the West

In the fall of 1881, a group of New York investors returned to a Dakota frontier hotel from Yellowstone Park to loudly celebrate gaining the promise of a lease on much of the public lands. They planned to build hotels, roads, and possibly rail lines. Even before they saw it, the group knew it was a good deal, but now, they saw the potential to make personal fortunes from it.

They overlooked the small, stern-looking man dining at the corner table. Novelist and journalist David Graham Phillips (1867-1911) wrote for the *Saturday Evening Post* that George Graham Vest tried to ignore the boastful group until he heard mention of Yellowstone Park. "Taking advantage of the ignorance of the people, this group of financiers had persuaded the U.S. Department of Interior to help them obtain quietly from the government a practically perpetual lease [on 500 square miles] of the nation's most magnificent park," Vest wrote later. "For a small sum [$2 an acre], Yellowstone was to be turned over to these individuals, and they were to have a free hand in enriching themselves."

The deal would give the group a monopoly on hotel, stage and telegraph rights.

It would have been easy for Vest to align himself with the schemers and make a fortune. Instead, he exposed the plan and went head-to-head with President Chester Arthur and Secretary of the Interior Henry Moore Teller (1830-1914), who argued that private investors would better maintain the park at less cost to the government.

Senator Henry Moore Teller of Colorado, ca. 1902. Library of Congress photo.

"Nothing but absolute necessity should permit the Great National Park to be used for money making by private persons, and in our judgment, no such necessity exists," Vest said. "The purpose to which this region, matchless in wonders and grandeur, was dedicated— 'a public park and a pleasure ground for the benefit and enjoyment of the people' —is worthy the highest patriotism and statesmanship."

When Vest entered the Senate in 1879, his fellow senators wanted a significant portion turned into a cattle ranch. He felt resistance to such schemes was his responsibility.

By chance, Vest was in Fargo's best—"a poor best"—hotel as he was in town to say goodbye to a dying friend.

Upon returning to Washington, Vest took his battle to the Senate floor. Wrote one observer: "He had the habit of drawing himself up almost as round as a big ball, and then he would unroll himself inch by inch, growing taller and taller, his eyes growing brighter and brighter, becoming as eloquent as his tongue."

In one of his first actions as a senator, he demanded the documents relating to the proposed lease, one of which would clear all the timber north of the Yellowstone River. In an outburst of oratory based on undisputed evidence, he revealed the proposed scheme to the Senate and the nation.

One of the ringsters, watching from the Senate gallery, recognized the steel-gray-haired man from the hotel and knew immediately that their champagne toasts and premature crowing had cost them their fortunes. Vest introduced a resolution calling on the Committee on Territories, of which he was a member, to investigate the need for legislation to protect the park and to enforce laws already on the books.

For more than a dozen years, Vest was able to keep in check every move by lobbyists to convert Yellowstone into a private domain, including the entry of railroads into the park. To Vest, an outdoorsman and conservationist, Yellowstone was his crusade. In return, Vest was maligned and slandered.

On January 15, 1883, Teller, pressured by Vest, instructed Superintendent Patrick Henry Conger (1819-1903) that neither sport nor subsistence hunting would be allowed in the park. So there would be no confusion about what "no hunting" meant, Vest penned the following:

> *"The regulations heretofore issued by the Secretary of the Interior regarding killing game in Yellowstone National Park are amended to prohibit absolutely the killing, wounding or capturing at any time of buffalo, bison, moose, elk, black- or white-tailed deer, mountain sheep, Rocky Mountain goat, antelope, beaver, otter, martin, fisher, grouse, prairie chickens, pheasant, foul hen, meadowlark, thrush, goldfinch, flicker, yellow hammer, blackbird, oriole, jay, snowbird, or any of the small birds commonly known as singing birds."*

In 1883, Vest made another five visits to what he called "a great breathing place for the national lung."

Arthur, a Republican who became president in the fall of 1881 following Garfield's death, had not held an elected office before being elected vice president on a ticket with Garfield in the 1880 election. Arthur had been a party hack most of his life, doling out patronage jobs to supporters and then hitting them up for donations for the next campaign. The presidency seemed to reform Arthur into a man who put his country first, going so far as to sign legislation for civil service reform designed to curb the practices in which he excelled.

Eventually, the colorful Democratic ex-Confederate Vest and the New York Republican ex-spoilsman Arthur would have something in common: Yellowstone Park. "I have no earthly interest in the matter except to protect this park," Vest said.

Shortly after becoming president, Arthur was diagnosed with Bright's disease, a kidney ailment now called nephritis. He tried to keep his condition private, but by 1883 rumors of his illness were circulating. He had become thinner and more aged in appearance, as well as less energetic in keeping up with the demands of the presidency. Some attributed it to laziness, and Arthur didn't try to dispel those rumors because they helped hide his condition. Arthur and some political friends traveled to Florida in April 1883, hoping to rejuvenate his health by getting out of Washington. The vacation had the opposite effect, and Arthur suffered intense pain before returning to Washington.

On April 19, Arthur suffered a chill, and when a lightened workload didn't seem to improve his failing health, Vest, at the suggestion of General of the Army Philip Henry Sheridan (1831-1888), approached the president with the idea of a summer trip to Yellowstone to "restore his vigor."

Vest, the "Self-appointed Protector of Yellowstone National Park," and Sheridan knew of Arthur's love of fishing. Sheridan and Vest convinced Arthur to try his hand at fishing Yellowstone's waters, with the ulterior motive that it would get Arthur to take up Yellowstone's cause. Sheridan arranged all travel arrangements, security details and communications for the presidential party. He arranged for the cavalry to transport the official daily messages released to reporters about the president's progress.

The White House announced that the trip would include installing a telegraph line to quell claims of the trip being a high-priced junket. It was "not a pleasure party for the benefit of the President, but an official exploration party" with the president as the guest of General Sheridan, for whom Yellowstone's Mount Sheridan is named.

A horse-drawn ambulance outside Bellevue Hospital in New York City, 1895.

By July 12, General Oliver Otis Howard (1830-1909) had mapped out the trip. They would ride the Union Pacific to Rawlins in the Wyoming Territory and then travel by wagon or army ambulance to Fort Washakie, Wyoming. They would continue from there on horses or mules. Couriers were stationed every 20 miles so the group could communicate daily with the world.

The group reached the Green River in early August. Along for the ride were President Lincoln's son, Robert Todd Lincoln (1843-1926), now secretary of war, who had been on an 1882 trip with Sheridan; Vest's son, George Jr.; Lieutenant Colonels James F. Gregory (1843-1897) and Michael Sheridan (1840-1918), the general's younger brother, who was in charge of writing daily reports for the media (each of which needed Arthur's approval); General Anson Stager (1825-1885) of Chicago, the co-founder of Western Union telegraph company; Montana Governor John Schuyler Crosby (1839-1914); Chief Justice Morrison Remick "Mott" Waite (1815-1888); Major William Henry Foxwood (1838-1915), a surgeon and naturalist, who had been on several previous trips; Daniel Rollins (1842-1897), a friend of Arthur and a surrogate (probate) judge in New York; and Captain William Philo Clark (1845-1884). A military escort and several guides, including Jack Barnett, a Yellowstone resident, accompanied them. Photographer Frank Jay Haynes (1853-1921), nicknamed "The Professor," documented the trip. Other travelers included former Secretary of the Interior Carl Schurz (1829-1906), Senators Conkling and Henry Laurens Dawes (1816-1903), Edmunds and Logan. Each was responsible for paying for his food and providing his clothing, fishing, and hunting gear. All but Arthur wrote at least one dispatch.

Haynes operated a photography studio in Fargo, North Dakota, and photographed Yellowstone's features for the Northern Pacific Railroad as part of its advertising campaign to entice tourists. General Sheridan met Haynes on the 1882 trip and was impressed with his work. The only restriction on Haynes was that he would not photograph the president while fishing (although it was okay for him to photograph the president's catches). While Arthur and Lincoln prohibited reporters from traveling with the company, they agreed to have Haynes photograph the expedition.

Self-portrait of F. Jay Haynes at the Missouri River, 1876.

The trip began with a week-long railroad journey to Green River, Wyoming. Though a few stops were made along the way, most of the group sped through the country. After an overnight stay in Green River, the "roughing it" part of the vacation began on August 6. It started with a two-day journey via "spring wagons" more than 150 miles to Fort Washakie to join the more significant military escort and Haynes. Arthur often preferred to ride with the driver during this trip. At Fort Washakie, the headquarters of the Wind River Indian Reservation, the Shoshone and Arapaho Nations performed a mock battle scene and danced for the group. Arthur met with the two head chiefs of each nation.

On August 10, the wagons were left behind, and the group continued on horseback, following Sheridan's previous route. Arthur and Senator Vest had a friendly competition to see who the best fisherman was. The pair took 105 pounds between them. Vest was credited with taking the most fish (mainly trout), but Arthur took the highest total by weight.

By August 23, the group was encamped at the northeast end of Lewis Lake. General Sheridan forbade sport hunting, despite the abundance of Richardson grouse, deer, antelope, and elk. Fishing remained unrestricted.

They used 108 horses to survey 350 square miles of the park's most rugged terrain over three weeks and arrived at Mammoth Hot Springs, camping in the superintendent's yard. Some of the party hinted that the "roughing it" phase had lasted too long. Physically, they were suffering from sunburn and mosquito bites; financially, they had been fleeced by Governor Crosby's consistent winnings at the nightly poker table.

During an afternoon campfire at Mammoth Hot Springs, Arthur chatted with everyone, including some Englishmen who could hardly believe the man with the sunburned nose and shabby clothes was president of the United States. That evening, dressed more formally, he "held court" at the hotel.

President Chester A. Arthur's party at Upper Geyser Basin in Yellowstone Park on August 24, 1883. Seated, from left, Montana Gov. Schuyler Crosby, Lt. Gen. Philip Sheridan, President Arthur, Secretary of War Robert Todd Lincoln (1843-1926), Sen. George Graham Vest; standing from left, Lt. Col. Michael Sheridan, Gen. Anson Stager (1825-1885), Capt. William Philo Clark (1845-1884), Surrogate of New York Daniel Gustavus Rollins (1842-1897) and Lt. Col. James F. Gregory. Photograph by F. Jay Haynes, Library of Congress.

Sheridan's troops set up the tents, cooked the meals, washed clothes, and ensured their guests' comfort.

At the journey's end, Arthur boarded the Northern Pacific Railroad in Cinnabar, Montana, headed to Chicago for a few briefings, and then returned to Washington.

President Arthur enjoyed his time away from the office, and the Yellowstone adventure did more for his health than his Florida vacation. He said he returned to Washington refreshed.

Sheridan wasn't so sure. "Though his cheeks are bronzed and healthy looking, he looks old and worn and stoops when he rides," Sheridan observed. "The long journey has evidently been too fatiguing."

Arthur retired from public life a year and a half later; in November 1886, he died.

The trip helped Sheridan and Vest to make a case for conservation, preservation of wildlife, and review of concessions and leases. Sheridan estimated that 4,000 elks had been killed the previous winter, and even under closer control, 2,000 more had been taken by skin hunters on the reservation's borders. New directives and regulations helped; some passed after Arthur's term and maintained Yellowstone and other national parks.

Haynes' photographs, perhaps, were the real success story of the expedition. His studio received hundreds of print orders, and he obtained the park's photography concession, a position he held until 1916. He was succeeded by his son, Jack Ellis Haynes (1884-1962), who was Yellowstone's photographer until his death.

The expedition provided the widest publicity the park had ever received. Because of the president's involvement, it was featured in the daily press for nearly a month, sufficiently fixing the Wonderland in the national psyche.

From 1872, when the park was established with the signage of the Yellowstone National Park Protection Act, until 1886, when it was put under the protection of the U.S. Cavalry, battles waged between railroad and mining interests and speculative forces on one side and preservationists on the other. Vest led the latter, aided by General Sheridan; George Bird Grinnell (1849-1938), the editor of *Forest and Stream*; and future President Theodore Roosevelt (1858-1919).

"There is nothing in the world just like it," said Vest. "Within its vast area, the Great Architect created scenes that give us pause and bring us to the sober thoughts of life and its meaning. There is gathered what we call phenomena, but they are merely the speech of nature in its grandest garb."

Two Missourians were among the first known persons of European descent to explore present-day Yellowstone—John Colter (1774-1813), who had been a member of the Lewis and Clark Expedition, in 1807, and Jim Bridger (1804-1881) in 1824—but few took seriously the claims they made of the sights they had seen. Wounded in a battle between the Crow and Blackfeet, Colter journeyed from Jackson Hole to Tower Falls and told of a place "where a man could catch a fish in one stream and cook it in another." People laughed at Colter's stories, and Bridger, known to stretch the truth on occasion, was labeled one of the greatest liars of his time.

"Nowhere can such geysers be found, nowhere lakes of such entrancing color, nowhere more beautiful or awe-inspiring mountains," Vest said. "The canyon, alone, with its falls, is a world wonder. The lake is another. Those prismatic pools stretch of Black Forest and the weird shapes of the volcanic formation are all but details of the mighty whole. Small wonder that the honest Colter and Bridger were not believed."

George Bird Grinnell

In 1894, Vest served on a committee that drafted the National Park Protective Act, which forbade hunting animals, limited fishing, and restricted leases to 10 acres each for 10 years.

Vest believed that his work on behalf of the preservation of Yellowstone Park was the most critical aspect of his public career. Throughout his long service in the Senate, anything about the park would receive consideration.

Jim Bridger, American mountain man, trapper, and Army scout, who was one of the first Americans to explore the Yellowstone region.

Vest was instrumental in securing the passage of an amendment that carried an annual salary of $2,000 for a park superintendent (Nathaniel Pitt Langford [1832-1911]) and $900 annually for 10 assistants appointed by the Secretary of the Interior to live and work in the park. "With a superintendent [in the park] only part of the year, much of the game has been killed and geysers destroyed," Vest said. "These geysers are the most wonderful, singular of all the productions of nature on this continent."

In fighting a proposal that would have segregated part of the park and opened it up to rail lines, Vest sarcastically supported its abolishment. "When [Montana, Wyoming, and Idaho] were territories and not represented in the Senate, I considered it the duty of every Senator, as this park belonged to all the people of the United States, to defend its integrity and to keep it for the purposes for which it was originally designed. Since Senators have come from those states, who, of course, must be supposed to know more

Nathaniel P. Langford, 1870, first superintendant of Yellowstone National Park.

about that park than those of us who live at a distance, and since they have manifested a disposition to mutilate it, I must confess that my interest in it has rather flopped. In plain language, I feel very disposed to wash my hands of the whole business," Vest quipped. "If the constituencies who are more benefited than any others can be in the park are willing to see it cut off, the best disposition of the matter would be to turn it over to the public, let the full greed and avarice of the country have their scope, let the geysers be divided out and taken for washing clothes, let the water of that splendid waterfall in the Yellowstone River be used to turn machinery, let the timber be cut off; in other words, destroy the park, and make it a sacrifice to the greed of this advanced age in which we live."

Plans to put railroads through the park were abandoned.

Vest visited the park five times, fought numerous schemes, and took any attack on the sanctity of the park as a personal affront. He impressed his colleagues that he became interested in Yellowstone by accident and felt it a duty to resist attacks on its integrity. "These geysers are the most wonderful, the most singular of all the productions of nature on this continent, have their eruptions at regular intervals," Vest said.

In 1887, Vest was responsible for doubling Yellowstone's yearly appropriation. "It is the most wonderful region upon this continent," Vest said. "It must be understood that this enormous extent of country, nearly 3,400 square miles, is utterly useless except for a park. Upon the south is a volcanic country covered everywhere with lava deposits. There are no minerals there, no agricultural resource, no grazing lands, fit for a park, and nothing else."

Following Vest's 1883 trip to Yellowstone, he advocated for Native Americans. He visited each tribe in Montana and would eventually earn the title of "white brother."

"I went to those Indian reservations with the opinion that the best Indian was a dead Indian," Vest said. "I came away with the impression that the great wrongs which have been inflicted upon this continent and those people are a stain" that has yet to be washed away.

Vest fought for Native American citizenship, minor reservations, individual land holdings, improved education, and more efficient courts.

Vest urged courts that would assure a full-blooded Indian trial be conducted by full-blooded peers or whatever other mixture a defendant might be. "It is vital to accustom the Indians to our laws, usages, and civilization," Vest said. "It was a mistake from the start that we have treated them as if they were foreigners and did not belong to the people of the United States."

Vest was one of the first senators to question whether the U.S. had authority or jurisdiction over Native American tribes and contented that, if it did, it owed members equal treatment under the law. "I am opposed to this bill because it is based on that namby-pamby sentimentality which distinguishes Indians and other persons subject to the government's jurisdiction," Vest said. "There is one law for the Indian and another for the white man. Let there be one law for white, black, and red."

The Choctaw in Mississippi was one of the first non-European ethnic groups granted citizenship. During the Civil War, they aligned with the Confederacy, so when the war ended, their lands were seized, and their tribal governments were dissolved. During Vest's time in the Senate, Choctaw sovereignty was still debated when the railroads wanted a right of way through more Indian land. In April 1882, Vest said: "Article 6 of the treaty of 1855 has been quoted here repeatedly, which gives the right to two railroads to pass, one east and west and the other north and south, through the Indian Territory, but excludes the right of any other railroad to pass through … [T]he railroads were put upon them at the point of a bayonet, forced on them by Congress in 1866 because a large portion of them had gone with the southern Confederacy.

"We have tried to impress upon them that civilization and the Christian religion went hand in hand with home, family, and the domestic circle. They told us repeatedly, 'We want to tenure in severity; we want nothing by a tenure in common; Earth is our mother, and we do not propose that her bosom shall be scarred with the chain of any surveyor.'"

Vest urged, "This is the sacred domain of five civilized tribes, and no white man shall enter it without our consent. They stand not as an impediment to civilization."

By denying the Indians the right to deny access, Vest said the Congress was telling them that the U.S. is a nation of robbers, "and we will hurl you back from your princely domain as the surf of the ocean is thrown back against the granite rock."

The Choctaw's sovereignty was not absolute, but no one questioned that the tribe's members were U.S. citizens; as such, they were bound to follow the rules of rights of way. "Nobody desires to break down their treaties; nobody wants to rob them of their land; all we ask is that they become amenable to the Constitution of the United States, to the rights of the people of the states of this Union—this and this alone," said Vest.

In 1884, Vest proposed legislation to establish legal jurisdiction and the ability to enforce criminal law within the boundaries of Yellowstone. "The state of things cannot continue," Vest said. "Recently, the park has been largely visited. Hotels have been constructed there, against my judgment. Still, they have been built, and a population has gone there, temporarily, it is true, but a population among which crime can be and is committed, and some punishment must be provided.

"The park is so far removed almost from civilization that parties of men have gone in there in numbers of five and 10 and even 20, armed to the teeth, to destroy the game to ship it to market." An estimated 2,000 elk were killed in one season. "There has been no authority there to resist these men," Vest said, recommending an additional 10 assistants be added to the park staff.

When Vest suggested the construction of narrow roads and bridges within the park, Ingalls objected, saying there was no way to estimate the costs of such a project.

Vest replied: "The Senator from Kansas is mistaken. I now hold the printed report of the engineer officer surveying the park, laying out roads, and locating bridges. The entire amount, as he specified, of the improvements to be made, if all of them are made, will reach $210,000.

"Thousands of persons are visiting the park, and the increase will be beyond calculation in the future. There were thousands there during the last summer, and it is fair to presume that there will be a great many more during the next and at each recurring season, and not to improve the roads in the park would be to say that persons should not travel in any comfort or with any convenience within its limits.

"If we have the park, let us treat it as a national park. If, on the other hand, we are to adopt the idea advanced by the Senator from Kansas and throw it open as part of the public domain, then as a matter of course, not a dollar should be expended upon it for any purpose. I am not afraid to say that every dollar paid to the National Park judiciously will be money well spent. In my judgment, it would be an outrage upon the American people to say that any man should be permitted to go there and put his homestead upon those geysers or upon that incomparable scenery of the great Yellowstone Canyon or Yellowstone Lake. Nowhere else upon this continent—indeed, and I believe not in the whole world—is such scenery to be seen.

"I have not yet come to that materialistic state of mind when I think that the Natural Bridge of Virginia should be macadamized, the great Mammoth Cave of Kentucky should be used as the incipient point for an underground railroad, or the waterpower of Niagara should be used for a mill. I believe that the people of the United States are entitled, on account of the magnitude and grandeur of their possessions, to have just such a place as it was intended should be set apart by the original act. While the act remains upon the statute book, there is but one duty for us to perform: to preserve that park and to carry out the intent and purpose of the approved legislation."

A bill granting a right of way through the park to the Cinnabar & Clarks Fork Railroad Company was introduced on February 4, 1884, by Senator Samuel James Renwick McMillan (1826-1897) of St. Paul, Minnesota, and on February 27, 1884, it was reported favorably. On May 27, 1884, it was debated at length in the Senate, and the powerful opposition that developed surprised Vest and unwelcomely shocked the railroad promoters.

Senator Samuel J.R. McMillan of Minnesota, who also served on the Minnesota Supreme Court. Brady-Handy Photograph Collection, Library of Congress, Prints and Photographs Division.

"I am aware that it is popular to assert in this country that nothing should exist in which there is not money, and anyone who proposes to preserve the great National Park in its original grandeur and beauty and preserve the game, which has almost ceased to exist upon this continent, is taunted with aestheticism and is sneered at, as being the proper spirit and ideas of the age," Vest began.

"I am not ashamed to say that my life has been largely devoted to field sports, that I have lived a large portion of my time in the woods, forests, mountains, and upon the rivers of the great West. I know whereof I speak when I say today, without any other interest or motive under heaven than that of an American citizen, that the construction of this railroad is the destruction of that park. Those who think that Mammoth Cave should be turned into a subterranean storehouse for mercantile purposes, that the Falls of Niagara should be used with their waterpower to turn a mill, that the wonderful geysers of Yellowstone should be devoted to laundry purposes and leased out to Chinamen in order to wash dirty linen, to such persons I have and can have no argument and no appeal to make. But to those who sympathize with me in the purpose to preserve one spot, at least, in which nature shall exist as it was originally, in which the great game, the elk and the bison, and the black-tailed deer, shall always be found for our children and our children's children, to such I now appeal most earnestly against this bill."

Senators Daniel Voorhees, Benjamin Harrison, John Alexander Logan (1826-1886) of Illinois, Omar Dwight Conger (1818-1898) of Michigan, Augustus Hill Garland

***Left:** Senator Daniel W. Voorhees of Indiana, ca. 1865-80. Brady-Handy Photograph Collection, Library of Congress, Prints and Photographs Division. **Center:** Senator John Alexander Logan of Illinois, ca. 1886. Photo by Dewitt C. Pratt courtesy Library of Congress. **Right:** Senator Omar D. Conger of Michigan, ca. 1865-80. Brady-Handy Photograph Collection, Library of Congress, Prints and Photographs Division.*

Right: *U.S. Attorney General Augustus Hill Garland of Arkansas. Brady-Handy Photograph Collection, Library of Congress, Prints and Photographs Division.*

Far right: *Wilkinson Call of Florida, ca. 1879-80. Brady-Handy Photograph Collection, Library of Congress, Prints and Photographs Division.*

(1832-1899) of Arkansas (with whom Vest served in the Provisional Confederate Congress in 1861), and Senator Wilkinson Call (1834-1910) of Florida, teamed with Vest in an oratorical phalanx that made so strong a showing against the bill that, when it was laid aside, it was not brought up again in that Congress, although it came back in 1887, 1889 and 1890.

"It is said this railroad is necessary to reach mines," Vest said in his continuing defense. "I shall not stop to discuss the value of these mines because, like all mining property, their value is prospective. They may amount to a great deal or nothing, with the chances largely in favor of the latter."

Vest urged the companies and investors involved to conduct a survey and propose an alternate route that would be less harmful. However, according to Vest, no one connected with the railroad had ever approached him about any compromise.

"I know that when any public man stands in the way of one of the speculative enterprises, the first thing is to cajole him or buy him, and if that cannot be done, the next thing is to destroy him," Vest said. "I do not expect to be exempt."

Vest's attack came in the way of threats to destroy the park he loved. "I have been notified repeatedly that unless I withdrew my opposition to the Cinnabar and Cook City Railroad, the park would be broken up," Vest said. "These men are in the employ of the speculators," who Vest theorized were seeking a buyout from the Union Pacific.

Vest did not believe the 65-mile railroad alone would destroy the park. Allowing the railroad, he thought, would open the door to other detrimental forces that could not be reversed. "There is another extraordinary provision in this bill," Vest continued. "It suggests that other roads might be constructed along this same river. This shall not be the only railroad that goes into the park.

"There was a bill pending here in the last Congress for constructing a road from Green River on the Union Pacific up by Lake Lewis to Cinnabar. That bill has not been presented in this session. It is held in abeyance and reserve, but just as soon as the present bill is enacted into law, this other set of speculators will come to Congress, and we are estopped from denying them the right to enter the park because we have given the privilege to the gentlemen now asking it. If we once break up the idea of this being a park exclusively, that is the end of [the Yellowstone National Park Protection Act of 1872]. And for myself, I shall have no more concern with that park or anything pertaining to it.

"I have spoken earnestly. I have no interest in this matter except as a citizen. I have no feeling except the feeling of one who knows the truth of what he says and desires to impress on his fellow Senators.

"I would not give one farthing for that park if this bill becomes law."

In 1885, Senator Preston Bierce Plumb (1837-1891) of Kansas offered a resolution asking President Cleveland to advise the Senate as to the status of certain unoccupied lands in the Indian Territory acquired from the Creek and Seminole in the Treaty of 1866 when each of the "civilized tribes" was removed from their lands and relocated to Oklahoma, much of the same land that would be claimed by the "Sooners" in 1889.

Senator Preston B. Plumb from Kansas (ca. 1865-80). Brady-Handy Photograph Collection, Library of Congress, Prints and Photographs Division.

"The President is sworn to carry out the law, and law as it stands absolutely prohibits the settlement of white men on that soil," Vest urged.

"Now, what is Oklahoma? Because I cannot reach the men who have gone in there, whether a single Senator listens to me or not, I have achieved something in the interest of law and order. Oklahoma proper is a country nearly 5,000 square miles in area. It is in almost the central part of what is known as the Indian country, and that Indian country, by law of 1834 of the American Congress, was declared to be all the lands west of the Mississippi River that were not entered, that were not surveyed, that were not assigned by the government or authorities of the United States."

Vest argued that the "Boomers" were living on land that the U.S. didn't own, and to make it legal, Congress should allow the tribes to convey the land rights. Senator Conger spoke to the resolution and substitute, expressing the belief they foreshadowed a movement to rob the Indians of lands they rightfully possessed.

Vest responded: "The Senator from Michigan has not considered his words. I will say that this resolution was not intended to rob any Indian but to protect the Indians. Emphatically and distinctly, I say I offered it to protect the Indians. This morning, the delegate from the Creek Nation wrote me a letter, which I have, thanking me in the name of his nation for what I said yesterday upon this floor on behalf of his people; and the Creeks and Seminoles have filed in the Department of the Interior two papers, asking that the very thing should be done which I propose in the resolution.

"My resolution says, and every impulse of my nature says, that these Indians shall be treated with the same standard of honesty as if it were the government of Great Britain with whom they were treating. So far from outraging the Indians, it protects them," Vest said.

During consideration of the $30,000 Indian Appropriations Bill of 1885, Vest contributed many personal observations from his visits to various tribes and reservations.

"Summer before last, I visited and held council with 1,100 men, women and children at Fort Assinniboine [in north-central Montana], which is on the edge of the British possessions and is the most northern of our line of forts," Vest said. "I was there in September. It is the bleakest, most inhospitable country and climate I have ever seen. Agriculture is simply impossible. The summer season there (they call it summer; I call it very fair winter weather) lasts about a month. They raise a few potatoes, a very few stunted vegetables, and that is all.

"The Assiniboine, a portion of the Gross Ventres, the Blackfeet, Bloods, and Piegans, all subsist upon the buffalo. If I had a map accessible, I could show the Senate what is called the buffalo country, extending through a portion of northern Montana into the Canadian Territory, over 149 miles of which I traveled in an ambulance with a military escort, from Fort Assinniboine (for whatever reason, the tribe is spelled with one n in the middle, and the fort is spelled with two) to Maple River on the Canadian Pacific. I now state that I did not see one living thing in those 149 miles. There were the bones of a buffalo, the wallows of the buffalo, a leaden sky, and a morning wind, and those Indians are expected to exist upon that, together with the meager rations the U.S. Government gives them.

John Two Guns White Calf (1872-1934) was the last chief of the Piegan Blackfoot Tribe.

"In this council that I held with them, one of the chiefs, John Two Guns White Calf [1872 -1934], rose and said through an interpreter that one of his children was then dying of starvation. I saw that poor emaciated creature dying for want of food in sight of the United States flag. I am no sentimentalist; I am a Western man, but it is a shame to this government. I went to the agent who lived 30 miles from there. He had no food. I then appealed to the military officer in command, and he issued rations.

"I hurried back as soon as I could get to the railroad. I made my way to Washington City; I went to the Secretary of the Interior Teller and the Commissioner of Indian Affairs [Hiram Price (1814-1901)] and appealed to them for relief for those Indians. 'The winter is coming on; that whole tribe will be exterminated; they will die for want of food.' Mr. Price said, 'I have no funds out of which to give those people anything; my rations will be exhausted in six weeks.' I said, 'Mr. Commissioner, exhaust them. Congress will meet within a month, and I pledge myself as a Senator of the United States that the Senate, and I believe the House, will make ample appropriations immediately upon the meeting of Congress."

The rations were doubled, and notwithstanding that, the post's commandant told Vest, the Indians would not have made it through the winter. Even with the extra food, they lost more than 350 members of the Iron Confederacy (northern Plains Indians).

In 1885, Samuel Thomas Hauser (1833-1914), governor of the Montana Territory, wrote that, unless assistance was sent, the Indians would run out of rations before March 1. "Their condition from exposure, destitution and starvation experienced during the past two years is utterly astounding," Hauser wrote.

Vest again pleaded with Congress. "It is useless for gentlemen to say, 'Let those Indians go to work.' You might as well say to a child in the cradle, 'Go to work.'" He reminded his colleagues that the northern Plains Indians had been self-sufficient on buffalo for centuries and were hunters, not farmers. "The buffalo have disappeared ... to hurl [the Indians] into the terrible struggle with civilization and tell them to work or die is simply to say die."

Vest's idea was to move the tribes south, away from the inhospitable climate, and to teach them to become self-supporting, which he admitted would take years. "In the meantime, the only thing for us to do as humane Christian people to say no more of it is to feed them and to see that they do not starve under our flag and at our door."

As early as 1885, more settlers were hovering on the Oklahoma border, held back by 20,000 Federal troops. "I have never, from the beginning of the discussion, believed those people have any right to go into that territory," said Vest.

Protecting the Yellowstone front also became more critical as the crowds there grew. "Captain [Moses] Harris [1837-1927] states in his report that persons are going there now and mutilating the cones around the geysers, which are artistic works of nature" and claiming them as souvenirs, Vest said. More than 10,000 people visited the park in 1886. The Territory of Wyoming claimed jurisdiction, but Vest argued that there was no jurisdiction in Yellowstone to punish murder or robbery, or any felony, which matched the opinion of Chief Justice Waite, a member of the 1883 expedition.

Chief Justice Morrison Waite of Ohio. Brady-Handy Photograph Collection, Library of Congress, Prints and Photographs Division.

In 1888, a Senate bill was introduced to provide compulsory education for Indian children. The bill included a $20,000 appropriation to educate school-age children in the Alaska Territory.

"I know nothing personally of the Indians of Alaska," Vest said. "I have a general idea that they are fish-eating Indians, much like the Chinooks on the coast of Oregon. Of course, their characteristics are greatly regulated and modified by the climatic influences around them. I suppose they are, in the main, like the Indians of Northern Montana, of which I happen to know something personally.

"The Senator from Connecticut [Joseph R. Hawley (1826-1905)] spoke of the sentiments of the officers of the Army regarding the Indians and particularly to General Grant and General [George Henry] Thomas [1816-1870]. General Sheridan has long been credited with having remarked 'that the only good Indian is a dead Indian.' As I have been informed from his lips, he never said anything of the sort. I traveled with him last summer 400 miles in the west, and we frequently conversed regarding the Indian question. His sentiments were as humane, as Christian, as those of anyone I have ever talked about."

Vest, who once ascribed to the "dead Indian" sentiment, grew more upset following each Western journey. In 1887, he went with Senator Dawes and Secretary of the Interior Lucius Q.C. Lamar, his old friend from the Confederate Senate, as a committee to visit Indian reservations. "We have robbed the Indians of this country," Vest told the Senate. "We have taken from them all they had. We drove them further and further west until last summer I witnessed scenes of absolute deprivation.

"If any man gave his life to the cause of elevating and educating the Indian, it would be the grandest mission to which he could devote every hour of his existence," Vest urged. "Anybody who seems to take any real interest in this matter is considered a sentimentalist. The prevailing idea in the West is that all an Indian is good for is killing him; he is a robber; he has taken land away from the whites."

The government aimed to select a reservation and agency sites to keep tribes away from the path of white settlement, meaning less desirable land. However, the definition of "desirable land" kept changing. By 1880, mining, farming, and ranching expansion made much of this previously undesirable land appealing. As a result, the federal government pushed tribes into ceding additional portions of their reservations in exchange for annuities and other benefits. Charles Arthur Broadwater (1840-1892), a contractor and partner in post trading at Fort Assinniboine, sought special consideration in redrawing the reservation lines. Using his considerable power in the Democratic Party, he asked Montana Delegate Martin Maginnis (1841-1919), a Democrat who pushed for the reduction of the size of Montana's Indian reservations, to arrange preferential treatment to improve business at the mercantile establishments that Broadwater controlled. Broadwater's actions typified most Euro-American Montanans' expansionist views regarding tribal land.

Chief Charlo, Native American leader and head chief of the Bitter Root Salish from 1870-1910.

One of Vest's missions was to meet with the Flathead Indians in Montana and convince them to follow the Treaty of 1872 with then-special commissioner General James Garfield, which they claimed to have never signed. After meeting with Flathead chiefs Charlo (1831-1910) and Arlee, Vest could see they were telling the truth and had no plans of leaving the Bitter Root Valley, which Vest called "the most beautiful land I ever saw."

Chief Charlo was described as "rugged as a granite cliff." He was sturdy with broad shoulders. His mouth was large, his forehead high and sloping. Jesuit priest Lawrence Benedict Palladino (1837-1927) said he was "quiet, yet firm—a true representative of his race, a thorough Indian, a brave and honest man."

Chief Charlo's branch, the Bitter Root Salish, had lived peacefully with intruding whites since 1855 following the preaching of "the Black Robes [Jesuits]," which the chief professed to believe. Other than Christianity, he disapproved of his people adopting the whites' ways.

Initially, Chief Charlo said, "This is my country; it belonged to my fathers; you can take me away from here, but you cannot take me away alive."

When Chief Charlo relented and said he would move to the Plains, Vest told him, "There are no Plains for you." Vest said, "The whites are like the leaves on the trees," and "You'll be better off on the reservation."

"Why should I believe you?" Chief Charlo said. "The paper you hold in your hand is a printed lie. You have robbed me of my land and taken away the houses given me by the President [Grant]. Now, you promise me more when you have not kept the promises you've already made?"

When Vest returned to Washington, he found the original 1872 treaty and saw that Chief Charlo was correct. His signature was not on the treaty, as many believed.

Indian Agent Daniel Shanahan said in his 1872-73 report that he promised Chief Arlee of the Nez Perce that he would recommend him to replace Charlo as head chief in exchange for his cooperation.

"Your Great Father, Garfield, put my name on a paper I never signed and that renegade Nez Perce, Arlee, is now drawing money to which he had no right," Chief Charlo said.

Vest visited and met with 11 Montana tribes: Assiniboine, Blackfeet, Chippewa, Cree, Crow, Gros Ventre, Kootenai, Northern Cheyenne, Pend d'Oreille, Salish and Sioux.

Vest was for Native American rights, but he believed the Indians should assimilate, which he said was impossible with large reservations. "Large reservations are simply an invitation to barbarism," Vest said. "With reservations of two, three, four million acres for 12,000 to 15,000 Indians, they're still just roaming savages, going from one end of the reservation to the other."

Vest's solution? "Until you put them on farms and teach them to support themselves, you can never make any advance. You can never take one step toward making them citizens of the United States as they should be."

Vest supported the work done by the Jesuits and said the Flatheads had advanced 100 percent more than any other tribe. The Jesuits taught girls sewing, housekeeping, teaching, and art. The boys were taught farming, herding, blacksmithing, and carpentry. It was done in a co-educational, boarding-school model. "They were kept away from the rest of the tribe," Vest said. "Eventually, they would marry each other. The Jesuits built them a house, broke some ground, and they quickly became the nucleus of a civilization of Christianity in that portion of the reservation they received.

"You must educate the sexes together so that one shall support the other, that they may go out and battle barbarism hand in hand," Vest said.

By 1889, Chief Charlo's people were destitute. "My young men have no place to hunt," said Charlo. "My women are hungry. For their sake, I will go." They moved from the Bitter Root Valley onto 558,000 of the 1.3 million acres initially marked off for them. Today, roughly 4,000 members of Flathead Nation live on the reservation. Another 2,800 members live elsewhere.

That many Native Americans live peaceful, non-assimilating lives would shock Vest, who believed they would perish. He fought diligently against those such as Teller who contended the Indians never owned the land and, thus, the whites had every right to it.

"They had this continent in fee-simple, absolute, as entirely and completely as I own today the house where I live," Vest said. "I know that the European nations announced that they had the right in the name of the Christian religion to come here and take this land from these people because they did not earn their bread by the sweat of their faces. That proposition I will never assent to."

While Vest never received the support he wanted for the tribes, he tried. "This amendment does not go half as far as it should. Let's try it. I will do anything I can to save a single human being from the degradation in which these people are placed," Vest said in 1888.

Vest's support of the Jesuits is significant considering his background.

"I was reared in the old Scotch Presbyterian Church— my earliest impression was that the Jesuits had horns and hoofs and tails, and there was a faint tinge of Sulphur in the circumambient air whenever one crossed your path," Vest said. But experience changed his prejudice: "Some of the best people I have ever known are members of that denomination, and I do not doubt that the Catholic Church has done more practical charity than any other denomination."

At the opening of the Fifty-first Congress, on December 4, 1889, Vest introduced a bill that made the north and west boundaries of the park coincide with state boundaries and extended to the east 35 miles and the south 15 miles "to include additional mountain land, heavily timbered, of no special value now in a commercial sense but of vast importance in protecting the water supply of the Northwest."

On February 20, 1892, Senator Francis Emory Warren (1844-1929) of Wyoming introduced S. 2373 to establish new Yellowstone boundaries. This was reported with amendments by Senator Orville Hitchcock Platt (1827-1905) of Connecticut on March 25, 1892, and debated and passed by the Senate on May 10. This bill made the Yellowstone River the boundary in the northeast to eliminate the railroad and mines controversy and eliminate the Montana and Idaho portions of the park, making significant additions to the south and east. In accepting this bill, Vest was "drinking gall and vinegar." He excused himself partly on the ground that Idaho, Montana, and Wyoming had become states, and he was inclined to submit to their senators on questions affecting the park. He confessed, however, "with humiliation," his defeat in his ongoing fight against disintegration and mutilation of the park and said he had found after 12 years "that a persistent and unscrupulous lobby can do almost what they please with the public domain." He said he submitted to this legislation "because I cannot help myself, not because my judgment approves it."

Senator Arthur Pue Gorman of Maryland, 1899.

Senators Call, Dawes, George Gray (1840-1925) of Delaware, William B. Bate (1826-1905) of Tennessee, party-switching Kentuckian John McAuley Palmer (1817-1900) of Illinois and Maryland's Arthur Pue Gorman (1839-1906) showed strong interest in the protection of the park, but there was no Logan to lead. Senators Platt and Teller supported the Wyoming Senators Warren and Sanders. Senator James Henderson Berry (1841-1913) of

Arkansas favored cutting the park into 100-acre tracts for settlers. Senator James Z. George (1826-1897) of Mississippi, as briskly as ever, wanted the park abolished and opposed any increase. On June 3, the bill passed on roll call 32 to 18, signifying the high-water mark of the railroad interest.

"The fact remains that legislation can be had for the park until the demands of these people are conceded," Vest said, denouncing the railroad lobby. "For years, the lobby has been trying to put a railroad into the park so the investors can turn around and sell it to the Northern Pacific for a huge profit."

The Northern Pacific enjoyed a virtual monopoly during and after Vest's lifetime. Within a decade of his death, the railroad would bring nearly 45,000 visitors to the park. Within 25 years, most tourists would arrive in cars.

On May 26, 1892, Vest pleaded with the Department of the Interior to humanely treat the Cahuilla Tribe in California, who felt the government (through Indian Agent Horatio Nelson Rust [1828-1906]) interfered with their rights to elect a tribal leader. "If one-tenth of what comes from reputable people about this man [Rust] is correct, he is utterly unfit for the position he holds," Vest said, claiming Rust was brutal and illiterate, neither of which was true.

Rust was primarily a photographer and spent much of his time capturing images of the day-to-day life of the Southern California tribes.

By December 1892, nearly a decade after his famous trip to Yellowstone, the Indian Territory had grown into what Vest called a "menace to civilization." He called the justice administered in the 71,000 acres "a farce, a blot, and a stain upon the judicial system."

The 1890 census showed that whites comprised a significant portion of the population, in some portions representing a 10-to-1 ratio. "It is evident from this enumeration that the time is speedily coming when history will repeat itself, between justice on one side and greed on the other," Vest said.

As it stood in 1892, the Indian Territory was a haven for criminals. "It has been a few months since in broad-open day, a peaceable community of Coffeyville, Kansas, was raided by the Dalton brothers from their depot in the Indian country, and men were shot down in the banks and upon the streets by these lawless banditti," commented Vest, who conceded that there were law-abiding white citizens within the Indian Territory, but not many. "It is a system of organized plunder," he said.

The fact that several members of the Dalton Gang were deputized as federal marshals made the system even more suspect. "We pretend that we want to teach these

Indians the habits of civilized life; we assert proudly that we are the great exemplars of a Christian civilization and an Anglo-Saxon jurisprudence," Vest pleaded. "How do we expect to teach these Indians when we treat them as savages; when we chase them down with foreign brigands; when we employ banditti as United States marshals to hunt like hares in the brush and drag them pinioned and manacled before a foreign tribunal in a distant State [either Paris, Texas, or Fort Smith, Arkansas], to be tried by an alien jury, and sentenced to certain death?"

Vest's solution: "If we want to show the Indians our jurisprudence, why not give him the same chance before the law given to a white man? Why not try him in his own country?"

As the 1893 Land Run approached, Vest urged caution to avoid a catastrophe, such as when Missouri opened the Platte Purchase in 1836. "The borders were crowded with white men who insisted that they must go in and they could not wait.

"Without regard to popular opinion, I have been the friend of the Indian. His fate has been a terrible one. The condition of the Indians in this country today is one of the darkest pictures in the history of our race."

"But let that go," Vest said. "In this case, we have treated the Cherokee fairly."

The Cherokee Strip was a portion of lands received by the Cherokee in 1835 when many were moved to present-day Oklahoma from western North Carolina and eastern Tennessee. Over time, the Strip had become unoccupied, and in 1879, a movement began to allow homesteading by the "Boomers." When President Benjamin Harrison forbade grazing leases after October 2, 1890, the Cherokee agreed to sell.

Benjamin Harrison, 1896, 23rd president of the United States. Pach Bros. photo, Library of Congress.

The Land Run began at noon on September 16, 1893, with 100,000 trying to stake claim to 40,000 homesteads. "Sooners" managed to sneak in early and take many of the best locations. Most of those in the Land Run could not secure a claim. Not all claimants found prosperity. Some found their free land unsuitable for farming, and many claims were quickly abandoned.

The fact that the Cherokee were paid for their land in 1893 Oklahoma is extraordinary. As recently as 2022, the Ute Tribe filed claims that the federal government violated the Fifth Amendment by taking its property within Utah's Uncompahgre Reservation without compensation, which would have gone against Vest's knowledge of land rights.

"We supposed in 1894 that we had settled this question after the long and acrimonious debate," Vest said. "We first passed a law recognizing the claims of certain citizens of Colorado who had gone into this [Ute] reservation and located claims on the gilsonite [a naturally occurring hydrocarbon used in drilling] lands. That bill passed and went to President Harrison and was vetoed upon the grounds that the settlers or persons who had gone there were illegally upon an Indian reservation, where they ought not to have been.

"Then it was proposed to put this land at auction to the highest bidder, which seems like the favorite idea now, as is done with unclaimed packages of an express company or the packages in the dead-letter office. It was proposed to put up these lands at auction without developing them and let any man bid and take his chance on finding gilsonite on what he bought or not finding it. There was some disposition to accept that proposition. The Senator from Colorado [Teller], not now here, opposed it so strongly that it also went by the board.

"Then in 1894, we placed in the appropriation bill (for it was the only place where legislation could be had), in a conference report, as a compromise between conflicting opinions, the provision of which the Senator from Arkansas [Berry] has so vehemently complained.

"Now, what was the result? The Secretary of the Interior [Michael Hoke Smith (1855-1931)] deliberately refused to accept that law. I called upon him repeatedly (and I will explain in a minute what interest I had in the matter), and he stated to me, after the commission made the report, that there were but about 10,000 acres fit for settlement. He explained that he had drawn up the proclamation for the President [Cleveland], who was then at Bar Harbor, to sign, and he took the proclamation there. The President then said that Congress was mistaken about the whole matter and that the land ought to be put up to the highest bidder, so there was another failure to settle this matter by law.

"I want to frankly state my connection with it for the last five or six years. There is a company in Saint Louis composed of reputable men, as you may find anywhere, who put $500,000 into purchasing lands outside of this reservation and have nothing to do with the Government. They have put up valuable works; they have surveyed a railroad 140 miles from their works to the Union Pacific; they have the money and are willing to build that road and give to the consumers of the United States the benefit of the increased production of gilsonite or asphaltum [asphalt]. Is that a crime? Are we to ban men willing to put their capital into enterprises of this kind? Are we to say to men who go out into the desert, where animal life cannot be supported, when they are willing to invest their money and make that desert available for civilization, 'You shall not do it;' if you do, you are denounced as speculators and thieves?"

Vest knew there was no need to buy the lands of a nomadic tribe.

"The facts are, as I happen to know by examination of this question over and over again, that the Indians want to live with the Uintahs," Vest said. "They are allied to them by blood. They belong to the same genetic family; they are all Utes. They do not want to live on the Uncompahgre Reservation of which we are now talking. There are only 10,000 acres, and they are separated from their people. They want to go back to the Uintahs. A great number of them are there now. There is no necessity for any government order to remove them. They roam over that whole country at will. As the Senator for South Dakota [Richard Franklin Pettigrew (1848-1926)] said, ample time is given to the amendment to the Government of the United States to make such rules and adopt such a line of conduct in the interests of humanity as may be necessary, which is the whole of it."

On February 17, 1897, in the Fifty-fourth Congress, Senator Vest secured the adoption of a Senate resolution calling on the Interior Department for information as to the installation of an elevator or other appliance to convey persons up and down the Yellowstone Canyon, which report was furnished by the interior secretary February 24, 1897. In this report, Assistant Secretary William Henry Simms (1837-1920) concluded that such an elevator would stay within the natural grandeur of the landscape.

Vest began the new century hopeful for a new chapter in relations between the U.S. and Native Americans. On April 9, 1900, he spoke on a bill to ratify an agreement submitted by the confederated bands of Utes in Colorado to sell their reservation.

"Nothing political or sectional is involved in this piece of legislation," Vest said. "Yet, I venture to say that upon no question ever brought before the American Senate has there been so much cheap philanthropy and rhetoric as upon the so-called Indian problem.

"With us in the West, it is a living, practical, real question, and it is time that this government should meet and grapple with the greatest question that has ever come before it in the present century and end it."

Vest introduced a pamphlet issued by Massachusetts Governor John Davis Long (1838-1915) that he said was full of gush and sentimentalism. "The last three generations of New England have had no Indian war, and they view this question by the light of the domestic lamp, not by that of the burning home."

For those so far removed, Vest said, they see the Indians in "the woodland tales of [James Fenimore] Cooper [1807-1882], the unerring rifle of 'The Deerslayer' [1841], the heroism of the Huron chief, and [Henry Wadsworth] Longfellow's [1807-1882] sweet 'Song of Hiawatha,' and

Henry Wadsworth Longfellow, 1868. Photo by Julia Margaret Cameron.

U.S. Agent Nathan Cook Meeker at the White River Indian Agency in western Colorado, who was killed by Ute warriors on September 29, 1879.

'shining water,' which have so enchanted the eastern press and pulpit that they profess to believe that the people on the border are principally occupied in first robbing the Indians and then murdering them."

Vest pointed out injustice toward Native Americans but said both sides had initiated abuses in the ongoing land disputes. "If this hostility exists in the halls of Congress, where it is seen, where is it felt? Look at the bill now pending before the Senate ... the principal object is it suffers the guilty to escape. I charge here today that the Ute Indians deliberately, for months before, prepared for this outbreak of hostilities and burned the grass between the Union Pacific Railroad and their reservation to prevent the advance of troops. Before they murdered the agent [Nathan Cook Meeker (1817-1879)] and 10 agency employees, they had secured three packages of Winchester rifles. General [Wesley] Merritt [1836-1910] reports that one Indian engaged in the White River Massacre [September 29, 1879] was captured with 12,000 rounds of fixed ammunition."

Between September 29 and October 5, 37 Utes and 24 U.S. Cavalrymen were killed.

"And yet these Indians today are to receive increased annuities from the government's bounty and to be removed to a more favorable reservation. Is this the hostility of the government?" Vest asked. "Sir, I say in all kindness that these [Massachusetts] gentlemen should read the history of their fathers; they should read of that first raid on Indian territory made by the so-called Pilgrim Fathers when they came to the shore of New England uninvited and unexpected. They resolved, 'first, that the earth with the fullness thereof belongs to the saints, and second, that we are the saints.'

"If they propose to carry out their philanthropy as they proclaim it from the lecture halls of Boston, in the name of justice, let it be carried to the full extent," Vest said. "If we propose to do complete justice, let us give back this continent to its original owners, or let us impanel a jury of nations and assess the damages and pay them to lineal descendants of the people we have wronged," Vest quipped, noting that neither party would dare, especially during an election year.

As Vest did best, he referred to history to explain the present. "I say it with no unkindness and with no desire to put any badge of inferiority on the Indian race, but in all animated nature, the rule prevails of the survival of the fittest; in all history, it has been so and will be so to the end. The very volume on the pulpits of the East, when preacher and congregation gush in the sentimentality of the wrongs done to the Indian, contains that wonderful history of the 40 years' pilgrimage by the chosen people of God, in which, under His immediate direction, they seized territory after territory and exterminated the inhabitant, smiting them hip and thigh, even to the destruction of men, women, and children. It has been so and will be so until the end of time. The expansive force of civilization will push aside the smaller." It was true, he said, of the Romans, the Normans, and the Celts.

"During the Revolutionary War, naturally and properly dreading the scalping-knife and the tomahawk ... our fathers sought the friendship of and attempted in every way to conciliate the Indian tribes then occupying the territory west of the Alleghenies, and extending from the Great Lakes of the north to the Gulf of Mexico on the south. We find in the annals of the Continental Congress an appropriation for 40,000 pounds sterling to purchase goods from Indian tribes. We find a resolution inviting Indian tribes to send their youth to Dartmouth, Princeton, and other colleges in the colonies."

Vest claimed that it wasn't until after the Revolutionary War that the new Americans began to look at the Native Americans as "the other."

Through education, such as provided by the Jesuits, Vest said there could be a new day in Anglo-Indian relations. "The old Indians are gone, hopelessly gone. The young Indian can be saved," he said. "There are 3,000 of them today in the Dakotas—in South Dakota, I believe—who are voters, exercising intelligently, as far as I know, the right of suffrage. Go to the Indian Territory, where there are the Five Civilized Tribes, and you will see what can be done by intelligent effort."

In February 1903, Vest was weak, wasting away, and nearly blind. He had to be helped to his seat and aided as he rose to speak. "The Indians," he said, "had been shamefully robbed."

While on the Committee on Indian Affairs, Vest visited the Indian schools of Wyoming and Montana. When President Theodore Roosevelt claimed the North American Indians had been treated with "great justice and clemency," Vest disagreed.

"I went to every Indian school, whether under control of the government or the Jesuits or others," Vest said. "I never saw a single government day school that was worth one cent to the Indians or did anything to advance them toward Christianity and civilization. I perfectly remember the visit I made to Fort Shaw in Montana. There were Crow, Blackfoot, and some Turtle Mountain Indians, 40 miles distant. A stockade surrounded it. I stayed there for two days and found [roughly] 890 children enrolled there, and there had not been 10 in attendance at the school on any single day unless it was 'ration day' when a meal was distributed among them.

"The agent was a superannuated clergyman from Rhode Island. Two teachers at this school were his daughters, and they admitted, as I learned personally on examination, that these Indians were taught nothing. Yet $2,800 was paid out of the Treasury of the United States to these teachers and reports made out at every session of Congress on behalf of day schools."

Where did we go wrong? Vest tried to correct the problem for three decades, but its roots began 40 years before he was born on the Kentucky frontier.

"In 1790, a year after the adoption of the Federal Constitution, in my judgment, the great mistake was initiated and has been since perfected under which we have come to our present position," said Vest. "The status of the Indian is unknown and undefined. We have attempted to civilize the Indian, yet we have excluded him from civilization."

But, said Vest, civilization "will come like the morning light slowly across the horizon and afterward mingling until it blazes like the noontide sun. It will come to these people; how soon we know not; but sooner or later, the Indian will be a citizen of the United States, and the divinity that presides over every home will lead him to a nobler and better future."

CHAPTER NINE

Vest on Jefferson

To understand George Graham Vest, especially the second half of U.S. Senate career, consider his views of founding father Thomas Jefferson. In what he thought was his best speech, Vest spoke at the Jefferson Club in Saint Louis, Missouri, on October 31, 1895, when a bronze bust of Jefferson by club member Benjamin Harney, Esq. (1866-1925) was unveiled.

Vest expressed his beliefs on what it meant to be an American, a citizen of a democratic republic:

Gentlemen of the Jefferson Club:

I have discharged with pleasure the duty which your kindness assigned me, and we now look upon the bust of him whose genius and prophetic foresight gave to our country the soil upon which this great city stands.

Jefferson wrote his epitaph. Amongst his papers, after death, was found a rough sketch in ink of an obelisk to be made in granite, eight feet in height, with the inscription:

Here was buried
Thomas Jefferson
Author of the Declaration of American Independence,
Of
The Statute of Virginia for Religious Freedom
And
Father of the University of Virginia

It is a significant epitaph and worthy of him who wrote it. Jefferson had been a member of the Virginia House of Burgesses and of the Continental Congress, Governor of Virginia, Minister to France, Secretary of State, Vice President, and President of the United States, but none of these honors nor titles are on the stone that marked his grave. True to his convictions, shown by every public and private act, the sworn enemy of parade, sham, and ostentation, the stern old Democrat wanted, living or dead, none of the tinsel and trappings of heraldic pomp or titular glory. He named himself his passport to immortality—the rights of man, religious liberty, and universal education.

Jefferson was charged by the enemies who pursued him during his life and assailed his memory after death, with being a communist who appealed to the ignorant and poor against the educated and wealthy. He was an aristocrat by birth, lineage, education, and association. Jefferson had in his veins the blue blood of the Randolphs, who, as Jefferson tells us in his autobiography, "trace their pedigree far back in England and Scotland, to which let everyone ascribe the faith and merit he chooses." Besides, he was born a land and slave owner, educated at the College of William and Mary, an institution established and endowed by royalty, and when a student in the old town of Williamsburg, the first capital of Virginia, was the favorite protege of Francis Fauquier [1703-1768], the royal governor from 1758 until his death, at whose table he was a constant guest. Passionately devoted to music, sculpture, and printing, an accomplished Greek, Latin, and French scholar, whilst in the higher mathematics, philosophy, and the sciences, he was without an equal amongst public men. Jefferson was naturally drawn by such tastes and pursuits away from the people, as they were then contemptuously called, and to the privileged classes who claimed by inheritance a monopoly of wealth, education and culture.

From Monticello, Jefferson went forth to make an untiring and relentless war upon tyranny and oppression in every shape. For nearly 50 years, his form towered in the front of every battle for civil and religious liberty, and there was not one single moment in which he ceased to struggle for human rights. It is almost impossible, after so many years and under the circumstances so changed, to realize the appalling difficulties that confronted the advocates of civil and religious freedom in the last century.

New Virginia was then but the gross caricature of old England. The Rakehelly cavaliers who fought under [Colonial Governor] Prince Rupert [1619-1682], the Duke of Cumberland, were reproduced in an exaggerated form in the young planters of the province. To primogeniture, entail, and the union of Church and State had been added the curse of African slavery, and to raise tobacco, clear more land, and buy more slaves, all to be at last squandered in riotous living, seemed to be the chief end of the Virginia gentleman.

Loyal to king and church, these foxhunting, deep-drinking, and gallant Virginians were ready to risk life and limb against any odds to defend the divine right of kings and the ecclesiastical supremacy of the Church of England.

From his four years' study of the law, and after mastering completely *Coke on Lyttleton* [Sir Edward Coke's 1633 commentary on Thomas de Littleton's (c. 1407-1481) treatise on land tenure], which he had read and re-read and carefully annotated, Jefferson stepped into a world of crystallized wrong and robbery, made up from ages of legal precedent, and sanctified by so-called religion; but not in vain had he studied the black-letter pages of that sterling old Whig textbook, of which Jefferson wrote: "Coke Lyttleton was the universal law book of students and a sounder Whig never wrote, nor profounder learning in the orthodox doctrines of the British Constitution, or in what was called British liberties.

"Our lawyers were then all Whigs. But when his black-letter text and uncouth but cunning learning got out of fashion, and the honeyed Mansfieldism of [Sir William] Blackstone [1723-1780] became the student's horn book, from that moment that profession (the nursery of our Congress) began to slide into Toryism, and nearly all the young brood of lawyers are now of that line. They suppose themselves to be Whigs because they no longer know what Whigism or Republicanism means."

When, therefore, in 1765, young Jefferson, fresh from Coke Lyttleton, stood at the door of the lobby of the House of Burgesses in Williamsburg and heard Patrick Henry [1736-1799] denounce in burning words the Stamp Act and the whole system of kingcraft, the seed fell into the ground well prepared for the truth.

SLAVERY

In 1769 Jefferson entered public life as a member of the House of Burgesses from his native county of Albemarle. His first measure was to provide for the gradual emancipation of slaves. Still, it resulted in utter failure and is now only valuable as indicating the settled opinions of Jefferson upon the subject of slavery and his fearlessness in grappling with the overwhelming public sentiment of his State in its favor.

Whilst a slave owner all his life, Mr. Jefferson was opposed to the institution and desired its gradual extinction. Like many intelligent men in the slaveholding states, he deprecated the existence of slavery. Still, he resented the statement that the people of these states were alone responsible for the evil or that those who had initially introduced slaves through their avarice had the right to interfere afterward with the property of the citizens to whom the slaves had been sold.

With prophetic vision, Jefferson saw the dreadful panorama of war and desolation which must accompany the end of slavery unless peaceful means were adopted for that purpose. Speaking of gradual emancipation, he says in his autobiography, written when he was 77 years old:

"It was found that the public mind would not yet bear the proposition, nor will it bear it even to this day. Yet the day is not distant when it must bear and adopt it, or worse will follow. Nothing is more certainly written in the book of fate than that these people are to be free, nor is it less certain that the two races, equally free, cannot live in the same government."

One portion of this prediction has been verified, and African slavery has been drowned in the tears and blood of both North and South.

At the same time, it is not difficult to realize how utterly beyond the imagination of any mortal man 50 years ago must have been the idea, not of emancipation, but that the emancipated slave would grasp the ballot and participate in the country's government.

We know now that the Negro race, with its strong local attachments, will never submit to colonization and that this philanthropic dream has vanished before the logic of events. The Negro is a component of our civilization and must so remain.

It is the very irony of history that of all the slaveholding States, Virginia should have suffered most in defending an institution forced upon her people by the greed of Old and New England in opposition to the judgment and wishes of her most distinguished men.

As far back as 1770, Virginia had protested the introduction of African slaves, but the royal edict silenced the protest, and the traffic went on.

In 1776, Jefferson framed with his own hand an indictment of the King of Great Britain, in the following words: "He has waged cruel war against human nature itself, violating its most sacred rights of life and liberty, in the persons of a distant people who never offended him; captivating them and carrying them into slavery in another hemisphere, or to incur miserable death in their transportation thither.

"This piratical warfare, the opprobrium of infidel powers, is the warfare of the Christian King of Great Britain [George III (1738-1820)]. Determined to keep open a market where men should be bought and sold, he has prostituted his negative for suppressing every legislative attempt to prohibit or restrain this execrable commerce.

"And that this assemblage of horrors might want no fact of distinguished die, he is now exciting those very people to rise in arms among us and to purchase that liberty of which he has deprived them by murdering the people on whom he has obtruded them, thus paying off former crimes committed against the liberties of one people with crimes which he urges them to commit against the lives of another."

These burning sentences were a part of the Declaration of Independence as originally written by Jefferson and reported to Congress, but so strong was the influence of South Carolina, Georgia, and New England, in favor of the slave trade, the words were stricken out, and the Declaration was adopted as we now see it.

In 1778, two years later, Virginia made it a felony to import slaves into her limits. In 1787, when she gave to the Union the Northwest Territory, the most princely gift in all "thc annals of recorded time," Jefferson prepared the ordinance. He incorporated in its provisions the condition "that after the year 1800 of the Christian era, there shall be neither slavery nor involuntary servitude in any of the said States, otherwise than in punishment of crimes, whereof the party shall have been duly convicted to have been personally guilty."

Again, in the Convention which framed the Federal Constitution of 1789, when the question of permitting further importation of slaves was under discussion, Mr. [George] Mason [1725-1792], of Virginia, said: "This infernal traffic originated in the avarice to British merchants. The British government constantly checked the attempt of Virginia to put a stop to it. Maryland and Virginia had already prohibited the importation of slaves expressly, and North Carolina had done the same in substance."

Declaring then in the strongest terms his opposition to slavery, he concluded by stating that "he lamented that some of our Eastern brethren had, from a lust of gain, embarked in this nefarious traffic."

Luther Martin [1748-1826] of Maryland declared the slave trade "to be inconsistent with the principles of the Revolution and dishonorable to the American character to have such a feature in the Constitution."

In this state of things, Gouverneur Morris, adverting to the circumstance that the sixth section of the same article, then under consideration, contained a provision "that no navigation act should pass without the consent of two-thirds of the members present in each house" — a provision particularly affecting the interests of the New England States — suggested that this, together with the fourth and fifth sections, should be referred to a committee so that a bargain might be formed between the parties out of these elements of special local interest on the one side and the other.

The suggestion was adopted, and on the second day afterward, the committee reported, extending the slave trade to 1800 and striking out the provision requiring a two-thirds vote to enact a navigation law.

When the report came up in the Convention, General [Thomas] Pinckney [1750-1828] of South Carolina moved to extend the slave trade to 1808, and the motion was seconded by Mr. [Nathaniel] Gorham [1738-1796] of Massachusetts.

Mr. Madison earnestly and eloquently opposed the motion, declaring it dishonorable to the American character, but his opposition was in vain.

Hand in hand, Massachusetts and South Carolina led the cohorts of slavery, and the motion prevailed, all the New England States, with South Carolina, Georgia, Maryland, and North Carolina voting for it, and Virginia, Pennsylvania, New Jersey, and Delaware voting against it.

Martin was a member of the committee to which I have alluded, and in a letter afterward to the Maryland House of Delegates, says: "I found the Eastern States, notwithstanding their aversion to slavery, were very willing to indulge the Southern States, at least with a temporary liberty to prosecute the slave trade, provided the Southern States in their turn would gratify them by laying no restriction on the navigation acts."

Even in her desolation, Virginia, noblest of ancient or modern commonwealths, can point to this record and hear in contemptuous silence the taunts and sneers of the political Pharisees, who "mock at her calamity."

DECLARATION OF INDEPENDENCE

Although Jefferson had failed in his attack on African slavery, he did not relax in his opposition to the arbitrary and oppressive measures of the British Ring.

In 1772 the people of Rhode Island began the Revolution by burning the British war vessel *Gaspie*, in Narragansett Bay, and when the ministers of George the Third claimed the right to transport the persons accused from Rhode Island to England for trial, Jefferson saw at once that the time had come for joint and concerted action between all the colonies. To concede this claim as to the humblest citizen was to surrender the liberties of all. In the early part of March 1772, Patrick Henry, Richard Henry Lee [1732-1794], Francis Lightfoot Lee [1734-1797], Dabney Carr [1743-1773], and Jefferson met at the Raleigh Tavern in Williamsburg, Virginia. He drew up the famous resolutions pledging Virginia to stand by Rhode Island and creating a committee of 11, whose duty should be to correspond with the other colonies and concert measures for the general defense.

It is singular with what pertinacity amidst all the passionate debates and resolves of this eventful period, Jefferson and his associates still clung to the idea of loyalty to the king. Not till 1775 did he reluctantly conclude that the colonies must separate from the mother country.

Thus had the Commons of England advanced step by step until the head of Charles the First [1600-1649] rolled from his shoulders before his palace at White Hall, and thus had the Girondists given place to the Revolution until Louis the Sixteenth [1754-1793] and Marie Antoinette [1755-1793] died beneath the axe of the Guillotine. In 1774, the people of Boston threw the famous shipment of tea into the harbor, and the King of England retaliated by closing the port. Again, Jefferson and his associates met at the Raleigh Tavern and resolved to stand by New England. Massachusetts and Virginia then stood shoulder to shoulder, and who could have believed that in less than a century, the same States would grapple with deadly conflict?

On June 21, 1775, Jefferson took his seat as a member of the Continental Congress, and in June 1776, wrote, in his own hand, the Declaration of American Independence, the most sublime enunciation, save one, ever made to the human race.

That "all governments derive their just powers from the consent of the governed" is a corollary from the divine injunction, "All things whatsoever ye would that men should do to you, do ye even so to them."

Together, these two great truths embrace all the rights and duties of mankind.

Having been reported to Congress, the Declaration was debated on the second, third, and fourth days of July and adopted on the afternoon of the fourth, every member present signing it, except Mr. [John] Dickinson of Pennsylvania [1732-1808], who abstained.

In after years, Mr. Jefferson related with great humor a ludicrous event connected with this solemn transaction. Near the hall in which Congress assembled was a large livery stable, and the weather was extremely warm; the bloodthirsty and aggressive flies, which swarmed through the open windows, attacked our patriotic fathers in abbreviated pants and thin silk stockings with such pertinacity as to terminate the debate.

So near to the sublime is the ridiculous, and so wonderfully do the most insignificant creatures influence the destiny of man!

REFORMING VIRGINIA

Thirteen States had now sprung into being, with institutions and laws not only varying between themselves but with some utterly opposed to the genius and spirit of the Declaration of Independence.

In none of the colonies were abuses so rife and firmly established as in Virginia.

Primogeniture and entail had created a class of thoughtless elder brothers and vagabond heirs who were reckless and self-indulgent to the verge of lawlessness.

The union of Church and State had destroyed the rights of conscience, and a licentious clergy, so far from "leading the way to Heaven," were merely adjuncts to the great houses, where high play and old madeira [rare wine] rewarded their complaisant ministry.

The world, for hundreds of years, had listened to the clanking of chains and shrieks of martyrs whilst fire and faggot [kindling] irradiated the deadly work of religious bigotry.

Even the Pilgrims, flying from persecution, "having landed on Pilgrim Rock, fallen on their knees and their faith on the aborigines," no sooner found themselves firmly established in New England, than they began to torture in the name of God.

To deny any book of the Old or New Testaments to be the word of God was punished by fire or stripes [from a whip], and blasphemy left the delinquent without his ears and his tongue bored by a red-hot iron. Men were pilloried, branded, and executed for nonconformity to the established church, and in but three out of the 13 colonies was there religious toleration — Rhode Island, Maryland, and Pennsylvania.

Mr. Jefferson graphically describes the condition of Virginia: "The first settlers of this country were emigrants from England of the English Church, at a point when it was flushed with complete victory over the religion of all other persuasions. Possessed, as they became, of the power of making, administering, and executing the laws, they showed equal intolerance in this country with their Presbyterian brethren who had emigrated to the northern government. The poor Quakers were flying from persecution in England; they cast their eyes on these new countries as asylums of civil and religious freedom, but they found them free only for the reigning sect.

"General acts of the Virginia Assembly of 1659, 1662, and 1693 had made it penal for parents to refuse to have their children baptized; had prohibited the unlawful assembly of Quakers; made it penal for any master of a vessel to bring a Quaker into the state; had ordered those already here, and such as should come thereafter, to be imprisoned until they should abjure the country; provided a milder punishment for their first and second return, but death for their third; had inhibited all persons from suffering their meetings in or near their houses, entertaining them individually, or disposing of books which supported their tenets.

"If no executions occurred here, as did in New England, it was not owing to the moderation of the church or spirit of the legislature, as may be inferred from the law itself, but to historical circumstances that have not been handed down to us.

"By our own Act of Assembly of 1705, if a person brought up in the Christian religion denies the existence of a God, or the Trinity, or asserts there more Gods than one, or denies the Christian religion to be true, or the scriptures to be of divine authority, he is punishable on the first offense by the incapacity to hold any office or employment, ecclesiastical, civil or military, or the second, by disability to sue, to take any gift or legacy, to be guardian, executor or administrator, and by three years imprisonment, without bail.

"A father's right to the custody of his children being founded in law on his right of guardianship, this being taken away, they may, of course, be severed from him and put by the authority of the court into more orthodox hands."

Amidst a storm of opposition and obloquy such as was never seen on this continent, Jefferson resolutely attacked primogeniture, entail, and the union of Church and State.

From October 11 to December 5, the battle raged daily in the Virginia Assembly. It resulted in a substantial victory for Jefferson, although the statute for religious toleration did not finally become law until 1786. When nearly 80 years old, Mr. Jefferson spoke of this as the most terrible contest of his long and stormy career. Against him were arrayed the wealthy families whose large estates were held by entail, the elder sons whose patrimonies were taken from them, and more than all, the clergy and established church, who resented the statute for religious toleration as a blasphemous attack upon religion and a personal outrage upon themselves. Jefferson was denounced as a communist, an atheist, and a foe of all religion, and the bitter enmities engendered by this conflict harassed him during life and assailed his memory after death.

No one knew better than Jefferson how unrelenting religious intolerance is and how dangerous the charge of infidelity or atheism to a public man, but so true was he to the rights of conscience that in his long life, and under all assaults, he made no reply to his enemies. He absolutely denied the right of any being, except his Maker, to call into question his religious belief, and thus, he lived and died.

In a private letter to Dr. Benjamin Rush [1746-1813], dated April 21, 1803, he wrote of his religious opinions: "They are the result of a life of inquiry and reflection, and very different from that anti-Christian system imputed to me by those who know nothing of my opinions. To the corruptions of Christianity, I am indeed opposed, but not to the genuine precepts of Jesus himself. I am a Christian in the sense in which He wished any one to be, sincerely attached to his doctrines in preference to all others, ascribing to himself every human excellence, and believing he never claimed any other."

To his young grandson [Thomas Jefferson Randolph (1792-1875)], when life had almost faded away, and he could feel upon his aged brow the breath of eternity, he wrote:

"This letter will be to you as one from the dead. The writer will lie in the grave before you can weigh its counsel. Your affectionate father [Thomas Mann Randolph (1768-1828)] has requested that I would address you with something which might possibly have a favorable influence on the course of life you have to run, and I, too, as a namesake, feel an interest in that course.

"Few words will be necessary with good dispositions on your part. Adore God. Reverence and cherish your parents. Love your neighbor as yourself, and your country more than yourself. Be just. Be true. Murmur not at the ways of Providence, so that the life into which you have entered be the portal to one of eternal and ineffable bliss. And if to the dead it be permitted to care for the things of this world, every action of your life will be under my regard."

If this be atheism or infidelity, what honest man or pure woman will not pray that the world be filled with unbelief?

To Jefferson, the doctrines of primogeniture, entail, and an established church was but part and parcel of the system which gave certain families the divine right to govern their fellow men, and against this heresy, with all its incidents and corollaries, he made untiring and relentless war until the end of life.

To him, there was but one creed in matters spiritual or temporal: "All governments derive their just powers from the consent of the governed."

In addition to the legislation abolishing primogeniture, entail, and an established church, Jefferson, at the same session of the assembly, introduced and passed a bill fixing the terms upon which foreigners should be admitted as citizens of Virginia, and this act became the model for the general naturalization law of the United States. Under a resolution introduced by himself in October 1776, he commenced the following summer, in connection with Edmund Pendleton [1721-1803] and George Wythe [1726-1806], a revision of the laws of Virginia, and in 1779, after three years of arduous labor, the work was completed.

But his great ambition was to establish a system of common schools, which should place a liberal education within reach of every child in Virginia, to create high schools, found a library at Richmond at the cost of 2,000 pounds a year, and change the College of William and Mary into a University. With indefatigable zeal, he perfected all the details, but the war absorbed the entire resources of the commonwealth, and long years of eventful history passed before he realized any part of his cherished plans.

GOVERNOR OF VIRGINIA

On June 1, 1779, Jefferson was inaugurated Governor of Virginia, succeeding Patrick Henry, the state's first executive. From the day of his inauguration to the hour when he retired from office, he was overwhelmed with difficulties before which an ordinary man would have shrunk appalled and hopeless.

Without navy, arms, or money, Jefferson was expected to defend an exposed seaboard, furnish supplies to the Virginia troops in the field, and prevent the horrors of an Indian war on the western border.

All that could be done by unflagging energy and the wisest forethought he accomplished, but in 1780, the storm of war burst with relentless fury upon Virginia.

[Major General Horatio] Gates [1728-1806] was defeated at Camden, and the traitor [Benedict] Arnold sailed up the James [River], burning and pillaging on either side, until he captured Richmond, whilst news came that Washington's army was on the eve of dissolution.

In 1781, [Lord Charles] Cornwallis [1738-1805] invaded Virginia from the South, and a troop of cavalry dashed upon Monticello to capture Governor Jefferson. Five minutes before their arrival, Jefferson escaped, and his faithful slaves refused, under bribes and threats, to give information about the route he had taken.

As always in the hour of national calamity, a scapegoat was necessary to appease the popular disquietude, and Jefferson was, in this instance, the victim. Conscious of his faithful discharge of duty, he chafed under these assaults as never before or after and, although acquitted by the unanimous vote of the Assembly, declared that he would never accept another public trust and that, with the close of the war, his political career had ended.

Surrounded at Monticello by his family, to whom he was tenderly attached, and with his books and flowers, Jefferson looked forward to years of quiet happiness, such as every man, worn with the battle of life, has pictured in his daydreams of the future. But Providence had destined otherwise.

In the spring of 1782, death robbed him of a wife [Martha] whose beauty and accomplishments gave Monticello the most charming mistress that ever blessed a Virginia home. From a stupor of grief, Jefferson awoke, anxious to leave the scenes that constantly reminded him of his irreparable loss.

He plunged into the vortex of politics, and in 1783, we find him at Annapolis, ready to take his seat in Congress, to which he had been recently elected. He devoted himself with untiring assiduity to public business and, as chairman of the Committee on Coins and Currency, gave his country and the world a system of coinage on the decimal basis, the most perfect known amongst men.

At the same session, he introduced the celebrated ordinance, enacted in 1787, by which Virginia gave the union the great states of Ohio, Indiana, Illinois, Michigan, and Wisconsin.

ENVOY TO FRANCE

On May 17, 1784, Jefferson was appointed Envoy Extraordinary to assist Mr. [John] Adams [1735-1826] and Dr. [Benjamin] Franklin [1706-1790], then abroad, in concluding commercial treaties with Great Britain, Holland, and other governments, on the "footing of the most favored nation," and on March 10, 1785, he succeeded Dr. Franklin as minister to France.

Jefferson remained in Europe for five years, residing in Paris and watching with deepest interest the great drama of the French Revolution [1789-1799]. He witnessed the fall of the Bastille [July 14, 1789], and the massacre of the Swiss Guards [August 10, 1792], but, like [British statesman] Charles James Fox [1749-1806], he saw through the blood and horror the outlines of liberty; and, unlike [Edmund] Burke [1729-1797], he beheld in the French queen not only a beautiful and unfortunate woman but the reckless, self-indulgent cause of her husband's ruin.

"This angel, as gaudily painted in the rhapsodies of Burke," he wrote 40 years afterward, "with some smartness of fancy, but no sound sense, was proud, disdainful of restraint, indignant at all obstacles to her will, eager in the pursuit of pleasure, and firm enough to hold to her desires or perish in their wreck.

"Her inordinate gambling and dissipations, with those of the Count d' Artois [1757-1836] and others of her clique, had been a sensible item in the exhaustion of the treasury, which called into action the reforming hand of the nation; and her opposition to it, her inflexible perverseness and dauntless spirit, led herself to the Guillotine, drew the king on with her, and plunged the world into crimes and calamities which will forever stain the pages of modern history. I have ever believed that, had there been no queen, there would have been no Revolution, no force would have been provoked or exercised."

Like John Knox [c.1514-1572], in the days of Mary Queen of Scots [1542-1587], Jefferson could not appreciate the beauty which looked, without pity, on the starving multitude and listened, without emotion, to the cries of her unfortunate people.

Jefferson looked with contemptuous amazement upon the French Court feasting and dancing at Versailles while the hungry people roared and surged through the streets of Paris.

"Slowly comes a hungry people, as a lion creeping nigher,
Glares at one that nods and winks behind a slowly dying fire."

The glamour of royalty did not seem to affect this stern republican, who rejected with scorn the divine right of kings.

In one of his letters, he writes thus of the Monarchs then occupying the proudest thrones of the earth:

"While I was in Europe, I often amused myself in contemplating the characters of the then reigning sovereigns of Europe. Louis the Sixteenth was a fool, of my personal knowledge, and despite the answers made for him at his trial.

The King of Spain was a fool, and of Naples the same. They passed their lives hunting and sending dispatches over thousands of miles through couriers to let each other know what game they had killed the preceding days. The king of Sardinia was a fool. All these were Bourbons. The Queen of Portugal, a Braganza, was an idiot by nature, and so was the King of Denmark. Their sons, as regents, exercised the powers of government. The King of Prussia, successor to Frederick the Great [1712-1786], was a mere hog in body and mind.

"Gustavus [III] of Sweden, and Joseph [II] of Austria, were really crazy, and George of England, you know, was in a straight-waistcoat. There remained then none but old Catherine, who had been too lately picked up to have lost her common sense.

"In this state [Napoleon] Bonaparte [1769-1821] found Europe, and it was the state of the rulers which lost it without a struggle. These animals had become without mind and powerless, and so will every hereditary monarch be after a few generations."

Every fiber of Jefferson's being sympathized with the unfortunate people whose sweat and blood had been wrung from them for centuries to feed these royal animals, and every hour in Europe added to his hatred of the monarchical system.

In February 1787, he left Paris and traveled incognito through France's fairest provinces, investigating the people's home life, houses, food, and modes of agriculture.

Besides attending to his diplomatic duties and making commercial treaties with all the principal nations of Europe, Jefferson found time to correspond with leading scientists upon chemistry, astronomy, geology, and natural history. He collected and shipped to the United States seeds and plants of all kinds suitable to our soil and climate and procured for [Counte de] Buffon [1707-1788], the great naturalist, specimens of the animals and birds peculiar to this continent.

When in France, Jefferson wrote and published his celebrated *Notes on Virginia*, which attracted universal attention and passed through several editions.

Whilst making treaties, writing philosophical essays, and watching the Revolution, this remarkable man invented an improved [moldboard] plough, which was awarded a medal by the Royal Agricultural Society of the Seine, and was exhibited to William Cabell Rives [1793-1868], Minister to France in 1853, as "The Prize Plough of Thomas Jefferson;" afterward Jefferson invented the revolving chair, now found in so many offices and households.

Rice was largely consumed in France, and anxious to know why the American article was unable to compete successfully with that raised in Southern Europe, he made a journey across the Alps in 1787, into the rice-growing districts [of southern France and northern Italy], and being unable to procure some improved seed rice, which he discovered there, on account of laws prohibiting its exportation, he filled the pockets of his coat and overcoat with the best rice, of the best rice-producing district of Italy, and sent it to Charleston. It came to hand safely, was distributed in quantities of 10 and 12 grains to planters, and, being carefully tended, furnished South Carolina with the best rice in the world.

SECRETARY OF STATE

After five years of unremitting toil for his country and mankind, Jefferson was compelled to give some attention to his private affairs and left Paris in October 1789 with his two daughters [Martha and Mary], expecting to return within a year. On November 17, 1789, he landed safely at Norfolk and found an invitation from Washington to become Secretary of State.

With reluctance, but acting under a sense of public obligation, he accepted the office and entered his duties.

Accustomed, as Jefferson must have been, to the uncertainty of political events and the mutations of public sentiment, he was profoundly astonished to find that a powerful party had come into existence in the United States, which distrusted the people, and favored a strong, if not monarchical, government.

At the head of this party was the Secretary of the Treasury, Alexander Hamilton [1755-1804], a man of rare ability and unquestionable courage, but without faith in republican institutions or any form of government not possessing monarchical features.

That such were Hamilton's opinions cannot be doubted.

In Madison's debates of the Convention which framed the Constitution, we find Hamilton saying that: "In his private opinion, he had no scruples in declaring, supported as he was by the opinions of so many of the wise and good, that the British government was the best in the world."

He declared that the Senate of the United States should be framed on the model of the House of Lords, and in speaking of the Chief Executive, said: "The English model is the only good one on this subject. The hereditary interests of the king were so interwoven with that of the nation, and his personal emoluments so great, that he was placed above the danger of being corrupted from abroad. At the same time, he was sufficiently independent and sufficiently controlled, to answer the purpose of the institution at home."

The notes written by Hamilton himself, from which he delivered this speech, can be found in his life by his son [James Alexander Hamilton, (1788-1878)], and in them are the following points: "Here I shall give my sentiments as the best form of government, not as a thing attainable by us, but as a model which we ought to approach as near as possible. British Constitution best form. … Society naturally divides itself into two political divisions — the few and the many — who have distinct interests … and if separated, they will need a mutual check. This check is a Monarch. … He ought to be hereditary and to have so much power that it will not be his interest to risk much to acquire more."

That there was a party in the United States disposed to monarchy is put beyond question by the statements of Washington, Madison, John Jay [1745-1829], John Marshall [1755-1835], and Monroe. Even Adams declared, "The proposition that the people are the best keepers of their own liberties is not true; they are the worst conceivable;

they are no keepers at all; they can neither judge, act, think or will as a political body. … Hypocrisy, simulation, and finesse are not more practiced in the Courts than in popular elections, nor more encouraged by Courts than people."

During the War for Independence, the Colonies had been held together by a common danger. Still, even then, it was evident that the Articles of Confederation must be set aside and a stronger government established. The power to levy and collect taxes, provide for the general defense, and act as Sovereign within its proper sphere were necessary attributes of government demanded by self-preservation itself.

This necessity created a tendency to centralization, and the excesses of the French Revolution, at which the world stood aghast, furnished what seemed a conclusive argument against popular government. Jefferson soon found himself almost alone in the elegant society of New York. The city's wealth, culture, and refinement were shocked at the atrocities committed in Paris, and Hamilton was their pet and idol.

"I had left France," Mr. Jefferson wrote long after, "in the first year of her revolution, in the fervor of national rights and zeal for reformation. My conscientious devotion to those rights could not be heightened, but it had been aroused and excited by daily exercise.

"The President received me cordially, and my colleagues and the principal citizens apparently with welcome. The courtesies of dinner parties given me, as a stranger newly arrived among them, placed me at once in their familiar society. But I cannot describe the wonder and mortification with which the table conversation filled me. Politics were the chief topic, and a preference for kingly over republican government was evidently the favorite sentiment.

"An apostate I could not be, nor yet a hypocrite; and I found myself, for the most part, the only advocate on the republican side of the question, unless among the guests there chanced to be some member of that party from the legislative houses."

It was impossible for harmony, nor any relation except that of antagonism, to exist between Jefferson and Hamilton. They were both men of great ability, with positive convictions and utterly irreconcilable views of the government.

Jefferson was the incarnate principle of democracy, pure and simple, without alloy.

Hamilton had no sympathy for the people or popular government. In February 1802, Hamilton wrote to Gouverneur Morris, his most intimate friend, and afterward his eulogist: "Mine is an odd destiny. Perhaps no man in the United States has sacrificed or done more for the present Constitution than myself, and contrary to all my anticipations of its fate, as you know from the beginning, I am still laboring to prop the frail and worthless fabric. … Every day proves to me more and more that this American world was not made for me."

Notwithstanding the great authority of Washington and the influence which his character exercised upon all who approached him, there soon occurred an open rupture between the Secretary of State and the Secretary of the Treasury.

In February 1792, Jefferson mentioned to the president his intention to retire from the Cabinet, and, when pressed for his reasons, frankly stated that it was impossible for Col. Hamilton and himself to continue together in the administration, and that now a proposition had been brought forward, the decision of which must definitely determine "whether we live under a limited or unlimited government."

"To what proposition do you allude?" asked the president.

"To that," replied Jefferson, "in the report of manufactures (by Hamilton), which, under color of giving bounties for the encouragement of particular manufactures, meant to establish the doctrine that the Constitution, in giving power to Congress to provide for the general welfare, permitted Congress to take everything under their charge which they should deem for the public welfare. If this was maintained, then the enumeration of powers in the Constitution does not at all constitute the limits of their authority."

If Jefferson should now revisit the earth, he would find the same doctrine advanced even amongst those who claim to be exponents of his principles and teaching.

In the meantime, all of Europe was preparing to attack France, and the question presented to Washington's Cabinet was whether the United States should remain neutral or assist the people who had assisted us in our struggle for independence.

On April 22nd, 1793, the Proclamation for Neutrality was issued. [For weeks, Citizen Edmond Charles Genét (1763-1834) had been visiting political groups, beginning in Charleston on April 8, to marshal support for the French. By the time he reached Philadelphia—then the capitol—Washington was outraged.]

He [Genét] was received with such tumultuous acclamation as was never before or since given to any ambassador or visitor to our shores. Public meetings, banquets, oratory, and music evidenced the deep feeling of the American people for the cause of France. A storm of indignation burst upon Washington and his Cabinet for refusing to immediately assist our allies of the War for Independence, then struggling against the combined despotism of Europe, led by England.

It is impossible for us to realize now the popular excitement of those eventful days or the clamor raised about the government, but Washington and his Cabinet stood firm, and the result justified the wisdom of their course.

Jefferson's correspondence with Genét and the English Minister [William Pitt, the Younger (1759-1806)], afterward published by order of Congress, stands today and will forever remain the most wonderful exhibition of learning, skill, and moderation to be found in the annals of diplomacy.

VICE PRESIDENT

Jefferson retired from Washington's Cabinet on January 1, 1794, the acknowledged leader of the Republican party, and with the compliments and plaudits of his countrymen.

Even his enemies were forced to admit that his correspondence with Genét had exhibited the highest order of ability and had shown him to be both patriot and statesman.

In 1796 he was called from Monticello to become Vice President, Mr. Adams having received in the Electoral College 71 votes and Mr. Jefferson 68, which resulted, as the Constitution then provided, in making the former President and the latter Vice President of the United States.

To the duties of this office, he brought the same industry and learning as to every other position.

When a young lawyer, beginning his public career as a member of the Virginia House of Burgesses, he had adopted the practice of noting down in a small leather-bound volume rules and precedents in parliamentary law, and upon this as a basis lie now prepared his "Manual of Parliamentary Practice," the highest authority in legislative proceedings known to the civilized world.

PRESIDENT

In the meantime, the Federalists and Republicans were marshaling their forces for the Presidential contest of 1800. Washington's conservative and mediatory influence had been withdrawn, and party spirit raged untrammeled.

The press was in the hands of the Federalists, and Jefferson the mark at which all their arrows were aimed. He was pictured as an atheist, libertine, a monster in human form. One of the favorite charges against him was that he was an ally of Napoleon Bonaparte, the Corsican tyrant.

The political preacher had already appeared in the Presidential canvass, and though not as alliterative as in modern times, was equally as sensational.

The great preacher then in New York was Dr. John Mitchell Mason [1770-1829], and he was shocked beyond measure to find from the *Notes on Virginia* that Jefferson had doubts about a universal deluge [Noah's Flood]. Some days before the election, Dr. Mason published a pamphlet entitled "The Voice of Warning to Christians on the Ensuing Election," in which he exclaimed: "Christians! Thus, a man you are expected to elevate to the chief magistracy insults yourself and your Bible."

We can imagine what sort of partisan this reverend politician must have been when we learn that in one of his sermons, he paused and, with uplifted hands and eyes, burst into prayer: "Send us, if Thou wilt, murrain [infectious disease] upon our cattle, a famine upon our land, cleanness of teeth in our borders; send us pestilence to waste our cities; send us, if it pleases Thee, the sword to bathe itself in the blood of our sons, but spare us, Lord God Most Merciful, spare us that curse—most dreadful of all curses — an alliance with Napoleon Bonaparte."

As Mason uttered these words, blood gushed from his nostrils, but putting his handkerchief to his face, he then waved it aloft as if a bloody banner in the coming contest.

Through all this scandal and vituperation, temporal and ecclesiastical, the people, as they always do, discerned the actual issue, and the Republicans were successful. Jefferson and Aaron Burr [1756-1836] each received 73 votes in the Electoral College to 65 for Adams, 64 for Pickney, and one for Jay, and after some weeks of great excitement, the House of Representatives ratified the will of the people by making Jefferson president and Burr vice president. The Alien and Sedition Laws had done their work, and the first Republican administration assumed control of the government.

The new president rode to the capitol on horseback, hitched his steed to the palings, and quietly took the oath of office. There was no procession, inaugural ball, show, or parade. Right or wrong, this was Jefferson's idea of a Republic and the commencement of a Republican administration. During the administrations of Washington and Adams, the absurd custom of Congress being opened by the president with a personal address had been adopted, in imitation of the English system, but Jefferson quietly transmitted his message in writing, and such has been the custom ever since.

He also refused to hold weekly levees, where a mob of sweating and uncomfortable people, in tawdry finery, torture each other and the president until life becomes a burden. Still, this travesty on common sense has since returned to plague the chief executive and disgust the sensible public.

Jefferson sought to simplify the government and relieve it from the display and extravagance by which monarchy aimed to dazzle the people and conceal the outrages inflicted upon them.

The Trinity of his political faith was a strict construction of the Constitution, economy in expenditures, and honest men in office.

His inaugural on March 4, 1801, should be treasured with Washington's Farewell Address.

"Equal and exact justice to men of whatever state or persuasion, religious or political, peace, commerce and honest friendship with all nations, entangling alliances with none; the support of the State Governments in all their rights, as the most competent administration for our domestic concerns, and the surest bulwarks against anti-republican tendencies; the preservation of the general government in its whole constitutional vigor as the sheet anchor of our peace at home, and safety abroad; a jealous care of the right of election by the people—a mild and safe corrective of abuses, which are lopped by the sword of revolution, when peaceable remedies are unprovided; absolute acquiescence in the decision of the majority, the vital principle of Republics from which there is no appeal but to force, the vital principle and immediate source of despotism; a well-disciplined militia, our best reliance in peace and for the first moments of war, till regulars may relieve them; the supremacy of the civil over the military authority; economy in the public expense that labor may be lightly burdened; the honest payment of our debts and sacred preservation of the public faith; encouragement of agriculture, and of commerce as its handmaid; the diffusing of information and the arraignment of all abuses at the bar of public reason; freedom of religion; freedom of the press; freedom of persons under the protection of the habeas corpus, and trial by juries impartially selected."

The first significant act of Mr. Jefferson's administration was to dispatch three frigates and one sloop of our small navy to the Mediterranean to overawe the Algerine pirates and terminate their daring attacks upon American commerce.

When Minister to France, he had been annoyed and irritated that the United States and other nations were compelled to pay tribute to these buccaneers. One bill sent to Mr. Jefferson for the ransom of an American crew was as follows:

> For three captains, $6,000 each, $18,000; for two mates, $4,000 each, $8,000; for two passengers, $4,000 each, $8,000; for 14 seamen, $1,400 each, $19,600; total, $53,600.

Jefferson was determined that this national disgrace should be obliterated, and history shows how well and thoroughly the gallant [Stephen] Decatur [1779-1820] carried out the instructions of his chief.

However, the most splendid achievement of Jefferson's administration was the acquisition by purchase from Napoleon of the Louisiana Territory, which extended our limits from ocean to ocean and gave us the mouth of the Mississippi.

When the treaty was signed in Paris, Mr. [Robert] Livingstone [1746-1813], one of the commissioners, said:

> "We have lived long, but this is the noblest work of our whole lives. The treaty which we have just signed has not been obtained by art nor dictated by force. It will change vast solitudes into flourishing districts, and from this day, the United States take its place among the powers of the first rank. ... The instruments which we have just signed will cause no tears to be shed. They prepare ages of happiness for innumerable generations of human creatures.
>
> "The Mississippi and Missouri will see them succeed one another and multiply, truly worthy of the regard and care of Providence, in the bosom of equality, under just laws, freed from the errors of superstition and bad government."

If the dead are permitted to care for the things of this world, with what satisfaction must the spirit of Jefferson today look down upon this vast domain acquired by his patriotic foresight; a land of plenty, filled with happy homes, and temples devoted to education, science, and art, such as this in which we now assemble!

After acquiring Louisiana, including the vast region stretching to the Pacific, Mr. Jefferson's next object was to ascertain the nature and resources of these possessions, and for this purpose, the expedition of [Meriwether] Lewis and [William] Clark [and 40 others] left Saint Louis in 1805, came up the Missouri [River], and for two years, four months, and 10 days was lost to civilization, and exposed to danger and hardships, the recital of which equals the stories of romance.

Not many months after the acquisition of Louisiana, intelligence reached the president of the treasonable design of Burr to seize upon the mouth of the Mississippi, invade Mexico, and establish a southwestern empire. After the death of Hamilton, Burr served out his term as vice president, presiding at the impeachment trial of Justice [Samuel] Chase [1741-1811], and then finding his public career ended, his restless ambition had conceived the scheme, which also ruined [Harman] Blennerhassett [1765-1831], and made himself an outcast and wanderer.

Party rancor attempted to make Burr a martyr and Jefferson a tyrant, but impartial history has long since entered the judgment that the president was right. Burr was guilty of the designs attributed to him.

The latter part of Jefferson's second term was clouded with the prospect of war with England and the distress caused by the embargo, which he enforced to the end of his administration, hoping to avert an expensive and ruinous conflict of arms.

In 1809, with the country four times greater in resources and territory than in 1800, his second term as president closed, and after 44 years of public service, he transferred the government to his friend, James Madison, and went back to Monticello and to the labor of love, which had been amongst the dreams of his early ambition. His whole energies were now devoted to establishing the University of Virginia, upon a system singularly illustrative of that equality and liberty which formed the leading characteristic of Jefferson's life and opinions. The University differs from other American colleges in these particulars: There is no president, and all the professors are of equal rank except that one of them is elected chairman of the faculty [that tradition continued until 1905]. The University is simply a group of schools, and the student chooses the studies he elects to pursue. Unlike other institutions, no rule requires a student to attend religious exercises, but his conduct is governed entirely by his sense of right.

The ruling idea in every detail is an absence of coercion and an appeal to manhood and conscience.

Jefferson lived 17 years after the close of his public career, and his last hours were embittered by the pressure of debts which he was unable to satisfy. His splendid library, a portion left him by George Wythe, was sold to the United States, and he was finally compelled to ask the Legislature of Virginia to authorize him to dispose of his lands by lottery to meet the harassing liabilities pressing upon him.

Although an exact man, Jefferson practiced the hospitality that prevailed in Virginia at that time, and he had never learned the modern methods by which a public official can, in a few years, become a millionaire upon a small salary. When he left Washington City, he was forced to borrow $10,000 to pay debts contracted for household expenses, and whilst we may deprecate the style of living that necessitated such outlay, we must admire the integrity that procured the money to meet the debt by a mortgage upon Monticello, rather than by a raid upon the public treasury.

On July 4, 1826, as the accentuating cannon and the glad acclaim of a free people saluted the birthday of American Independence, Jefferson's life ended peacefully and serenely at Monticello.

On the same day, at his home in Massachusetts, Adams passed away. No longer rivals nor political opponents, they met together the last enemy of all our race.

Gentlemen of the Jefferson Club, you have taken the name and are pledged to the principles of him who established the Democratic Party [as it existed in 1878]. No responsibility can be greater, for the defeat of these principles and the destruction of the organization based upon them, means the end of free institutions upon this continent.

We now hear strange doctrines from some who claim to be Democrats. We are told that if the party fails to declare in its national platform for affirmative action on a single issue, its members should desert the flag and "follow after strange gods."

No Democrat who honestly reveres the doctrines and teachings of Jefferson can be a Republican or Populist.

The Republican Party of today is the lineal political descendant of the old Federalists and holds to the doctrine of Hamilton that this is a government of unlimited powers and that Congress can do anything it deems necessary for the general welfare.

The Populists believe that the government is a great eleemosynary institution and should support the people instead of the people supporting the government.

The Democratic Party holds that there should be no partnership between the government and any individual or class, but that all the benefits and burthens of the government should be equally and justly distributed, every citizen being protected in life, liberty, and property, and made the architect of his own fortune.

It holds that all property should be taxed in proportion to the protection received from the government. It does not believe in the system under which Mr. [Cornelius] Vanderbilt [II] [1843-1899] pays no more upon his hundreds of millions to support the National Government than does the poorest citizen who must, in war, risk life and limb to protect these millions.

The Democratic Party is national, not sectional. It is coexistent with the whole union and our government's autonomy.

The Democratic Party is the only obstacle to the supremacy of Hamilton's federalist ideas, and the man who deserts its flag gives aid and comfort to those who malign the character and teachings of Jefferson.

No greater calamity could come to this country or the world than the disruption of the great organization founded by the author of the Declaration of American Independence.

Upon the canvass of the past, Washington and Jefferson are the central figures in our struggle for independence. The character of the former was so rounded and justly proportioned that so long as our country lives or a single community of Americans can be found, Washington will be "First in war, first in peace, and first in the hearts of his countrymen."

To Washington, we are more indebted than to any one man for national existence, but what availed the heroism of Bunker Hill, the sufferings of Valley Forge, or the triumph of Yorktown if the government they established had been but an imitation of the monarchy from which we had separated?

To Jefferson, we owe eternal gratitude for his sublime confidence in popular government and his unfaltering courage in defending, at all times and in all places, the great truth that "All governments derive their just powers from the consent of the governed."

The love of liberty is found not in palaces but with the poor and oppressed. It flutters in the heart of the caged bird and sighs with the worn and wasted prisoner in his dungeon. It has gone with martyrs to the stake and kissed their burning lips as the fire-tortured spirit winged its flight to God!

In the temple of this deity, Jefferson was high priest!

For myself, I worship no mortal man living or dead; but if I could kneel at such a shrine, it would be, with an uncovered head and loving heart, at the grave of Thomas Jefferson.

CHAPTER TEN

History is Written by the Victors

Soon after his second re-election to the Senate in 1891, Vest bought a house on P Street near Twelfth Avenue in northern Washington, a 15-minute walk from the Capitol Building. His official address was listed as Kansas City, but he spent much of most summers in Sweet Springs, midway between Kansas City and Columbia, in a cottage he had built in 1882. He had first seen the place in 1853 while deer hunting.

The cottage was about 50 yards from a spring the peculiar-tasting water of which he liked. This mineral water, Vest claimed, did him more good than any other water he had tried.

During the 1892 presidential campaign, Vest declared he was ready to address the tariffs imposed under the Tariff Act of 1890 anytime, anyplace, and did speak on them more than he had on any other single topic. He attempted to show there had never been such poor relations between employees and employers. To make his point, he used 21 essential products with high tariffs and a long list of strikes compiled from newspapers nationwide. He claimed the tariff act, engineered by then-Congressman William McKinley (1843-1901), had led to iron, steel, and clothing strikes. "One cannot shoot a gun, bury a corpse or physic himself without paying [a tariff]," Vest said.

Early in Vest's senatorial career, he declared his party stood for "revenue [from tariffs] as the principle and protection [of American industries] as the incident," while Republicans the opposite. Dawes concluded: "After having had experience in framing tariff legislation, Vest was convinced that the whole system for protection was utterly indefensible and false in fact and theory."

Vest believed the tariffs were "legalized robbery, naked plunder" and an "interdependent mutuality of greed." Tariff laws taxed one class for the benefit of another, he said, making it unconstitutional. "The cornerstone of our government is 'equal rights to all, exclusive privileges to none,'" Vest said.

In 1892, after Cleveland was re-elected to the presidency, Vest spent the day with him at his cottage in Lakewood, New Jersey. "When leaving his cottage in the evening for New York, I said, 'Mr. President, I did not come here today to ask for an appointment at your hands. Still, I cannot keep from saying that Wade Hampton deserves a position under your administration that will enable him to pass his declining years in comfort. He would fill the place of Railroad Commissioner with honesty and ability."

Cleveland did not hesitate, assuring Vest he would appoint Hampton to the suggested post. Hampton served four years under Cleveland and a year under McKinley, who told Vest he would have kept him longer if not for the pressure to appoint a Republican.

A volatile issue of the 1880s was whether the U.S. currency should be backed by silver and gold, or gold alone. Because silver was worth less than its equivalent in gold, taxpayers paid their government bills in silver. At the same time, international creditors demanded gold, depleting the nation's gold supply. The issue cut across party lines, with western Republicans and southern Democrats joining the call for the free coinage of silver and both parties' representatives in the Northeast holding firm for the gold standard.

In the Lakewood meeting, Vest and Cleveland discussed silver. "He agreed with me that it was a dangerous point before our party and that it should be adjusted satisfactorily, if possible, so as not to divide the party," Vest said.

During Cleveland's first term (1885-1889), he and Treasury Secretary Daniel Manning (1831-1887), who served from 1885 to 1887, stood firmly on the side of the gold standard and tried to reduce the amount of silver that the government was required to coin under the Bland-Allison Act of 1878.

Angered Westerners and Southerners advocated for cheap money to help their poorer constituents. In reply, Richard Parks "Silver Dick" Bland (1835-1899) of Missouri, one of the foremost "Silverites," introduced a bill in 1886 requiring the government to coin unlimited amounts of silver, which would inflate the then-deflating currency. While Bland's bill was defeated, so was a

Senator Wade Hampton of South Carolina, later governor of that state. Brady-Handy Photograph Collection, Library of Congress, Prints and Photographs Division.

Grover Cleveland, 22nd and 24th president of the United States. National Archives photo.

Congressman Richard P. Bland of Missouri, ca. 1865-80. Brady-Handy Photograph Collection, Library of Congress, Prints and Photographs Division.

bill the administration favored that would repeal any silver coinage requirement. The result was a retention of the status quo and a postponement of the resolution of the free-silver issue.

In 1890, the Sherman Silver Purchase Act provided for the monthly purchase of silver at the discretion of the Treasury. Vest, a long supporter of silver coinage, believed that "discretion" prevented parity. "Making it a commodity is the worst measure for silver," he said, which proved correct as its value declined.

In Cleveland's first message after his second election in 1892, he urged Congress to repeal the purchasing clause of the Sherman Silver Purchase Act, which permitted the free and unlimited coinage of silver with the same intrinsic value and purchasing power for every dollar coined. The act provided for the monthly purchase of 4.5 million ounces of silver with Treasury notes, which Vest called a "cowardly makeshift evasion of the real issue"—bimetallism, the coinage of both silver and gold.

When the bill to repeal the purchasing clause of the Sherman Act passed the House of Representatives and reached the Senate, Voorhees was chairman of the Senate Committee on Finance. "From the commencement of his public career, he was known to have been an earnest and devoted friend of bimetallism," Vest wrote. "Those of us who favored bimetallism had no doubt he would be found acting with his old friends against the bill."

In a conversation with Voorhees at Healing Springs, Virginia, in the summer of 1892, the two agreed the purchasing clause of the Sherman Act should have disastrous long-term ramifications.

On August 22, 1893, to the surprise of his friends, Voorhees sided with Cleveland and voted for the bill. "He delivered an elaborate and expansive speech, giving his reasons for supporting Cleveland's recommendation that the purchasing clause be repealed," Vest wrote.

Ten days before Cleveland's second inauguration on March 4, 1893, Vest met with the president-elect in New York. He was asked to covertly meet with Bland to see if he would be open to reenacting the Bland-Allison Act as a compromise. "I saw Bland three days later at my House in Washington, and after a long conversation [more than three hours], Bland agreed to the compromise, although he did not believe the Goldings, as he called them, would assent to any such legislation."

Vest wondered aloud what Jefferson would think of a system whereby a dozen New York financiers could so control the currency of a nation to produce a money famine and then exact their own terms.

The Panic of 1893 struck the stock market, and the country soon faced an acute economic depression. The panic was worsened by the acute shortage of gold resulting from the increased silver coinage, and Cleveland called Congress into a special session to deal with the problem. The debate over the coinage was heated, and the effects of the panic drove more moderates to support repealing the coinage provisions of the Sherman Silver Purchase Act.

Even so, the "Silverites" rallied their following at a convention in Chicago, and the House of Representatives debated for 15 weeks before passing the repeal by a considerable margin. In the Senate, the dissolution of silver coinage was contentious. Cleveland was forced to lobby Congress for repeal, against his better judgment. He convinced enough Democrats to go along with eastern Republicans to form a 48–37 majority. Depletion of the Treasury's gold reserves continued at a lesser rate, and the subsequent bond issues replenished the gold supplies. At the time, the repeal seemed a minor setback to "Silverites," but it was the beginning of the end of silver as a basis of American currency.

One of the distinct differences between Cockrell and Vest was in public relations. In Washington, Vest was all business and resented being called from the floor for trivial exchanges, while Cockrell shook every hand. When the repeal of the Sherman Act was pending, a prominent Democrat from Clay County, Missouri, who was visiting the House, commented that he planned to visit Vest in the Senate.

"You may go," said the congressman, "but you won't see Vest."

"What do you mean?" asked the Democrat.

"Vest won't come out to see you."

"Well, I bet a supper he does," said the Democrat.

The congressman, probably Kentucky-born Armstead Milton Alexander (1834-1892), accepted the bet and agreed to accompany the visitor to the Senate. The visitor gave his card to a page and asked him to deliver it to Vest on the Senate floor. When he returned, the visitor asked, "What did he say?"

"Nothing," said the page.

"Did you hand him my card?"

"Yes, sir, I did," the page said.

The pair then visited the gallery to see if Vest was present. "There sat Vest, crouched low at his desk, indifferent to the galleries and everything except the legislation."

While Vest generally ignored his constituents' visits, he was alert to their needs and desires, and presented pension bills and more than the average number of bridges, federal buildings, and river improvements.

Vest generally favored immigration, but in May 1892, he made it clear he did not view the Chinese as good for the country. "They do not assimilate with the American people," Vest said. "To use a better word, they do not homologate with our people at all." Vest's opposition to Italian immigrants was because, he claimed, they were largely illiterate and penniless, similar to the condition of his Scot-Irish ancestors when they arrived on the North American shores in the 1600s.

Vest enjoyed taking on "rank hypocrisy" when he recognized it. One such opportunity came over two months in 1892 when William Alfred Peffer (1831-1912) of Kansas proposed prohibiting "intoxicating liquor" from the grounds of the World's Columbian Exposition in Chicago.

"Why not include cigarette smoking?" Vest quipped. "We all know the bad effects, the loss of human life, the immoral influences of cigarette smoking, especially with the young, are much more deprecated than a glass of beer or wine."

Vest challenged the Senate to ban alcohol from the Illinois state Capitol. "Everyone knows you can order a "cold tea" and openly drink bourbon whiskey in the Senate restaurant," he said.

"But our silken conscience and our delicate olfactories are torn and outraged with the idea that a visitor to the World's Exposition should have a glass of beer or wine on a hot day when he is exhausted by a survey of the exhibition.

"What will a foreigner think of this country if he comes here and travels on our railroads, where he can order, in one of the palace cars of the Pennsylvania or New York Central Road, a glass of champagne, brandy, whiskey, anything he wants, if when he strikes the Exposition, he is told that he cannot have any alcoholic liquor whatsoever? He may come from the southern part of France, where the people drink nothing but wine; he may be German, who has been unused to water all his life and has drunk beer, but he is told that in coming to the Exposition, he must give up all his natural habits. He is compelled to drink lake water exclusively inside the Exposition. It is true he can go out, and by taking a carriage or walking a mile, he can strike the saloons of Chicago.

"This simply puts the visitors to the inconvenience of leaving the Exposition and going down into the streets of Chicago.

"There is not one of us who can look another in the face and not recognize the meaning of all this. All our opinions as practical men, even the temperate men, are to be subordinated to the cry in the extreme for a measure that we know to be utterly impracticable and useless. Public sentiment will not sustain this sort of work. We all know what the effect of it will be, and to pass such amendments as are proposed here now will bring the whole matter into ridicule."

When an amendment was filed that would close the grounds and exposition building on Sunday, Vest offered an amendment that would shut down all machinery and restrict labor, but the grounds should remain open, and a building should be adapted for religious purposes. "An idea struck me with great force that the great exposition of works of art and works of beauty, all those things that would tend to elevate and instruct man, ought to be open on Sunday to that large population who have no other day on which they can afford this peculiar aid to enjoyment as well as improvement."

Vest relayed an exchange with a Cook County representative during a visit to Chicago. "He said, 'It would be a good thing if the whole population of Chicago was shut up on the Exhibition grounds on Sunday; they would spend their time there much more innocently than if left at large.'"

Vest was consumed with the idea: "The city contains a large population who will find no other way to spend the day, who would be improved by spending the day inside the Exposition grounds."

The longer Vest stayed in the Senate, the more often he fought against temperance legislation, such as a provision prohibiting the sale of intoxicating liquors within a mile of the National Soldier's Home, established in 1851 for wounded and disabled veterans. Vest opposed the proposal and suggested a bar be put inside the home. "If you put the limit at a mile, the old soldiers will go there with the appetite for a drink upon them," he said, "and rather than walk the mile back and for another drink, they will go have two drinks or three, and then it is a mere question of capacity, for after the third drink the limit is entirely taken off."

The problem was not, Vest argued, intemperance but the "cormorants worse than vultures" who lurked around the home, especially on the days the soldiers received their pensions. "You soon see them [the soldiers] lying around the immediate limits in a state of insensibility."

Senator George Frisbie Hoar of Massachusetts, ca. 1870-80. Brady-Handy Photograph Collection, Library of Congress, Prints and Photographs Division.

Vest argued that the greater the distance, the greater the temptation to overdrink. "If we put the limit at a half-mile, we remove grogshops with the villainous mixture called alcoholic stimulants away from the immediate vicinity of the home, and yet sufficient distance not to expose these men to the temptation that would necessarily arise if it were right at hand."

On February 27, 1893, Senator Hoar offered an amendment making it unlawful to sell intoxicating liquors to the patients anywhere; Vest responded, "If we propose here to put these old soldiers on the same footing with minors and habitual drunkards, then this amendment is absolutely proper," said Vest, "but I, for one, have never intended to put them in such a category."

❖ ❖ ❖

Most of the clashes between Vest and Hoar centered on alcohol, and no one realized more fully than Vest the price he paid for his consumption.

Once, when Vest arrived in the Capitol lobby looking more haggard than usual, Hoar chided him for missing an important vote. "You're a fine young man to absent yourself at such a time and leave us old fellows, Cockrell and me and the rest, to handle these matters."

Hoar was four years older, and Cockrell three years younger than Vest.

"You'll never be as old as I," Vest said, "if you live 50 years longer."

"Bless you," Hoar said. "I was born in 1826 and was preparing for college when you came into the world."

"If you'd been born in 1726, you would be as old as I feel. You and Cockrell may see more years, but you'll never see my age. You haven't lived as lively as I, and I wish sometimes I hadn't," reported the *Saint Louis Post-Dispatch.*

Born in bourbon country and coming of age among brewers, it's not surprising Vest was a supporter of the alcoholic beverage industry. Like his friend Adolphus Busch, many of his constituents were involved in Missouri's largest industry. He denounced prohibition as "crank legislation" promoted by "pseudo philanthropists who had nothing else to do."

He urged people who loved personal liberty to fight the issue.

On regulation of liquor traffic in the District of Columbia and Alaska, Vest said: "Unless you have public sentiment and public opinion to maintain your laws in favor of temperance, the evil is but intensely aggravated."

To prove his belief that human nature rebels against restraint, he said: "If the Mississippi River ran whiskey, if every stone on its banks was a lump of sugar and every shrub a mint and everybody could go there and drink without hindrance, fewer people would drink than if you put up a fence with placards upon it declaring no man should touch the liquid in that river."

Vest knew the dangers of excessive drinking and called it "the greatest evil that ever afflicted humanity," citing an illustration that a drink called Russian brandy contains "'50 murders in every pint.' It is the fabled Pandora's box, out of which comes all the crimes known to civilization," Vest said. "If I had the power … to destroy the last drop of alcoholic stimulant upon the face of the earth, I would do it with the greatest pleasure and alacrity, but it cannot be done, and the experience of the whole human race shows it."

Vest predicted, correctly, that prohibition, if it ever came to pass, would do nothing to curb the alcoholism problem; it would just drive the traffic for liquor into "dens and purlieus."

Senator John Griffin Carlisle of Kentucky, ca. 1870-80. Brady-Handy Photograph Collection, Library of Congress, Prints and Photographs Division.

On October 30, 1893, the purchasing clause of the Sherman Act was repealed, but the gold reserves continued to decrease. When Cleveland entered into a contract with John Pierpont "J.P." Morgan (1837-1913) to purchase gold, the Senate called for a committee to investigate the transaction. Vest was one of the five committee members.

The committee, after interviewing Secretary of the Treasury John Griffin Carlisle (1834-1910), went to New York to meet with Morgan and August Belmont (1816-1890). When they refused, under attorney's advice, to disclose who purchased the bonds and for what price, Vest wanted to push for contempt charges. He was alone in his stand, and the investigation ended.

In December 1893, the Senate heard a report from James Henderson Blount (1837-1903) about possible annexation of the Hawaiian Islands. The annexation movement was led by Hoard and William Pierce Frye (1830-1911) of Maine. Vest questioned whether the traditional policy of the United States was being forsaken and a "great expansive, territory-acquiring government" was being instituted? "We want a compact republic in which every section is represented, a compact republic with no islands out in the ocean around which we are to gather an enormous fleet and upon which we are to place expensive fortifications—a pawn to be seized in the event of war with a great power."

When the Wilson-Gorman Tariff Act came to the Senate from the House in 1894, it was referred to the Finance Committee and then to a sub-committee consisting of Vest, Isham Green Harris (1818-1897) of Tennessee, and James Kimbrough Jones (1839-1908) of Arkansas. "We labored diligently for nearly three weeks in revising the House bill, hearing Senators and parties interested in the provisions, until we had prepared a measure which we considered a tariff such as the National Democratic Convention of 1892 recommended," Vest said.

A Democratic caucus was then called to review the bill. "The result was three days of wrangling and acrimonious debate such as I had never heard before and hope never to hear again," said Vest.

The sub-committee's draft was assailed as "absolutely destructive" to Eastern wool manufacturers and Louisiana sugar interests. Louisiana Senator Edward Douglass

Senator Edward White of Louisiana, 1905, who served as the ninth chief justice of the United States from 1910-1921. Photo by Frances Benjamin Johnston.

White (1845-1921) had recently been appointed an associate justice of the U.S. Supreme Court and confirmed by the Senate but retained his seat to participate in the tariff legislation. White said the bill was the equivalent of marching into his state with a Bowie knife in one hand and a torch in the other.

William Whitman (1842-1928), treasurer of Arlington Mills in Lawrence, Massachusetts, responded to a charge made by Vest that the profitable wool manufacturers were collecting the duty and pocketing the proceeds before it could reach the growers. Whitman was outraged by Vest's claims at first but then softened, claiming Vest had been misled by the young Massachusetts Democrats. Whitman offered to open his books to Vest and invited him to visit Arlington Mills to learn the truth.

The truth, according to Vest, was that Whitman was singularly responsible for the wool provisions outlined in the modified Wilson-Gorman Tariff Act. The House significantly cut tariff rates on imports and exports and eliminated tariffs on coal, iron, lumber, and wool imports. The provisions eliminating tariffs on these products greatly angered American businesses as it would hurt profits.

"After three days, the caucus instructed the sub-committee to prepare a bill that could be passed through the Senate," Vest said. "With this nebulous, uncertain, and unsatisfactory result, we were left to grope through the difficulties presented by local and sectional selfishness."

Vest was determined to resign from the sub-committee, leaving what he called a thankless and humiliating task to someone else. "We were compelled to make such concessions to the protective interests as would render the measure utterly unacceptable to ourselves and the Democratic Party," said Vest, who reminded Senators Harris and Jones of the "storm of calumny and slander that was already being poured on them

__Right:__ Senator Isham Harris of Tennessee, who also served as the 16th governor of that state. Brady-Handy Photograph Collection, Library of Congress, Prints and Photographs Division.

__Far right:__ Senator James Kimbrough Jones of Arkansas.

by the newspapers and our enemies, and that this storm would increase in fury if we reported a bill such as would secure a majority in the Senate."

Vest knew they could lose no more than three Democratic votes to pass the bill and suggested that they talk to President Cleveland and Secretary Carlisle, a Kentucky Bourbon Democrat, to confirm that they would back whatever bill the group would be compelled to report.

Harris and Jones called a carriage and went directly to the White House while Vest contemplated his resignation. Carlisle told the pair that passing some tariff bill was necessary or the Democratic Party would be discredited. "He [Carlisle] said he would support us in any legislation we might be able to enact," Vest said. "I told Harris and Jones I would not be satisfied until we heard from the President. The following morning, I saw him [Cleveland] and reported he fully endorsed what Carlisle had said and that he would accept his part of the responsibility for any bill we could pass."

"Reluctantly, I agreed to go on with the disagreeable task placed upon us, but I did so under a sense of duty without any expectation of enacting a tariff law that would meet my wishes or that of the party."

The bill passed the Senate 39-34, but when the House refused to concur, a conference committee was called. It included Vest, Harris, and Jones from the Senate; and from the House, William Lyne Wilson (1843-1900) of West Virginia, Benton McMillin (1845-1933) of Tennessee, and Kentuckian Alexander Brooks Montgomery (1837-1910), who called the amendments un-Democratic.

"We agreed with what they said and explained that the President and Secretary of the Treasury wanted a bill that would pass, and it was the best we could do," Vest said. "I ventured to illustrate the conditions confronting us by telling a story about my experience at a variety theatre and saloon-adjunct in the Far West, which I attended when I was a young man. After the first act of a thrilling drama, the proprietor, dressed in typical costume of the frontier, wearing a flannel shirt, with his trousers in his boots and a large 6-shooter suspended from his leather belt, appeared before the dropped curtain and announced in stentorian tones that Miss Lillie Dale, the celebrated prima donna, would now sing 'Down in the Valley.' A drunken miner shouted, 'Miss Lillie Dale is no good and can't sing worth a damn!' Fixing his eyes upon the offending party, and without any change of countenance or voice, the proprietor repeated, moving his right hand significantly toward his six-shooter, 'Nevertheless and notwithstanding, Miss Lillie Dale will now sing 'Down in the Valley.' And Miss Lillie Dale did sing 'Down in the Valley' without interruption."

After two more weeks, the conferees were unable to agree. President Cleveland sent a letter to the House saying, "The Senate bill then pending was an act of treachery and dishonor to the Democratic Party."

Vest said, "It would have been infinitely better for the country and party if President Cleveland had vetoed the bill and given his reasons plainly and distinctly for doing so. As it was, he furnished the Republicans with an unanswerable argument against all that we could say upon the tariff question."

Vest viewed the experience as a nightmare. "Before the conference ended, three of the conferees broke down under the constant strain," Vest said. "Wilson was attacked by facial erysipelas, and in a few days, I became a victim of the same malady. We sat opposite each other, our faces discolored by iodine—ready for a war dance."

Senator Harris went on the sick list and blamed overwork and constant anxiety. Senator Jones was stricken with angina pectoris. Said Vest, "I have never recovered from the exhaustive labor to which I was subjected during that terrible struggle."

Always up for an exchange with Vest, Hoar taunted him, saying he had missed his aim. Instead of hurting New England manufacturers (as intended), he wounded the corporations of Pennsylvania and West Virginia.

"I am reminded of the man who threw a stone at a yellow dog and instead hit his mother-in-law," Vest said. "While he was sorry he missed the mark, he was glad his effort was not altogether in vain."

In 1894, following "The Panic of 1893," which led to a four-year depression the likes of which the country had not seen, the Senate braced itself for the first March on Washington.

Led by Massillon, Ohio, businessman Jacob Sechler Coxey (1854-1951), it included unemployed workers from across the United States. Nicknamed "Coxey's Army," the march aimed to protest unemployment and lobby for the government's creation of public works jobs.

Jacob S. Coxey, Sr. of Ohio, who twice led unemployed workers across the United States in protest of the lack of jobs in 1894 and 1914.

Senator William Vincent Allen (1847-1925) of Nebraska, the recognized Populist leader in the Senate, introduced a resolution in anticipation of the visit by Coxey's Army:

"Whereas it is currently reported that unarmed, law-abiding and peacefully disposed but unemployed citizens of the United States are about to peacefully assemble in the city of Washington and to 'petition the Government for a redress of their grievances;" and

"Whereas threats of arresting such persons have been made upon their entering the District of Columbia; ..."

Vest was the first to gain recognition following the reading. "I deprecate the introduction of resolutions on this subject from any quarter," said Vest. "It seems that the persons alluded to in the resolution should be treated like other persons in this country. If they observe the law, as a matter of course, they will not be molested. If they violate any law—national, state or municipal—they should be punished."

Vest was offended that such a fundamental right—the right to assemble—must be explained and justified. "That they have the right to come here to visit this capital, to enjoy all the immunities and privileges of other citizens of the United States, is so plain, so unquestioned, that any suspicion regarding it is a reflection upon the intelligence and patriotism of the people of the whole country."

Allowing lawlessness to be linked with protest, Vest said, would divide the country and lead to its destruction.

"If citizens want to come here, employed or unemployed, and visit this capital, inspect the public edifices, or see the operations of the lawmaking department of the country, it goes without saying that they will be protected," Vest said.

Six thousand jobless men made it as far as Colmar Manor, Maryland, but when Coxey and other leaders were arrested for walking on the grass of the United States Capitol, the protest rapidly dwindled.

Vest was not so supportive of 500 followers of William Hogan commandeering a Northern Pacific Railway train for their trek to Washington. "How can you peacefully assemble when your group includes men who have trampled upon the laws, seized private property and undertaken to secure transportation to this city by force of arms?" he asked.

Federal troops apprehended the "Hoganites" near Forsyth, Montana. "Those who have violated the law must abide by the consequences," Vest said.

In August 1894, Wilson read the letter from President Cleveland calling the Senate tariff bill an act of treachery and dishonor to the Democratic Party. "To Vest, this was a tactless act," wrote Dawes. So angered, it led Vest to, in his own words, shine "a calcium light" on the Senate.

According to the *Globe-Democrat*, Vest spared no one. Speaking to a crowded chamber, he presented his defense and vindication. The Wilson-Gorman Bill became law without the president's signature on August 27, 1894. Vest believed that Cleveland should have vetoed the bill.

From 1895 until his death, Marcus Alonzo "Mark" Hanna (1837-1904) was to the Republican Party what General Grant was to the United States during the Civil War. "He possessed none of the qualities necessary to succeed as chairman of the National Republican Committee," Vest said. "The fact that Senator Hanna was a practical businessman who had accumulated a large fortune by his own exertions gave him the entire confidence of the great corporations and capitalists."

According to Vest, Hanna viewed the Declaration of Independence and Washington's Farewell Address as relics.

After McKinley became president in 1896, Hanna was appointed by Ohio Governor Asa Bushnell (1834-1904) to the Senate to fill the unexpired term of John Sherman, who was named secretary of state. "It was my fortune to meet Senator Hanna in debate when he delivered his first prepared speech on the Ship Subsidy Bill reported by the Senate Committee on Commerce, of which we were both members," Vest said. "He was not an orator, but his terse, epigrammatic, and incisive arguments commanded the earnest attention of all his colleagues, and from that time, he was recognized as one of the strongest debaters in the Senate."

Vest said Hanna overlooked the bill's constitutionality. Hanna wanted the $150 million paid by taxpayers to foreign ships for carrying their exports abroad to go to American shipowners to equalize the difference in cost between building ships domestically and abroad. "He dwelt on our coastal trade [being] the largest in the world, and he attributed this to the exclusion of foreign-built ships from the trade between American ports."

Vest spent the summer of 1895 abroad, trying to revive his poor health, and wisely missed a silver convention held in Pertle Springs, Missouri. Vest, a long-time Silverite, believed the United States should take the lead and show that bimetallism could work. "It is generally conceded that England will not alter the gold standard," said Vest from Carlsbad, California, where he attended a monetary conference.

On September 18, the press broke the news that free coinage supporters had lost Vest as an ally because he had changed his mind on silver, which was not true. Upon arrival in New York, Vest said the "damned newspapers had falsified and misrepresented" his actions and opinions. When asked if he would support a candidate running on the gold platform, he said, "I will not be driven from the Democratic party by any set of men. I have given my life to its principles. I shall die in its faith. I will go into that [1896 Democratic Party] convention and do all I can to secure the nomination [for president] of someone who believes in bimetallism and the free and unlimited coinage of gold and silver."

Vest unenthusiastically nominated Bland and eventually threw his support behind William Jennings Bryan (1860-1925), who lost to McKinley.

In February 1896, Vest's logic won recognition of the Cuban Republic.

Senator George Gray (1840-1925) of Delaware called Vest's plea one of the most eloquent addresses ever given in the Senate. "If the independence of Cuba could be achieved by eloquence, it has been this afternoon by the burning words that have fallen from the lips of the Senator for Missouri," Gray said. "No one could have heard him without sympathizing with the feelings with which his heart was throbbing and without giving favorable response to every aspiration that he has uttered for liberty in Cuba."

Gray and Senator Stephen Mallory White (1853-1901) of California argued that Cuba had not reached the proper stage in its struggle to warrant recognition of independence.

"If France had acted upon the doctrine announced by the Senator from California and waited until our fathers had achieved their own independence, the result would have been far different, and we today would be English subjects instead of free citizens of a free country," Vest said. "If we, as the great Republic of the world, mean to stand by those people who are imitating us and endeavoring to make a government for themselves like that of this country, we must help them in their hour of need."

Vest denounced Spain's treatment of Cuba and compared it to a toothless old she-wolf with one cub sitting at the "dark door of despotism."

Several senators asked if recognition of Cuban independence would not eventually mean annexation. Vest's response: Maybe. "While I resisted on the Hawaiian question, the project which was brought here to annex Hawaii to the United States, I did it upon the ground that it would necessitate an immense naval force to keep it an integral portion of the United States. Jefferson stated, and I believe it to be true, that no navy would be necessary to hold Cuba as a state. If that be so, it is simply a question as to the fitness of the population of that island to become citizens of the United States and take upon themselves the responsibilities of citizenship."

Others asked if the president's declaration would spark retaliation from Spain.

"Are we," Vest pleaded, "a Christian and God-fearing people, to stand silent and dumb while the Spanish general declares that he intends to pen up the people of Cuba and butcher them into subjection to the Spanish throne? Sir, if we do, God will curse us ... Liberty lives with the poor and oppressed."

Vest's resolution passed 64-6, but President Cleveland ignored it, and conditions went from bad to worse.

In 1896, Vest was in Kansas City for the dedication of Swope Park, a 1,300-acre gift to the city by Colonel Thomas Swope, Vest's classmate at Centre College in 1848. "In these days of greed and selfishness, where the whole world is permeated with the feverish pursuit of money, it is refreshing to find a millionaire who is thinking of humanity and not wealth," Vest said during the two-hour speech. "Tom made his fortune and has been compelled to fight many unscrupulous and designing men, but he has risen above the sordid love of gain and shown himself possessed of the best and highest motives."

Before the park gift, Swope, Kansas City's largest landowner, was more known for his frugality—he commuted to work by streetcar until a month before his death. "Intellectually, he has few superiors," Vest continued. "The public has never known his literary tastes, culture, and love of the good and beautiful. The world assumes no man can accumulate wealth without being hard and selfish, which is too often the case, but not so with Tom. In these gifts, he repays himself with the consciousness of a great, unselfish act."

When's Vest's friend died a decade later, his sudden death became the focus of one of the most publicized murder trials of the early 20th century.

In 1897, Cushman Kellogg Davis, a senator from Minnesota and an imperialist, became chair of the Senate Foreign Relations Committee and was closely involved in the sequence of events leading to the Spanish-American War, which lasted for four months in 1898 and expanded the U.S. presence in the Caribbean. The Treaty of Paris, which Davis signed, resulted in the U.S. acquisition of the Philippines.

"When the treaty was submitted to the Senate, the Democrats who opposed its ratification thought it impolite to hold a party caucus, appointed a committee of three Senators—Jones, Gorman [Arthur Pue Gorman (1839-1906)] and myself—who were instructed to confer personally with every Senator not known to be favorable to the treaty and ascertain his position as to its ratification," Vest said.

Gorman, a founding member of the original Washington Nationals and an early baseball star, was a Bourbon Democrat credited with getting Cleveland re-elected.

The committee reported a deadlock, with most Republicans favoring and four Republicans joining the Democrats and Populists in opposition. But then Vermont Senator Justin Smith Morrill (1810-1898), a Republican who strenuously opposed taking the Philippines, died. His successor, Jonathan Ross (1826-1905), appointed by Vermont Governor Edward Curtis Smith (1854-1935), favored ratification.

Bryan, a colonel in the Spanish-American War, resigned his commission and came to Washington to urge his political friends to vote for the treaty. He said that, once approved, a joint resolution could be adopted against the colonial system and give self-government to the Philippines. If the treaty were rejected, the war between the U.S. and Spain would be renewed, leading to heavy losses.

"I told Colonel Bryan that I would, under no circumstances, vote for the Paris Treaty; that there could be no continuation of the war because Spain was utterly helpless, and any joint resolution adopted by the Senate would be thrown into the wastebasket by the House," Vest said.

The Senate eventually ratified the treaty 57-27. An amendment declaring that the U.S. pledged itself to give the people of the Philippines the right to govern themselves

Left: *Vice President Garret Hobart, who died in office on November 21, 1899. Davis and Sanford photo, Library of Congress, Prints and Photographs Division.* ***Center:*** *U.S. Secretary of State William Jennings Bryan of Nebraska, 1913. Harris & Ewing, photographer, Library of Congress, Prints and Photographs Division.* ***Right:*** *Senator Justin Smith Morrill of Vermont, ca. 1855-65. Brady-Handy Photograph Collection, Library of Congress, Prints and Photographs Division.*

ended in a 29-29 tie. Vice President Garret A. Hobart (1844-1899) voted against the resolution.

Bryan, "The Great Commoner," would become a fierce opponent of American imperialism. He was the Democratic nominee for president in 1896, 1900, and 1908, and served as Secretary of State from 1913-1915 under President Woodrow Wilson (1856-1924).

As for Morrill, elected five times to the Senate and considered one of his generation's "purest" public servants, Vest said, "He had no ambition except to perform his official duties honestly and faithfully. It was my good fortune to enjoy his confidence and friendship during the 20 years I had served with him in the Senate."

Morrill died on December 28, 1898. Said Vest: "If all those to whom he did acts of kindness could whisper across his grave, it would make an anthem sweeter and more sonorous than any that ever pealed through a cathedral aisle."

Within a year of passage, the Wilson-Gorman Tariff Act failed to pass judicial review. Due to the financial depression, inept leadership, lobbies and greed, the law was never popular with the public, prompting McKinley to call a special session of Congress in 1897, leading to the Dingley Tariff, which raised protective rates to their highest point since the Civil War—in Vest's view, another example of "outrageous oppression on the common people just to feed the cormorant greed of the trusts."

Vest told the *Kansas City Times* that, after a trying session on the tariff question, he, Nelson Wilmarth Aldrich (1841-1915) and Matthew Stanley Quay (1833-1904) were riding the railcars home from the debates when a poor, raggedy, under-nourished newspaper boy boarded the car. Vest refused to buy a paper. Aldrich (a Republican) remarked as he started fumbling for some pennies, "Oh, come, Vest, let's encourage the infant industry.'" But the Rhode Islander could find no pennies, so he asked Vest to loan him 3 cents. As Vest did so, he grumbled, "Yes, that's the way with you Republicans. You are always willing to encourage infant industries at some other person's expense."

In January 1899, Vest and industrialist Andrew Carnegie (1835-1919) penned paired articles against imperialism and the annexation of the Philippines in *The North American Review*. Carnegie was a determined foe of what he called "territorial aggrandizement" in "Americanism versus Imperialism." Vest believed it was hypocritical for a country that broke away from an empire to create one of its own.

American industrialist Andrew Carnegie, 1913. Photo by Theodore Marceau.

Vest, in part, wrote: "I am opposed to annexing the Philippines because such annexation makes the people of those islands ultimately citizens of the United States, and necessitates the admission of the territory thus acquired as a State.

"The idea of conferring American citizenship upon the half-civilized, piratical, muck-running inhabitants of 2,000 islands, 7,000 miles distant, in another hemisphere, and creating a State of the Union from such materials, is so absurd and indefensible that the expansionists are driven to the necessity of advocating the colonial system of Europe, against which the American Colonies revolted when the King of England attempted its application to them."

Vest argued that it insulted our ancestors who suffered and died so the U.S. could consider adopting a colonial system when they fought for seven years to break free of Great Britain.

"The fact is ignored that the first four years of the Revolutionary War were fought against the colonial system of Europe, which was based upon the cardinal principle of monarchy, that millions of people could be held as colonial subjects, governed by laws in the making of which they had no part, and under whose exaction they were impoverished by unjust and excessive taxes," Vest wrote.

Vest continued, "Our fathers took up arms against the most powerful nation in the world. In 1776, Jefferson framed the Declaration of Independence, the foundation stone of which is the sublime truth that 'all governments derive their just powers from the consent of the governed.'"

Vest cited five Supreme Court cases to support his position that annexation was unconstitutional and noted that the Articles of Confederation contained no provision for acquiring new territory. James Madison, Vest wrote, argued in adopting the Constitution of 1789 that Congress was preserving principles of freedom for which it raged against England. "The ordinance of 1787, providing for the government and disposition of the Northwest Territory, established self-government for the people in the ceded territory, and the same enactment is found in treaties made with France, Spain, Mexico, and Russia for the cession of Louisiana, Florida, the northern part of Mexico and Alaska," Vest wrote.

In short, Vest wanted nothing to do with the Philippine Islands: "I would oppose annexation if, instead of paying $20 million [which the U.S. agreed to pay Spain for the island nation], we could receive five times that sum for taking them."

Based on federal efforts to educate Native Americans, Vest claimed the U.S. would spend at least $100 million without certainty it would make the Filipinos law-abiding and intelligent citizens. Vest questioned the revenue that proponents claimed could be generated by the Philippines. "Assuming that the United States would degrade itself by licensing gambling, lotteries, cockfighting, and the sale of opium," he wrote, Vest claimed enterprising carpetbaggers and hungry political appointees would eat up any possible gains delighted with a "new field of plunder."

Vest claimed that colonialism brings war, noting that only two years of Queen Victoria's long reign (1837-1901), which began when the Senator was a 6-year-old on the Kentucky frontier, had been in peace. "Why should we now disregard the counsel of Washington, that: 'The great rule of conduct for us regarding foreign nations is, in extending our commercial relations, to have with them as little political connection as possible?'"

In 1900, Senator Hanna took charge of the Republican presidential campaign and attacked the Democratic platform that denounced imperialism and trusts. "There are good and bad trusts, the latter largely predominating," Hanna said.

"When I met Senator Hanna afterward in Washington, I congratulated him upon his courage and candor," Vest said. "I told him that I was opposed politically to the Republican party, collectively and individually, but I had much more respect for a man who was consistent and logical."

Senator Mark Hanna of Ohio, 1896. Photo by W.J. Root.

Vest said that he grew to admire Hanna's qualities. "He was brave, frank and without the taint of hypocrisy," Vest said. "He was a hard fighter and a strong and bitter partisan, but he never struck below the belt, and there was never any doubt about his position on public questions."

In 1900, *The Chicago Journal* pronounced Vest "that great big little fellow with a tremendous intellect in a body so small and emaciated." It asserted that he was "still half the brains of the Democratic side of the Senate."

In Vest's version of the quote, which appeared in the Baltimore newspapers, he said, "I am a short, broad man, but my enemies say my speeches are both long and narrow."

On March 14, 1900, the gold standard was firmly established. Wrote Dawes, "Though feeble and scarcely able to stand, he [Vest] made his last valiant but ineffectual fight against what he called 'the vilest monopoly ever created.'"

In his autobiography, Massachusetts Senator Hoar said of Vest: "No list of the remarkable Senators of my time would be complete which did not contain the name of Senator Vest of Missouri. He was not a frequent speaker and never spoke at great length. But his oratorical powers are of a high order. On some few occasions, he has made speeches, always speaking without notes, and I suppose without previous preparations so far as expression and style go, which have deeply moved the Senate, though made up of men who have been accustomed to oratory and not easily stirred to emotion."

Hoar, a Republican who served in the Senate from 1877 to his death in 1904, described Vest as brave, sincere, spirited, and straightforward. "He has many of the prejudices of the old Southern secessionist ... his chivalrous nature will not permit him to abandon a cause or an opinion to which he has once adhered, while it is unpopular."

"He gradually acquired power and became the Democratic leader by sheer intellectual force," wrote the *Saint Louis Post-Dispatch* in 1902. "No man on the Democratic side had more qualities fitting him for leadership. He knew men, their strength and weakness; he could dazzle with oratory or shine with repartee; his memory was prodigious, and the facility with which he drew upon his stores of information won him the admiration" of Democrats and Republicans alike.

Vest was wedded to the "Lost Cause" and lashed out at anyone disparaging the South and its antiquated leaders, living and dead, decades after the war ended.

On April 20, 1891, in a convention speech given to Missouri's former Confederates, Vest said, "In all revolutions, the vanquished are the ones who are guilty of treason, even by the historians, for history is written by the victors and framed according to the prejudices and bias existing on their side."

The phrase "history is written by the victors" lives on more than 130 years after Vest's utterance.

Bryan and McKinley met again in the 1900 election, but Vest's health prevented his active participation. Instead, he conducted interviews on the veranda of his massive Sweet Springs cottage. He sat in his rocker, the image of a Kentucky colonel, railing against imperialism. He predicted a Republican victory based mainly on a conversation he said he overheard at a Sweet Springs barbershop between two local farmers:

"Bill, what'ya think of the election?"

"Dunno, Jim. You know I've always been a Democrat. Dad was before me and Grandpap before him. But, Jim, I'll tell ya, I'm getting $32 more a head for my mules than I ever did. Derned if I don't think I'll have to put one in for Bill Kinley this time."

"I reckon you're right, Bill. I doin' better on hogs than I've ever done. I don't want anything to spoil a good thing. I don't want no change."

"There has been no other personality in public life like unto his," wrote Henry M. Rose (1859-1932), chief clerk of the U.S. Senate, of Vest in 1902. "He has been a leader in national affairs, no less than in his party councils—wise, conscientious, industrious, patriotic, faithful, and brave. With all these characteristics, there is no wonder that he has a large and delighted audience on the floor whenever he addresses himself to the Senate. At the same time, crowded galleries were constantly at the point of enthusiasm as their occupants caught his every word.

"He has been universally regarded as the most entertaining and attractive orator in the Senate," Rose said. "His speeches are remarkable for brilliant oratory, purity of diction, pungent sarcasm, sparkling humor, and historical reminiscence."

As in his days in the Confederate Congress and Senate, Vest was at home in the U.S. Senate, surrounded by friends and acquaintances from his youth, including Kentucky Senator Joseph Blackburn, an 1857 Centre College graduate who, as did Vest, attended Sayre's academy. Blackburn, the younger brother of Kentucky Governor Luke Pryor Blackburn (1816-1887), married Sarah Therese Graham (1833-1899), Vest's cousin, in 1858. Blackburn's career, like Vest's, would be marked by support of the free silver issue and the Panama Canal.

Vest's senatorial career, according to more than one biographical account, was characterized by a reluctance to recognize new developments and issues in American life; he adhered largely to bygone principles and precedents.

One example was his uncompromising views on women's suffrage. "What man can, without aversion, turn from the blessed memory of that dear old grandmother, or the gentle word and caressing hand of that blessed mother gone to the unknown world, to face in its stead the idea of a female justice of the peace or township constable?" Vest asked. "For my part, I want, when I go to my home, when I turn from the arena where man contends with man for what we call the prizes of this paltry world, to go back, not to be received in the masculine embraces of some female ward politician, but to the earnest, loving look and touch of a true woman. I would not, and I say it deliberately, degrade a woman by giving her the right of suffrage. Woman as she is today, the queen of the home and hearts, is above the political collisions of this world and should always be kept above them."

During the debate, Vest quoted women who were opposed to woman suffrage. Hoar declared Vest was refuting his own argument. "Everybody knows," said Hoar, "my honorable friend from Missouri is one of the most brilliant men in this country. He is a logician, an orator, a man of large experience and a lawyer, and yet when called upon to put forth this great effort of this afternoon, what did he do? He furnished the gush and eloquence, but when he came to any arguments, he had to call upon two women to supply that."

Vest also opposed the election of senators by popular vote. He claimed it would create new temptations of fraud and corruption. "Who pretends to say," Vest asked, "that this body—90 in number—is not equal in integrity, in intelligence, in all the great qualities of a representative capacity" to any group selected by popular vote.

Vest quoted Madison, Hamilton and Jefferson to support his stance. "I probably belong to a past school of public life, but I think the Constitution should be approached carefully," Vest said. "I believe the men who made the Constitution prescribed the form to be adopted to avoid this desire on the part of demagogues to achieve their purposes by flattering the people.

"If the fountain is impure, so will the stream be ... yet we are told that if we change the form of the election, we will get rid of the impurity."

To Vest, Dawes concluded, the argument was futile, reminding him of another story.

"I am," Vest explained, "a Western man, and so I will use a Western illustration of the countryman who, on a hot day, was taking a bag of corn to the mill. He saw that his horse was laboring under the heat and the burden placed upon him, and in order to relieve the animal, the rider got off, took the bag of corn upon his own shoulder, got back upon the horse and congratulated himself that he found a solution."

Former Missouri Governor William Joel Stone (1848-1918) was slated to replace Vest in the Senate, and Vest did not like the feeling that his days were numbered. During a Florida fishing trip with Amos Jay Cummings (1838-1902) to Quay's St. Lucie, Florida, home, Vest called Cummings' attention to a buzzard perched upon a snag in the tidewater, watching a wounded, floundering fish.

Senator William J. Stone of Missouri. National Photo Company Collection, Library of Congress, Prints and Photographs Division.

"Cummings, you are unable to see in this spectacle what I do," Vest said. "The reason is because you are unfamiliar with Missouri politics. That wounded fish there is your humble servant, G.G. Vest, and that ravenous buzzard with those protuberant eyes is Bill Stone. I can't help but hope some other buzzard will sweep down and get that fish when it dies."

According to Dawes, Quay was one of Vest's warmest friends and a frequent fishing partner. "Senatorial duty was stronger than friendship," she wrote. In April 1900, it fell to Vest to decide an embarrassing situation, which he told the *Boonville Weekly Advertiser* was one of his most "painful incidents." In 1899, Quay's second term, he failed for reelection because he was under trial for gross misapplication of Pennsylvania state funds. His attorney pleaded the statute of limitations had expired, and Quay was acquitted, yet the legislature refused to reelect him to the Senate. Pennsylvania Governor William Alexis Stone (1846-1920) appointed Quay a senator during the adjournment. The following winter, the U.S. Senate had to vote on whether to seat or reject him. A roll call vote was tied 32-32, and the decision came down to Vest.

With head bowed and in an almost inaudible voice, Vest voted to reject Quay.

"Such devotion to duty was highly praised in the newspaper," Dawes said.

Several years later, Senator Julius C. Burrows (1837-1915) of Michigan said, "Do you remember Vest's vote in the Quay case? They were as brothers; Senator Vest made an exhaustive examination of the law, and he concluded that Quay had no right to the seat. Many would have found it convenient to remain away from the Senate, but when the vote was taken, Vest's rigid honesty would not allow such an evasion."

While Vest was hampered by his allegiance to Southern ideals, the only link between him and Senator John Tyler Morgan, a 30-year senator from Alabama who is considered largely responsible for creating the Jim Crow Era, came with them on opposite ends of an item close to Vest's heart and adopted state. In May 1900, Morgan strongly

Senator John Tyler Morgan of Alabama, ca. 1901.

opposed a bill to provide a $5 million government loan to the upcoming 1904 World's Fair in Saint Louis, which would commemorate the centennial of the Louisiana Purchase and the Lewis and Clark Expedition.

Other than the Panama Canal, Morgan opposed most measures that didn't center on forging his ideology of white supremacy or the forced migration of Blacks out of the United States.

"Our people are not in a condition to pay this amount of money, levied upon them by the tax collector, for the glory and honor of any place, and more particularly, is that a fact when we get no sympathy from Saint Louis or Missouri and no assistance, as far as we know, upon which the resurrection of the South depends," Morgan said. "We have no encouragement, no sympathy, no assistance."

Vest's immediate response: "I do not know to what measure the Senator refers when he says Missouri has no sympathy with the South. Missouri showed during the war and since the war her deepest and earnest sympathy with the South and solicitude for her interests. There has never been a measure before the Senate that I have not supported earnestly and vigorously to rebuild the Southern people and bring them back to prosperity."

Vest questioned the length of Morgan's memory. "I stood here at the expense of my health and risk of my life to prevent legislation that I thought, and the Senator from Alabama said, would ruin his state and the entire Southern people. I was under the impression that I was of the South and that I was doing all I could to rebuild her ruined industries and desolated fields."

Vest proposed that the government would share in the profit of the World's Fair, receiving as much as $11 million. "Sixteen states and territories are included in the Louisiana Purchase, with more than 20 million people, and valuations of billions of dollars, paying thousands of millions of revenues to the Treasury of the United States each year," he said.

"Are we asking too much, when we consider what Chicago received?" Vest asked, referencing the 1893 World's Columbian Exposition, commemorating the 400th anniversary of Columbus' arrival in the Western Hemisphere. Chicago received $4.7 million and minted 2.5 million souvenir half-dollars sold for $1 each. Vest reported that the citizens of Saint Louis had committed $11 million, and the Senate's $5 million was "not out of proportion."

Vest's career was winding down, so he urged reconciliation in the still-divided country. "My public career will end in a very few months, and I had fondly expected after the Spanish-American War that the men of the North and of the South, who stood like brothers against a foreign foe, would continue to stand like brothers in this time of peace," he said. "Those of the South are sincere mourners at the graves of Lincoln, Grant, and McKinley, and no more honest tears were ever shed than those dropped upon the bier of our last president [McKinley, who was assassinated in 1901], from the eyes of men who had faced in battle the soldiers of the North during four long years. People of the North should remember that the South, too, has produced great and good and patriotic leaders.

"They should remember Washington, Jefferson, Lee were slave-holders and differed widely upon that question with their brothers in the northern states. I shall never cease to feel kindly toward the present occupant of the White House [Theodore Roosevelt] for what he said in the broad spirit of statesmanship and as a historian of the life of Thomas H. Benton, regarding Lee. He said Lee was by far the greatest general that ever came from English-speaking races."

On April 11, 1902, Vest rose and, tremblingly, stated: "I hope I may be pardoned if I speak briefly of Wade Hampton, whose memory will live for centuries to come among the people not only of the South but of the whole country. I knew him well and loved him sincerely. He was the highest type of Christian gentleman: patient, brave, honest, and unselfish. He was not depressed by adversity or unduly elated by prosperity. Having lost all except life and honor, he bowed submissively to the result of the great war, in which he shared the fortunes of his people."

Massachusetts Senator Henry Cabot Lodge (1850-1924), one of the most informed statesmen of his time, praised Vest's speech, especially when he spoke of Roosevelt, Lee and Hampton: "Everyone must share with me the feeling of deep emotion with which we have this morning listened to his eloquence, always beautiful and impressive, but never more than on this occasion."

In July 1902, *The Sedalia Sentinel* reported Senator Vest was totally blind. "His mental faculties are unimpaired, however, and he rarely misses a day in the Senate," the newspaper wrote. Vest's rapid decline began in early November 1902. *The American Times-Recorder* reported on November 8, 1902, that George Jr., the private secretary to his father, died between 3 and 6 a.m. the previous morning. The desk clerk at the Columbia Hotel in Washington said he saw George Jr. at 3 a.m. when he asked for ice water and complained of not feeling well. When the clerk checked on him again after 6, he was dead. The attending doctor, Frederick Henry Morhart (1875-1947), ruled the cause of death as "convulsions due to acute gastritis." George Jr. was 42.

In 1902, the *Saint Louis Post-Dispatch* said of Vest: "He is a little man, big only in mentality." According to the paper, Vest played the role of minority leader well. "Vest has strongly influenced all legislation on which the party had a decided policy. His part in the tariff battles, his fight for silver, and his failure to defeat colonial policy have affected history strongly. Leading a minority, he could not gain the fame of positive victories, but by restriction and limitation, he accomplished much of permanent value."

With George Jr. gone, the weight of ongoing battles fell heavier and heavier on Vest, especially points of order, which were often disregarded.

On February 16, 1903, Vest declared, "My experience in a great many years' service in this body is that the Senate of the United States, that is, the majority, generally does what it wants to do without regard to the rules. I have never known an instance when the sentiment in the Senate was decidedly in favor of certain legislation, that the rule was not overridden and disregarded if the Senate could possibly get a vote as to the rule."

In early March 1903, Senator Hanna came to Vest's seat. "He expressed in the kindest terms his regret that I was about to leave public life and hoped that my health would be restored so I could return to Washington," Vest recalled. "I thanked him and said that I considered my public career closed, that from present indications, he might be out of the Senate and in the White House if I ever came back to that capital." Hanna responded that he had no intention of running for president. "If in good health, I should esteem it my duty to accept the office of President if tendered by my party, but I am suffering greatly from rheumatism caused, as the doctors tell me, by a chalky deposit in my joints, and I do not think I should live six months if made President of the United States.

"Besides," he said, "I am not superstitious, but the history of presidents from Ohio is gruesome. William Henry Harrison died one month after his inauguration; Hayes was elected only after a terrible struggle, by a majority of one vote in the Electoral College; and Garfield and McKinley were assassinated. No, I shall devote the remainder of my public life to healing the breach between capital and labor, which is the burning issue of the day."

By the end of his senatorial career, Vest had earned numerous friends on both sides of the chamber, including Hanna. "I know of no other instance in our political history where a man came directly from the counting room to the United States Senate without any training or experience in public affairs and stepped at once into the front rank as a debater and was also unquestionably the most influential citizen of the country in public affairs, not excepting even the president," Vest said of Hanna.

Vest effectively retired from the Senate on a bitterly cold day in January 1903.

A national coal strike had ended, but the controllers of coal banded together, creating a near monopoly. While the price should have fallen because of increased production, a tariff made importation impossible. It was winter, and demand outpaced supply. Public opinion favored the removal of the tax.

Vest presented a bill to remove the tariff duty from hard coal, which had sent the price of coke from $3 a ton to more than $16 per ton.

"The Senate was in an animated, almost hysterical session," reported *The Saturday Evening Post*. "The leaderless, planless, and helpless Democratic minority lounged listless and feeble at their desks.

"Among the minority, facing the unnerved lions, stood, or instead was propped, a mere mite of a human being. His body was so small and shrunken that his head was scarcely a foot and a half above the level of his desk. His black clothes hung in bags upon his wasted body, and it seemed to be able to stand only because it was wedged between chair and desk.

"A splendid brow adorned his light, white hair; a skin of waxen pallor; eyes deep set in dark sockets and beneath lids that seemed to have risen for the last time; a snow-white mustache shading a mouth that seemed set in the rigor of death. And a few feet behind the propped figure stood a watchful attendant [James "Jimmy" Edwards], ready to catch it should it become loosened from its propping.

"Such was the astounding spectacle which the galleries watched with amazement. The lions gazed as if fascinated, and their looks concentrated upon this strange and corpselike apparition of insignificance."

Vest spoke in a thin, clear, high voice. "There was power in that voice, there was something unrelenting and supremely dangerous in its ominous calmness and evenness," the *Post* reported. "And each word it sent with the deliberation of the trained marksman into the ranks of the majority caused a quiver or a flush. How was it possible for this one man, standing in the grave itself, to produce such an effect upon these men of might? Why were they shrinking in terror before this incarnation of helplessness?"

From all reports, Vest had spent a month arming himself for this last Senate fight. He waited for the moment to take on Rhode Island Senator Nelson Wilmarth Aldrich (1841-1915), the grandfather of Nelson, David, and John D. Rockefeller, who supported the tariff staying in place.

"His speech was calm and simple, a passionless arraying of merciless facts—the monopoly, the tariff, licensed extortion, the suffering of the people," wrote the *Post*. Aldrich struggled to respond as if the diminished figure of Vest cast a spell over him, taking the glibness from his tongue, the plausibility of his objections. Senator Hoar argued the Senate lacked the Constitutional right to originate Vest's measure but quickly fell under the same spell in response to his life-in-death appearance.

Vest demolished the plea of technicality and renewed his demand. His voice was tranquil and logical, with his rapier steadfastly aimed at the craven and quaking heart of "the interests."

Vest proclaimed that the nation was not on the verge of a coal crisis but was already in one. "Consumers are being plundered day by day and hour by hour," he said.

According to the *Post*, a succession of speakers addressed Vest's arguments, but each struggled. Their tongues tripped, their sentences entangled, and their rhetoric faltered, fizzled, sputtered, and expired as the galleries leaned in breathless disbelief.

It was clear to Aldrich that while Vest, who again put principle above pocketbook, was in the minority in the Senate, he was in line with the desires of most people. Aldrich quickly offered to sacrifice one "interest" to avoid cutting all "the interests" out of the tariff. The duty was taken off coal; the coal crowd quickly lowered prices before importation could begin. The public knew Vest was behind the tumbling prices.

It was Vest's last Senate appearance. Once the issue was resolved, Edwards helped Vest from the hall back home to his bed.

Vest's last act as a senator was having Edwards, with whom he'd briefly served in Sterling Price's Army in 1861, named Senate doorkeeper, a post he held until 1917, a dozen years after Vest's death.

"We were friends," Edwards said.

CHAPTER ELEVEN

The Great Missourian

Indiana Senator C.W. Fairbanks (1852-1918) said Vest ended his Senate career with the "cordial personal esteem of every member of the Senate, Republican, Democrat and otherwise."

After leaving the Senate, Vest spent time at the Saint Louis home of his daughter and his "beloved cottage" in Sweet Springs, which he had built in 1882 at the zenith of his political career. When built, Sweet Springs was a retreat for many of Missouri's prominent citizens—both in the political and business arena—who frequented the hotel or the cottages. In addition to Vest, Missouri Governors Lon V. Stephens and John Sappington Marmaduke (1833-1887), a former Confederate general, had cottages there. They were drawn by the springs. Vest, who thought the proper water could cure most any ailment, searched the world over, and visited the principal watering places of Europe, drinking and bathing in the springs of Germany, Italy, and Switzerland, never to find any he liked more than in Sweet Springs.

"I met him the last time at Hot Springs, Arkansas," said T.T. Crittenden, who said Vest was trying to restore his health. "He was then greatly depleted, only weighed 89 pounds. Still, there were at times a gleam of the old Vest whom I had known for so many years. He said to me in one of our social talks, 'Crittenden, I am making a hard fight for life, and death may be the victor in the end;' and it was.

"Seeing him in that enfeebled condition made me love him the more, made me cast behind the little ill tempers of the past. Had I 10,000 more causes for resentment, the sight of the great man at that time would have dissipated into thin air all those causes."

During Vest's lifetime, Sweet Springs, named for its sweet-tasting magnesium springs, saw its peak as a summer vacation destination and then fell almost into obscurity. Fire destroyed the hotel. The lawns and roadways become unkempt, and many of the cottages were in tumble-down condition. All that remained were the springs and a beautifully shaded and unusually cool retreat. It was Vest's favorite place, and it was there that he chose to retire and write a "charming series" of articles for *The Saturday Evening Post* (1903-04). It was a return to his roots as a correspondent for one newspaper and the founder of another.

Judge Philips visited Vest at Sweet Springs. "He was blind, beyond the capacity to read, his emaciated body unable to support him even in a chair, his physical forces gone, he lay in his bed, unaided by amanuensis or recourse to memoranda, and thought out his subject," Philips said. "When his mind became aware of the matter, he asked for a stenographer, the son of an old, cherished friend [William Muir (1825-1872) of Boonville]. His voice was so feeble that the stenographer had to sit close to the bed; he dictated with exactness as to dates, historical facts, and apposite quotations."

Assisted by stenographer Hugh Draffen Muir (1869-1950), Vest worked daily from 9 a.m. to 9 p.m., recalling a wealth of incidents, quotes, and dates from memory, including the letter from Jefferson Davis. "His memory was as clear as the crystal water of his loved springs, and his mind as keen as the best days of his political career," wrote *The Saint Louis Republican.*

"When this was done, scarcely a word or phrase needed correction or revision," Philips said.

Vest dictated his memoirs to Muir, who had 53 years of experience as a court reporter. Muir transcribed and edited his notes to send to the magazine.

While he didn't live to see it, Vest predicted that silver would not be an issue in 1904 and that Bryan would never be president. "But" added Vest, "Our party is not dependent on the fate of any one man. It survived the death of Jefferson and will the disappearance of Bryan," Vest told *The Saint Louis Republican.*

Adolphus Busch, president and co-founder of Anheuser-Busch. Vest represented the brewing industry before the U.S. Supreme Court against the state of Kansas in 1887, a case that they won.

On his passing, the typical story read: *George Graham Vest, U.S. Senator, C.S.A. Congressman, Confederate veteran, conservationist, and champion for the rights of Native Americans, died on August 9, 1904, in Sweet Springs, Saline Co., Mo. He was buried in Bellefontaine Cemetery in Saint Louis.*

Before Vest's death, while visiting his daughter, Mollie Jackson, in Saint Louis, Adolphus Busch, who with Eberhard Anheuser built the Anheuser-Busch brewing dynasty, offered him the use of a private railcar—*The Adolphus*—to tour the country.

"When a man is in office, he has many friends; when out, few do him any reverence," Vest told his daughter and son, Alex, after the meeting. "Mr. Busch is the kind of a friend that sticks whether one is in or out."

Vest's friendship with Busch began March 7, 1861, when Vest and city councilman and omnibus proprietor Erastus Wells (1823-1893) crashed the social event of the year—the double wedding of brothers Adolphus and Ulrich Busch Jr. (1833-1925) to sisters Elizabeth Lilly (1844-1928) and Anna Anheuser (1838-1916), the daughters of Adolphus' partner, Eberhard Anheuser (1806-1880).

"He [Adolphus] asked me as a favor to him to take this car and travel about anywhere I wanted to go, California, Florida—anywhere—and to take my family and stay as long as I wanted," Vest said. He declined the offer but said it and another offer, a gift of $100,000, were among the sweetest gestures in his life. According to Vest, Busch said: "I have plenty. My heirs will never miss what I give you."

"I answered him that my means were sufficient to care for my family," Vest said. "I thanked him from the bottom of my heart." When Vest died, Busch was the only non-family member in his will: "My cane, which is a silver snake, shall be delivered to my friend, Adolphus Busch, and my other canes are to be distributed among my friends as my executors may think appropriate."

By the standards of the day, Vest was a wealthy man. According to the *Saint Louis Republican*, his estate was valued at close to $200,000 ($6.67 million in 2024 dollars), built on several wise investments in Kansas City real estate and stocks in solid Washington institutions. Not a bad rebound for a man who was penniless in 1867.

As a young man, Vest said he "earned money like a gentleman and spent it like a thoroughbred."

The bulk of his estate went to Sallie. The rest was evenly divided among Mollie and her three children; the children of his deceased son, George; and Alex and his daughter.

About four days before his death, Vest was unable to speak and at times was unconscious. At 5 o'clock in the morning of August 9, he passed away at his cottage. Messages of condolence came from all parts of the United States, and extra help was added to the telegraph force to manage the incoming messages.

A service was held at 4:30 the following afternoon with the Reverend John C. Shackleford (1847-1911), an intimate friend of Vest, presiding. After the service, his body was taken on a private car to Saint Louis, arriving at Union Station on August 11. More than 800 mourners, including the board of directors of the World's Fair and a committee appointed by Missouri Governor Alexander Monroe Dockery (1845-1926), met the car on its arrival.

The casket was opened at the train station, and once friends had paid their respects, he was taken to Bellefontaine Cemetery.

Vest died amid the World's Fair in Saint Louis, an event he and his godson, immediate past Governor Lon Vest Stephens, helped Missouri secure before Vest left the Senate the year before. All public buildings were closed, and Governor Dockery ordered flags raised to half-staff and suspended state business in Vest's honor. "Since the admission

Congressman Champ Clark, ca. 1900-10. Photo by Harris & Ewing, Library of Congress, Prints and Photographs Division.

of Missouri to the Union, her sons have borne a conspicuous part in all great controversies, but among them, none achieved greater distinction than our distinguished, departed Senator," Dockery said. "Indeed, it was more than mere distinction. He rose to greatness."

Congressman "Champ" Clark, another Missouri transplant from Kentucky, said Vest was among the best and brightest of the 22 men who served Missouri in Congress in its then-83 years of statehood. "He was at times witty as [State Senator] Thomas Black Reed [1819-1899] and as humorous as Mark Twain," Clark said. Clark went on to say Vest was as sarcastic as Charles Maurice de Tallyrand-Périgord (1754-1838) of France and John Randolph (1773-1833) of Roanoke, Virginia.

"A finer storyteller never lived," Clark said. "If all the books and newspapers could be destroyed tonight and the printer's art forgotten, centuries hence Missourians would repeat Vest's anecdotes to 'point a moral or adorn a tale.' Where he got them all must forever remain a profound mystery."

Clark said Vest and Cockrell—who served together in the U.S. Senate for 24 years—were the best senatorial team Missouri had ever seen. "Vest was one of the crack orators of his generation, and Cockrell was one of the most indefatigable workers who ever lived," Clark said. "Both were effective, strong speakers, Vest being witty, humorous, sarcastic, eloquent and lathered the Republicans up with vitriol to infuriate then almost into apoplexy, while Cockrell confined himself to historical facts and made a specialty of arithmetic."

Among Vest's other mourners was Dan Porter (1852-1927), his longtime caretaker and valet, whose two sons—Finis and Woodson—worked as Vest valets for a time. Porter said that if Vest had been given "his desserts," he would have been president. Said Porter: "I have been for Vest from the first time that he ran for governor, and in the respective races for the Senate. I would have voted a dozen or two ballots each occasion had that been possible."

Porter; Sallie; Alexander; Mollie and her husband, George P.B. Jackson; and Vest's physician, Dr. James W. McClure (1843-1933), were at his side when he died.

Of his death, *The Republican* devoted most of three pages. "Senator Vest was only 74 years old, but so frail was his physique . . . that he lacked the necessary recuperative powers to recover" from a seizure suffered a month earlier, the newspaper said.

"Proof was abundant that as long as he was conscious, he retained complete possession of his mental faculties, though interest in life and the world in which he stood so proud a figure had left him days before the end," *The Republican* reported. "At 2 o'clock this morning [August 9], while his relatives were all gathered about his bedside, the aged statesman sank into a comatose state, from which he did not rally. From Saturday morning, he could not speak and, at times, was unconscious or semiconscious. During the last 36 hours, respiration was scarcely perceptible, and the pulse was so weak that it became almost lost many times."

That the end came quickly would have been in keeping with Vest's views on death, or at least those expressed in his 1898 eulogy of Republican Senator Justin Smith Morrill, best known for his legislation establishing land-grant universities, with whom Vest worked closely on the Yellowstone legislation.

"It is said that death is the great enemy of our race, but under certain circumstances and environments, this is not true," Vest said. "When the young, vigorous, ambitious and hopeful and stricken down, we stand shocked, as if before some unfinished painting or statue where the pencil or chisel has fallen from the nerveless hands of a great artist, but when life's work is done, when the task is finished, and we simply wait for the inevitable end, death is oftentimes a friend.

Let me not live
After my flame lacks oil, to be the snuff
Of younger spirits, whose apprehensive senses
All but new things disdain …

"Every intellectual man will appreciate these lines of Shakespeare. He meant that he did not wish to live after passion and appetite were dead, when life had become an everyday, hand-to-hand conflict with disease and pain, and when we were about to sink into that stage of senility and second childhood when we become objects of pity, if not of contempt."

The Republicans of Missouri called Vest a man of "unquestioned integrity and unsullied honor," which was echoed by Republican Senator George Frisbie Hoar of Massachusetts, who said, "He was brave, sincere, spirited and straightforward." Other Republicans were of similar opinion, agreeing that if a Democratic statesman must exist, Vest should be the model.

Said Crittenden, who served as an honorary pallbearer: "Whatever coolness may have existed between us has long since passed away and grown into a reminiscence even into a sweeter recollection. I have seen great stalwart oaks of the forest gradually dying, gradually growing weaker, from trunk to bough, and at last fall as the monarch falls, leaving a large vacancy in smaller trees; so fell Senator Vest … serenely pure, yet divinely strong."

"The thing that makes Vest's story different is his individualism—his ability and personality, rather than his achievements as a constructive leader," Dawes wrote. "If the only requirement for a statesman was that he be versed in governmental affairs, Vest could take his place with the best of the lesser group. But the final test of a statesman is his influence upon government's policy. As he was in the minority, 22 of the 24 years in the Senate," yet he influenced more than the creation of Yellowstone, if that weren't enough.

"It is a true saying that no man is indispensable," said historian Albert Jeremiah Beveridge (1862-1927). "But there are some whose ability is so distinguished, whose integrity and instincts are so true, whose course is so firm that to replace them when they drop out of life requires time and careful patriotic selections. Such a man is Senator Vest of Missouri."

The Washington Press Correspondents praised Vest as being "the easiest man in the Senate to follow." Vest, they said, knew what he wanted to say and said it. One reporter characterized him as a "great student, poet, orator, and sage; great as a statesman, delightful as a man."

Sallie detected early on that her husband was influenced by the crowd in which he found himself.

According to his friends, in private life, there was no party line, and some of his most devoted friends were his political opponents. He was "at home," said one of his friends, with the prince or the pauper, whether it was in the Senate cloakroom discussing architecture with Morrill, or Shakespeare and international law with Cushman K. Davis, or on the Gulf coast fishing with Quay. He was happy around the campfire with President Arthur; or touring "Republican Alaska" with former Secretary of War J. Donald Cameron (1833-1918); conversing about silver with Broadhead in the Swiss Alps; or in Saint Louis' Southern Hotel talking cattle with Richard Coke (1829-1897); or on the veranda of his Sweet Springs home talking to a random farmer about Missouri mules; or displaying his skill as a billiard or poker player in some rendezvous.

Judge Philips said Vest was the "most interesting conversationalist I ever knew."

Dr. J.W. McClure, Vest's family physician and friend for more than 40 years, wrote in a 1904 tribute that "He loved Missouri because Missourians love him and were ever responsive to his laudable ambitions. He was a greater man than Benton, because from the exalted position he won in the affairs of his country, he never forgot or looked down with contempt upon those beneath him. He loved natural nature unadorned the most, as he despised the deceitful veneering of the artful.

"He loved dogs because of their honest and faithful friendship.
"He loved little children for the innocence of their prattling tongues.
"He loved the old wayside wells for their unceasing flow of kindness.
"He loved the friends of the forests for their generous gifts and gratitude."

Sallie died at her daughter's Saint Louis home of pneumonia on May 21, 1906, after a short trip to Philadelphia, where she visited her daughter-in-law, the widow of her son, George Jr.

Alexander Sneed Vest died February 28, 1931, in Kansas City, and Mollie died at Sedalia on May 8, 1933.

Vest's impact is commemorated on two historical markers in Kentucky—one in his hometown of Frankfort and another in Owensboro. Vest Avenue, once a section of Twentieth Street in the Saint Louis subdivision of West Bremen, is named in the senator's honor.

Resources

Primary Sources

1—Western Historical Manuscript Collection, letter from Vest to the editor of *The Savior*, March 30, 1903.

2—*Vestonia: Senator Vest at his Best*, selected, compiled, and edited by Henry M. Rose, chief clerk of the U.S. Senate, December 1, 1902.

3—Daviess County (Kentucky) Public Library Collection, *The Owensboro Gazette.*

4—George Graham Vest: Champion of the Dog, Edwin French, 1930, Boston.

5—Old Drum: Being an account of George Graham Vest and his now famous Eulogy to the Dog, Daisy Kramer, The Printery, 1970-71, Kirkwood, Mo.

6—Letter from Josiah Turner Jr. to his wife, dated December 4, 1864, Duke University Rare Book, Manuscript, and Special Collections Library.

7–Daviess County Deed Book 74, pages 426-427.

Secondary Sources

1—"The Senatorial Career of George Graham Vest," by Elaine Dawes , A.B., submitted in partial fulfillment of the requirements for the degree of Master of Arts in the Graduate School of the University of Missouri, 1932.

2—Sketch of George G. Vest, read by Henry Lamm, ESQ., at the Missouri Bar Association at Saint Louis, Mo., 1904.

3—*The Kansas City Star*, "The Senator As A Member of Missouri's Wartime Legislature," Tuesday, January 27, 1903.

4—The Red Ranger, "Senator Vest's Tribute to a Dog," an excerpt from the *Saint Louis Republican*, reprinted August 1926.

5—*Missouri News Magazine*, "The Story of Old Drum, a Senator and a Law Suit," by Luke Chase, June 1956.

6—*Missouri Historical Review*, "The True Story of Old Drum," by Walter L. Chaney, Volume 19, January 1925, reprinted from *The Breeder's Gazette*, December 16, 1915.

7—*The Glasgow Globe*, "A Famous Speech by Senator Vest," August 4, 1904.

8—*Offbeat Kentuckians: Legends to Lunatics*, by Keven McQueen, McClanahan Publishing, 2001.

9—"Who Shot Old Drum?" by Dr. John A. Horner.

10—*The Kentucky Encyclopedia*, John E. Kleber, editor, University Press of Kentucky, 1992.
11—Kansas City Journal, *"Vest's Early Career," Feb. 1903.*
12—Vertical file, Saint Louis, 1906; Saint Louis, the Fourth City, Vol. 2, pp. 752-3; *Encyclopedia of the History of Saint Louis, Vol. 2*, pp. 1016-1116.
13—Story of Enduring Friendship between Senator George Graham Vest and Adolphus Busch, by James C. Espy.
14—*Missouri Historical Society Bulletin*, "Historic Preservation in Missouri;" Vol. 32, page 225.
15—*Missouri Historical Review,* "Senator Vest's 'Dog Speech'" by H.H. Crittenden; page 513-516.
16—Missouri Historical Society Vertical File, Associated Press report of April 8, 1927.
17—*Kansas City Times*, "Missourian's Tribute to the Dog is Chief Memorial of a Notable Career," by Frank T. Moriarity, March 26, 1955.
18—*V.F.W. Magazine*, "Senator Wasp Saved Yellowstone" by James K. Anderson; December 1927, pages 20-22.
19—*Journal of the Missouri Bar*, "George Graham Vest" by Hugh P. Williamson; July 1955, Vol. 11, No. 7, pages 99-100.
20—"Historic marker at courthouse honors dog's best friend" by Keith Lawrence, *Owensboro Messenger-Inquirer*, February 28, 2002.
21—Correspondence from Transylvania University Librarian to Miss Marian E.M. Dawes, Saint Louis, Mo., dated January 6, 1932.
22—"When A Woman Attacked George Graham Vest," *Journal of the Missouri Bar*, July 1955, "George Graham Vest" by Hugh P. Williamson.
23—"They Tried to Crucify Me or The Smoke-Screen of the Cumberlands" by John W. Langley (former congressman), Pikeville, Ky., 1929.
24—Interviews with George Vest Triplett IV, July 1, 2002, and October 12, 2002, Owensboro, Ky.
25—"John Colter's Hell" by Lynn Colter, *Sky: A Traveling Magazine*, May 2002.
26—"The Career of George Graham Vest," *Saint Louis Post-Dispatch*, January 4, 1902.
27—"Vest on Death," *Saint Louis Post-Dispatch*, January 4, 1902.
28—Numerous stories, *Saint Louis Republican*, August 10, 1904
29—*Biographical Register of the Confederate Congress*, Ezra J. Warner and W. Buck Yearns, Louisiana State University Press.
30—*The Papers of Jefferson Davis, Vol. 10*, October 1863-August 1864, Lynda Laswell Crist, Kenneth H. Williams, Peggy L. Dillard, Louisiana State University Press, 1999.
31—"Old Put: The Story of a Sunday Pigeon Hunt," by G.G. Vest, *The Saturday Evening Post*, July 2, 1904.

32—"An Honorable Defeat: The Last Days of the Confederate Government," by William C. Davis, Harcourt, Inc., 2001.
33—"Alexander H. Stephens," by G.G. Vest, *The Saturday Evening Post*, published September 5, 1903.
34—"Pictorial and Genealogical Record of Greene County, Missouri: Together with Bibliographies of Prominent Men and Other Portions of the State, Both Living and Dead."
35—"Rise and Fall of the Confederate Government" by Jefferson Davis, 1912 edition.
36—"Jesse James: Last Rebel of the Civil War" by T.J. Stiles, Random House, 2002.
37—"The National Cyclopedia of American Biography."
38—"Concise Dictionary of American Biography," Scribners, 1977.
39—"Pulitzer: A Life" by Denis Brian, John Wiley & Sons, 2001.
40—"Yellowstone: A Wilderness Besieged" by Richard A. Bartlett, University of Arizona Press, 1985.
41—"History of the Frankfort Cemetery" by L.F. Johnson, 1921.
42—"A Corner in Celebrities" by Alice Elizabeth Trabue, 1922.
43—"Senator George Graham Vest and the 'Menace' of Mormonism, 1882-1887," *Missouri Historical Review*, by M. Paul Holsinger, April 1971.
44—"The Discovery of Yellowstone Park," 1870, Second Edition, by Nathaniel Pitt Langford, J.E. Haynes Publisher, St. Paul, Minnesota.
45—"The Road to Confiscation," *The Yale Law Journal*, Feb. 1916, Vol. 25, No. 4.
46—"Senator Vest: Champion of the Dog" by Edwin M. C. French, The Meador Press, Boston, 1930.
47—*Wade Hampton: Confederate Warrior, Conservative Statesman*, by Walter Brian Cisco, Bassey's Inc., Washington, D.C., 2004.

Assistance

Western Historical Manuscript Collection, Columbia, Mo.
State Historical Society of Missouri, Columbia, Mo.
The University of Missouri, Columbia, Mo.
Johnson County Historical Society, Warrensburg, Mo.
The Kentucky Room, Daviess County Public Library, Owensboro, Ky.
Duke University Manuscript and Special Collections Library, Durham, N.C.
Hagan Memorial Library, University of the Cumberlands, Williamsburg, Ky.
The Kentucky Historical Society, Frankfort, Ky.
The Library of Congress, Washington, D.C.

Special Thanks

Editor and friend Ted Sloan; Frankfort historian Russ Hatter; Gene Burch; publisher Doug Sikes; editor Randy Baumgardner; designer Frene Melton; researcher Sheryl Vanderstel; historian David G. Vanderstel, Ph.D.; historian Thomas E. Stephens; the staff of *Kentucky Monthly*, including Michael Embry, Patty Ranft, Brooke Raby and Lucy Saunderson; Vince Staten; Sheila Heflin of the Daviess County Public Library, Owensboro, Ky.; B.J. Gooch, Transylvania University Archives, Lexington, Ky.; Kentucky Senator David Boswell of Owensboro, Ky.; Judge George Vest Triplett IV, Owensboro, Ky.; The Jefferson Davis Association, Rice University; Janie C. Morris, research services librarian, Duke University; Ru Story-Huffman, Hagan Memorial Library, The University of the Cumberlands (Ky.); The Johnson County Historical Society, Warrensburg, Mo.; Jacklyn Dré Marceau, Columbia, Mo.; The State Historical Society of Missouri, Columbia, Mo.

About the Author

Stephen M. Vest

Stephen M. Vest is the editor and publisher of *Kentucky Monthly*, a Governor's Awards in the Arts (Media) honoree. Founded in 1998, *Kentucky Monthly* has more than 100,000 readers.

He is the author of *Unexpected Inheritance* (Butler Books, 2014), a memoir about being raised by older parents and a hard-to-please grandmother; two collections of columns, including *THAT Kind of Journalist* (2008), and the publisher of the 2012 anthology *Kentucky's Twelve Days of Christmas* with editor James B. Goode.

Vest holds journalism and English degrees from the University of Louisville and Murray State University (MFA-Creative Nonfiction).

His work has appeared in publications nationwide, including *The Journal of Kentucky Studies*, *Still*, and the anthology *Of Woods and Waters* (2005) by Ron Ellis.

A frequent speaker, Vest teaches communications at Campbellsville University, public speaking at Midway University, and feature writing and storytelling at Eastern Kentucky University.

He and his wife, Kay, live in Frankfort, Kentucky. They have four grown children—Christopher, Katy, Molly and Sydney.

The author and subject are third cousins, four times removed. Virginians John Daniel Vest (1705-1765) and Charlotte Ann Bakes (1709-1770) are their common ancestors.

Index